Still Surviving

ALSO BY NANON M. WILLIAMS

The Ties that Bind Us

The Darkest Hour: Stories and Interviews from Death Row

*The Darkest Hour: Shedding Light on the Impact of Isolation
and Death Row in Texas Prisons*

Still Surviving

Nanon M. Williams

goodmedia press
Dallas, TX

goodmedia press
An imprint of goodmedia communications, llc
25 Highland Park Village, 100-810
Dallas, Texas 75205

Second Edition

Book and cover design by goodmedia communications, llc
Cover photo by Adolfo Cantu-Villarreal and TZOM Films

The text in this book is set in Garamond and District.

Manufactured in the United States of America

Library of Congress Control Number
2012952840

ISBN: 978-0-988-3237-2-8

To all people who stand up to injustice in this world.
Your efforts do make a difference.

Contents

Foreword   ix

Alone in the Dark   1

Arrival on Death Row   12

From Dusk Till Dawn   25

J-21 The Sign of Blood   30

My Twenty-Second birthday   40

Stand by Me   51

Through Hell and Back   58

The Shadow of Death   67

Sergeant None of Your Business
and Solitary Confinement   76

Ax Man   93

Welcome Back   106

Revolutionary Education   119

Pope Joan and Li'l Dez   128

Bench Warrant   137

Reflections on the AmeriKKKan Nightmare   152

The Legal Eagle   160

Run, Run, Run   168

The Great Escape   176

A Reason to Live   186

Words of Encouragement   192

Something Real   200

Memories are Made of This   217

The New Millennium Arrives in Hell   227

Still Holding Strong   232

Acknowledgments   238

About the Author   240

FOREWORD

On January 31, 1865, Congress passed the thirteenth amendment to the United States Constitution. The amendment reads: "Neither slavery nor involuntary servitude, except as a punishment for crime whereof the party shall have been duly convicted, shall exist within the United States, or any place subject to their jurisdiction." Abraham Lincoln, and the abolitionists of the time, rightly believed that all people were created equal by their Creator and deserve equal and fair treatment under the law. They rightly believed that when our founding fathers wrote the following excerpt from the Declaration of Independence "all men" were not limited to only white men: "We hold these truths to be self-evident, that all men are created equal, that they are endowed by their Creator with certain unalienable Rights, that among these are Life, Liberty and the pursuit of Happiness." With the greatest and noblest of intentions, the writers of the thirteenth amendment and those who worked tirelessly to ensure its passing, fell short of their goal. By including the caveat of "punishment for a crime" the thirteenth amendment left open a window for racism and injustice to remain woven into the fabric of our society.

One hundred forty-seven years after passing this important and profoundly necessary Constitutional amendment, the United States has turned mass incarceration into a modern-day form of slavery. The United States has more African-Americans enslaved and locked in cages than it had enslaved and working on Southern plantations in 1850. Rather than being a social justice atrocity exclusive to the South, African-Americans are now systematically incarcerated throughout the United States at a rate of thirteen times that of white people.[1] African-Americans comprise only twelve to thirteen percent of the United States population, and yet they make up seventy-two percent of the more than two million people incarcerated in the United States.[2] Of the two and half million people incarcerated in American prisons, ninety percent are men, which makes the above statistic even more alarming when you consider that African-American men represent only six percent of the population in the United States but almost seventy percent of the prison population. According to the Bureau of Justice, one in three black men will go to prison in their lifetime. The devastating impact the War on Drugs has had on African-American men cannot be overstated, and we must not overlook the impact their incarceration has had on their families, their communities and our nation.

One hundred years after the passing of the thirteenth amendment, Martin Luther

King, Jr. and other civil rights activists continued to fight for justice, leading a nonviolent movement to bring the equality promised by the Declaration of Independence to *all people*. In 1968, the same year Martin Luther King, Jr. was tragically assassinated, the Nixon Administration launched the War on Drugs. This war, waged almost exclusively in densely populated, African-American, urban ghettos, is the most costly (the federal government spends an estimated $500 per second), ineffective war—in terms of both lives and dollars—ever fought by Americans.[3] According to the National Center for Biotechnology Information and the U.S. National Library of Medicine National Institutes of Health, the number of people incarcerated in the United States has increased five-fold since 1972 without a comparable decrease in crime or drug use.

Yet, to most middle class Americans, the War on Drugs seems to be more of a public relations initiative associated with Nancy Reagan's "Just Say No" campaign than an actual war. Why? Because the war—waged by the American government on American citizens—occurs in slums, barrios and ghettos, where no middle class Americans live. Both the drug users and drug sellers are carted off to massive prison complexes built in rural areas many miles from roads or highways. They are out of sight and out of mind for most Americans. The War on Drugs is very much a war, but a more appropriate title would be the "War on African-Americans and Poor People" because the government is not rounding up white, middle and upper class drug dealers and users. There are no air raids at expensive private schools where drugs are sold and bought in ample supply. There are no police SWAT teams barging into the homes in white, middle- and upper-class neighborhoods where a stop by the local bar or country club would mostly likely yield as much drugs as the convenient store parking lot of the ghetto.[4]

Prior to meeting Nanon Williams, I was the middle class American who had given little thought to incarceration. Prison and prisoners were not a part of my life, nor were they a part of anyone's life I knew. Or so I thought. It is not that I was callous to the suffering of others. Rather, I had never thought to make myself aware. Even though many people I know, as well as many of our United States Presidents, at some point or another experimented with drugs in their youth and/or young adult life, I did not know anyone who had ever been arrested for drugs, much less incarcerated. My education about prison came from televisions shows such as *Law & Order* and *Breakout*. I was naive to the realities of incarceration in this country. I did not know that while the United States represents only five percent of the world's population, we incarcerate twenty-five percent of the world's prisoners. *The United States—home of the free and brave—incarcerates twenty-five percent of the world's prisoners.* Now consider this: sixty percent of the people imprisoned in the United States are incarcerated for nonviolent crimes.[5] The majority of people in prison are not serial killers, rapists and child molesters. No, they are drug addicts (i.e., seriously ill individuals in need of treatment) and people who are so economically disadvantaged they often have no other source of income than to sell drugs in order to put food on the table and keep the electricity on. Imagine if, during the days of prohibition, we incarcerated—locked in six by nine cages—everyone who drank illegal moonshine or bathtub gin. Is marijuana, cocaine or crack that much different than hard liquor? The answer is no. One is currently legal; the others are not. And at one point in history they were all legal, and at other points in history they were all illegal.

And then there are those individuals like Nanon Williams—those who are innocent of the crimes for which they are charged. According to the Innocence Project, an estimated two to five percent of all people incarcerated in the United States are innocent. To put that in perspective, fifty thousand to one hundred twenty-five thousand people are incarcerated in the United States for crimes they did not commit. This statistic should make the hair on your arms stand up and prompt you to ask yourself, "What can I do to change this?"

Nanon, an African-American man who grew up in the gang-infested streets of Los Angeles, found himself entrapped in the economy of drugs. At seventeen years of age with a promising football career ahead of him, Nanon had never consumed a single drop of alcohol or drugs. As the oldest male in his family, he wanted to contribute financially to his household. Foolishly, he got involved in the economic opportunities available to him—the drug dealing activities he saw on just about every street corner in his neighborhood.

By his own account, he was "no choirboy," but he also was not a murderer. He was an impoverished, African-American boy who grew up with challenges so extreme few middle class Americans could imagine. He got involved with the wrong crowd who did not hesitate, at the hands of an over-eager, career-zealous prosecutor, to point the finger at the least experienced and youngest boy in the group. Nanon Williams has now been incarcerated for over twenty years—more than half his life—for a murder he did not commit while the man who actually committed the murder lives freely in our society.[6]

But that is not the end of the story. It is only the beginning. Amidst violence that rivals the worst of battlefields, daily brutality, extreme isolation, racism and inconceivable injustice that are standard operating procedures in America's prisons emerged a young man dedicated to shaping the minds and hearts of fellow Americans in order to create a better tomorrow for us all. Nanon wrote *Still Surviving* when he was twenty-nine years old. At the time, he had been incarcerated for twelve years, three while awaiting trial in Harris County and nine on Texas' notoriously cruel death row. He was rightfully angry, but even in his anger you will see a wise young man, whose only protection was to shield himself in muscles and tattoos, desperate to find his way in a world that drives even the toughest men mad—a world few live to tell about.

Ten years after the first printing of this book, Nanon continues to fight for his freedom. Along the way, he has met with hard-fought successes and bitter disappointments. And he has grown into a man committed to exposing the injustice, abuse and inhumane conditions that have largely resulted from America's most failed war—the War on Drugs—and society's lack of awareness about it. He has also grown into a man with the desire to positively influence and improve others' lives so that in a world of madness, there can be meaning. In order to improve the world, we must be educated about the darkest shadows within it.

Still Surviving provides an intimate look into a world so horrible and unjust you may be tempted to put the book down and look away. I encourage you to look deep within yourself to find the compassion and courage necessary to bear witness to the suffering of others. Allow Nanon Williams' wrongful conviction and two decades of imprisonment, and the fifty thousand or more others just like him, to spark in you the same passion for justice that slavery sparked in Abraham Lincoln and the abolitionists responsible for the passing of the thirteenth amendment.

In his book, *The Power of One*, Bryce Courtenay wrote, "I have found in life that everything, no matter how bad, comes to an end." Each and every one of us holds within ourselves the power to change the world. As Gandhi so wisely instructed, "Be the change that you wish to see in the world." You will no doubt be surprised by how much one determined person can truly accomplish.

Robyn Short
Publisher
goodmedia press

Endnotes

[1] Kain, E. (2011, June 28). The War on Drugs is a War on Minorities and the Poor. *Forbes*. Retrieved January 15, 2013, from http://www.forbes.com/sites/erikkain/2011/06/28/the-war-on-drugs-is-a-war-on-minorities-and-the-poor/

[2] Human Rights Watch. (2000). Punishment and Prejudice: Racial Disparities in the War on Drugs. *The UN Refugee Agency*. Retrieved from http://www.unhcr.org/refworld/pdfid/3ae6a86f4.pdf

[3] Office of National Drug Control Policy. (2013, January 16). Drug War Clock. *DrugSense*. Retrieved from http://www.drugsense.org/cms/wodclock

[4] Gorski, P. (2008). The Myth of the Culture of Poverty. *Poverty and Learning, 65*(7), 32-36. Retrieved January 16, 2013, from http://www.ascd.org/publications/educational-leadership/apr08/vol65/num07/The-Myth-of-the-Culture-of-Poverty.aspx

[5] Schmitt, J., Warner, K., & Gupta, S. (2010, June). *The High Budgetary Cost of Incarceration* (Rep.). Retrieved January 16, 2013, from Center for Economic and Policy Research website: http://www.cepr.net/documents/publications/incarceration-2010-06.pdf

[6] Amnesty International. (2004, January 21). *USA: Dead Wrong: The case of Nanon Williams, child offender facing execution on flawed evidence | Amnesty International* (Rep.). Retrieved January 16, 2013, from Amnesty International website: http://www.amnesty.org/en/library/info/AMR51/002/2004

1

ALONE IN THE DARK

THE WINTER NIGHT WAS dark and rainy. I fell asleep in my bunk at the Harris County jail. When I awoke, cold air was storming through the corridors like a freezing gas that paralyzed the nervous system. For a brief moment, it seemed as if I had awoken from a nightmare. But no, as I stared out of the steel cage, I realized that this was no nightmare. This was a reality that I wished like hell was not true. It was the reality of a new life, a new pain, and a new tomorrow that I wished I could go backward in time to escape.

When dawn broke and light erased the darkness, I knew that at any moment I would be handcuffed, shackled, strapped with chains around my waist and transported to a new place, a new prison and a new hell that would make the Harris County jail seem like a boys' camp, where kids met on weekends to enjoy new adventures in life. However, the place I was headed for was no boys' camp with wonderful adventures to enjoy. I was headed to death row, a place where joy and hope were left behind and where life ended altogether.

I will never forget the tears streaming down my mother's face and the feeling of helplessness that tortured her because there was nothing she could say or do. There was no comfort she could give that would take away the death sentence. When I visit that memory, I feel a rage and sadness so jointly connected that a strange calmness is born, asking to be aborted.

As I reflect upon these memories etched so deeply in my mind, memories of the very hour my terrifying journey to death row began, the echoes of life resound louder than ever before.

"Clear the corridor!" a Harris County deputy yelled through the jail's housing facilities. The moment of actual transportation to death row was here, and my mind felt paralyzed. I felt as though I could not gather myself. The stillness broke as the deputy entered the corridor and shouted, "Nanon Williams, what cell are you in?"

Unable to respond with any degree of self-control, I just tapped the bars signaling to the guard as he walked towards me.

"Get ready for transport." He spoke cautiously as he looked me up and down. I was a six-feet, one-inch tall, muscular, two-hundred-twenty-five-pound young man with a massive chest and arms. As I looked down at the deputy, who was several inches shorter and at least fifty pounds lighter, he appeared to be afraid of how I would react to the news of my transfer. In my mind everything changed, and I was thinking to myself, *Fuck it!* My breathing grew heavy and hard and adrenaline stormed throughout my body.

He threw the door open, and there I stood, stripped down to my boxer shorts and staring with a faraway look in my eyes that unnerved the deputies gathering around the cell door.

"Bend over and spread 'em!" a lieutenant called from behind the mechanical doors that rolled open the cells into the corridor. He spoke with a redneck, Texas drawl, a sound that will always be a nightmare to me.

I understood him, but I responded, "Do what?"

"Bend over and spread your ass cheeks and cough, Inmate!" he repeated.

"I'm not bending over to spread shit, so do what you gotta do." Before I could finish my sentence, they exited the corridor and left me in the open tank.

Those Bastards! I thought. *Who in the hell do they think I am? Do they really believe I am going to bend over and spread my ass cheeks for them? Fuck that!* I would not allow them to subject me to that degradation, even if I was headed for death row. Some might think that I was copping an attitude to appear tough, but they would be wrong. My sense of dignity was the only thing that could not be taken from me, and I was not going to give that away. Whatever happened would just have to happen. I would not willingly degrade myself.

"Corridor opening!" the deputy yelled again through the holding tank. I could see the metal helmets, steel batons, taser guns, and the padded vests they were wearing as they came into the corridor, walking in a straight line like an army platoon. I knew what was about to happen, so I backed away to the farthest corner of the holding tank, my back touching the concrete structure.

"Inmate! Bend over and spread your ass cheeks, or physical force will be applied!" An oily smirk spread over the lieutenant's face.

"Fuck you!" I replied. "I ain't bending over and spreading my ass like an animal for your pleasure!" But before I could finish the words, the taser gun was fired and hit my left thigh, sending a shockwave through my body that made me extremely dizzy. My vision blurred. I smelled the burned flesh of my thigh, and I braced myself against the concrete wall for support as I slid to the floor.

I attempted to rise to my feet again, but I was hit again in the chest with the taser gun. The metal ball that shot out this time didn't seem to affect me, so I lunged toward the lieutenant with all my might, knocking him to the floor as my fist crashed against his chin. Before I could strike him again, the other deputies wrestled me to the floor and all of them piled on top of me. When I was handcuffed and shackled, lying on my stomach, the lieutenant began choking me, repeatedly screaming, "You dumb son-of-a-bitch! This is how it will feel before they kill you! Feel it, you stupid motherfucker!" He continued to yell as I drifted in and out of consciousness.

What seemed like hours later, after the handcuffs were taken off, a nurse woke me up. I was on a mattress in the infirmary. She asked me how I felt. I looked up at her. Tears were welling in her eyes as she looked down at me. I glanced down at the shackles that still chained my ankles together.

"Young man, I don't know what happened to cause the incident in the holding tank," she said softly, "but I advise you to call your attorney and get pictures taken of yourself."

"I'm on transport to death row," I replied, "so I won't be able to make any calls for security reasons. But thank you for being concerned."

She continued to ask me if I was alright and even volunteered to make a call for me. That was against regulations. I assured her that I didn't have an attorney worth calling. She then volunteered to call my mother, but the last thing I wanted was to cause my mother more worry and heartache than she already had. I continued to gratefully decline the nurse's offers of help.

I knew it was a matter of time before they came to get me, so I asked the nurse how long I had been in the infirmary. She said I had only been there about twenty minutes. I thought it was much longer, but of course I was unconscious so that time slipped away.

"Young man, if you don't mind me asking, how old are you?" the nurse asked. "You look awfully young."

I told her my age and that I had been incarcerated since I was seventeen years old, waiting to go to trial on a capital murder charge.

She looked appalled. "You mean to tell me you were a teenager when you were arrested and now you're going to death row?"

"Yes."

Her expression was one of the saddest I had seen. She continued to stare at me until I felt uncomfortable beneath her gaze.

"Well, I'll keep you in my prayers, and you make sure to pray for yourself," she told me. "We need no one except God, and when you feel down and out, ask Him to give you strength. You look like you need it." Her smile was sincere and helped to impress her words into my mind. "You take care, you hear?"

All through the entire conversation with the nurse, I did not really think about the bruises that plagued my body with pain. The only noticeable injury that I could see was the bandage around my thigh and the bright red mark across my chest. They didn't hurt too badly and looked worse than they felt. When I heard the deputies enter the infirmary to take me to transport, I stood up and pain shot through my back as if I was being hit over and over again. They had viciously assaulted me, but being unconscious didn't allow me to feel much of anything as it was happening. While some people may believe I deserved my injuries for hitting the lieutenant, I wasn't going to voluntarily let anyone degrade me. I stood up for myself in the only way I knew how.

I was handcuffed, shackled and a leather belt was strapped around my waist that locked my arms across my torso. I could only imagine what any onlookers thought of me, but I didn't really care at that moment. The time had come when death row was no longer a nightmare that lay ahead. It was swiftly becoming reality. I was going to hell today. Those thoughts circled round and round my weary mind. I had a million and one questions in my mind about existing among four hundred and fifty convicted killers. Would I simply become prisoner number four hundred fifty-one? Would I be just another prisoner consumed by the inferno of the hellhole I was about to enter? The world I once knew and loved was now of a different lifetime. I was a condemned man on my way to Texas' death row.

The chain bus was extremely uncomfortable. The wheels spun loudly as the van maneuvered in and out of traffic, causing the shackles to bite into my ankles when I tried to brace myself to keep from sliding all around the metal bench that was bolted to the floor. No matter how hard I tried to anchor myself to the seat, I could not maintain my balance. So I just rolled with the punches and stared out the window. The air was cold, and I could tell by the frost still falling from the windowsill that the hard breeze caused everything to freeze up, but who really cared about the weather. I should have been thinking about what death row would be like, but instead I was looking outside at the white puffy clouds, the frost, and anything else that could serve as a brief distraction.

The van turned off on to a winding dirt road. A large sign hung over the entryway that read, "Welcome to Diagnostics—Huntsville, Texas." I was now lying on the floor of the bus because I had fallen off the metal bench one too many times. I thought, *Who cares where we are. I just wish these pigs would get me out of this van!*

A guard screamed from the tower above the entryway, "Where you coming from, Chief?" One of the deputies replied with that nightmarish East Texas drawl, "We're from the Harris County Sheriff's Department." He exuded an attitude of superiority over the guard. "We got a death row prisoner for y'all!" The gates rolled open, and the van rolled into a huge building that looked more like a warehouse than a prison. The doors of the van were flipped open.

"You ready to go, Inmate?" a prison guard asked, helping me to my feet. "Take it easy, okay? This is just diagnostics, and I'm going to run you through classification and medical as quickly as I can. Then they'll take you to your prison unit in a couple of hours."

I tried to block out his words. He seemed to behave more humanely than the others I had experience with, so I cooperated as best I could. He searched my clothing and dressed me in a thin cloth that resembled a hospital gown.

"How's that? That fit you alright?" he asked, trying to be friendly.

"Yeah, it fits alright," I responded. But who really gave a damn if it fit or not? All they had to do is handcuff me and strip me naked if that was what they wanted to do. After all, I had no choice. However, I chose to reply as cordially as I could because the guard was treating me respectfully. I believe that if anyone treats you with respect, you should give that same respect back. If they treated me disrespectfully, well, that would be the beginning of a long, long day for all of us.

"Here at Diagnostics I will be your escort, and we basically will run you through dental, then to the doctor, and take you to Classification to get pictures of your tattoos, scars, fingerprints, etc. It shouldn't take too long, as you are a high security risk, and we have to run you through as quickly as possible," the guard continued to explain to me. Sometimes I responded rather coldly to his questions, but I quickly put myself in check. This guy was just doing his job, at least he didn't have an attitude. Most law enforcement officials attempt to wave their authority in prisoners' faces. This guard was different, and it relaxed me just a bit.

The heavy steel door that opened another section of the prison stood ajar as we entered. In a bewildered daze, I'm sure I seemed once again overwhelmed at the idea that death row was just hours away. Still, no matter how many other things distracted me, nothing seemed to hold my attention.

"Williams, Williams, Williams," the doctor said tiresomely as he called my name. "Are you Nanon Williams?"

"Yeah, that's me."

"Well, I just want to run you through a few simple tests and check your reflexes, eyes, lungs and basically just make sure you're in good health."

As he ran his tests, I wondered, why in the hell they would care if I was in good physical health? After all, they were going to strap me down on a gurney, stick needles in my arm and pump poisons into my body so that they could watch me die right before their very eyes. Trying to be sure that I was in good physical health was a sadistic joke—a sick and twisted game the state of Texas plays. I told him I was in good shape and that I was through running tests. He glanced at the guard to see if I would be allowed to do that, and the guard just nodded. He took me up a flight of stairs that entered into a dormitory of sorts.

From a short distance I heard loud voices and guards steadily yelling, "Be quiet!" over a microphone. No one seemed to be paying attention. I could still hear voices clustered together as we got closer to the end of the hallway. As we approached an open door, I saw a large group of prisoners, approximately sixty or seventy men, who were naked and lined up against the wall just outside the door. They were told to get out of the way, and we entered into the dormitory. Some of the prisoners attempted to cover themselves, but others just let their private parts swing as if they were accustomed to being a part of a crowd of naked men every day. It seemed to me that all prison was going to be was a bunch of guards wanting to watch prisoners get naked, day in and day out. As I thought of this, I couldn't help but wonder why there were so many prisoners getting raped in prison and men committing sexual intercourse with one another voluntarily. The constant nudity was awkward and felt unnatural. However, as I soon came to learn, the lack of privacy and the lack of modesty were simply more strategies the state uses to take away a prisoner's individuality, dignity and self-esteem—another method of breaking the spirit.

After looking around, feeling disgusted and disrespected, I was taken to a desk where a female guard sat. She had the brightest smile I had seen in a long time. She was immensely enjoying her position in a roomful of naked men.

They will not break my spirit! I kept thinking to myself. *If they think I'm going to get naked in front of everybody, well, these bastards have another thing coming!*

"Could you un-handcuff the inmate?" the woman asked the guard, grinning pleasurably. I looked at her with a feeling of repulsion. *If this tramp thinks I'm going to get naked for her, she's goddamned sure got another thing coming!*

When the guard reached for the handcuff keys, I hurriedly stuck my hands forward and my eagerness somewhat shocked the guard. I felt if I was un-handcuffed, I had a better chance of protesting, compared to being shackled, handcuffed and standing in a light blue hospital gown with nothing on but my boxer shorts and a bandage wrapped around my thigh.

"Okay, Mr. Williams," the sluttish woman breathed, attempting to sound sensual. "Do you have any scars or tattoos on you?" When she cooed my name that way— "Mr. Williams"—I knew that she really enjoyed her job because it had been a long, long time since anyone had called me "Mr. Williams." *I could get used to that*, I thought.

"Yeah," I said, letting her know that she was invading my privacy against my will. "I got quite a few tattoos. But I don't know what you mean by scars. I don't have any major scars."

"Could you please take off your shirt and show them to me?" She asked the questions with so much seductiveness that I could understand for a moment, but only a brief one, why the other prisoners were standing with pride so the woman could get a good view of their manhood.

"I can't do that with handcuffs on," I said.

"Oh, I don't have enough security with me today to take off the handcuffs, Ma'am," the guard politely stated. "He's a death row prisoner, and we're suppose to run him through the classification process as soon as possible."

"Well, how am I going to do my job if he's handcuffed?" she replied again, exhibiting a great disappointment that my nakedness would not be displayed for her pleasure. "It will only be for a few minutes."

"Still, Ma'am, I don't think it's best to take the handcuffs off." The guard was becoming annoyed, tired of explaining things to her. While he was speaking, I looked around, wondering how she could safely stay in this dormitory style building alone with so many prisoners, but when I looked up, I saw a glass window, and several guards stood behind it. I realized that the security was not as lax as I first thought.

"Excuse me! Hello? You there!" The woman attempted to get my attention. "I'm going to have to lift up your shirt and see the tattoos you've got, and I'll try not to be rough." She lifted my shirt, and I heard her gasp. "Mr. Williams, why do you have so many red bruises on your back? What happened to you?"

"Ask the Harris County Sheriff's Department. But what difference does it make anyway? What's done is done. Now, can you hurry up and finish?" I responded coldly. I was in no mood for some woman who used her position as a part of the system that wronged me, to ogle my body and behave seductively toward me.

"I see you have a tattoo on your back and on your arms, Mr. Williams. Do you have any more somewhere else?" she asked, her eyes dropping toward my boxer shorts, obviously hoping that I would pull them down.

"Nah, I don't have any more."

She continued writing in her record book, but I could not help wondering why she did not take photos with the camera behind the booth or ask about the bandage around my thigh. Still, the less information they had, the better it would be, right?

"Well, Mr. Williams, that's it for now. Take care of yourself, and I hope your appeal goes okay for you," she said, still smiling in her usual way. "Next in line," she said, dismissing me as the other prisoners argued over who would be next in line.

As I was leaving I looked back and shook my head, wondering how they could argue about something so insignificant, but I didn't really give a damn one way or the other. I just wanted to get the hell out of Diagnostics and get to the crueler reality I knew death row would present. Once I faced the worst and knew how it would be, then I would know what to do and how to act.

As I was escorted to another holdover cell, I was given a set of all white clothing that looked like a servant's uniform. *Who the fuck cares?* I thought. *It's not like I'm going to a fashion show or anything.*

"Say, Williams," the same officer who had been escorting me most of the day said, "I forgot to run you down to dental. Do you need to see the dentist?"

"Nah" I said lazily. "I just want to get to wherever it is you're taking me next."

"Well, go ahead and relax a little bit, and there's a sack lunch on the stool if you want it. The boys from death row will be here to get you shortly," he said. "We called fifteen minutes ago to let them know we're done with you."

After lying asleep in the corner for a while, I awoke from a nightmare. "This is how it will feel when they kill you," I heard the lieutenant yelling in my ear over and over again. *I'll see you again, you bastard!* I thought. But I didn't say that out of anger or the wish to retaliate. I said it as a challenge that he presented to me, in order to show his sorry ass that death row would never kill me.

"Williams," the guard said in a low tone. "They're here to get you, Bud, so be cool, alright?"

Although I appreciated the guard's friendliness, I wasn't his "bud." I was someone he would help drag to the death chamber if he were assigned to that task, so I tried to keep in perspective what was happening and what role the guards play in this whole process. The door flew open and several guards entered with chains, a shotgun and a mask. I knew that the time had come at last. I had been trying to prepare for this moment. Now it was here.

"Okay, Williams, strip off your clothes, and put them on the bars," said the guard who had just arrived from death row.

Here they go with that "get naked" shit again! I thought to myself.

2

ARRIVAL ON DEATH ROW

THE SUN BEGAN TO set just before the white prison van pulled up into a closed structure to be inspected by other prison guards. Everywhere I looked I was surrounded by barbed wire fences that begged to be touched, so blood could run slowly down the razor-sharp embrace in order to lubricate the rusty pieces that fell to the ground when strong winds came. As I waited in the van, the closed structure finally opened by the electric gate, and under its passage a sign read: "WELCOME TO DEATH ROW—ELLIS ONE UNIT."

When the van skidded to a halt by the careless driver, more prison guards were waiting at the entryway of the building. Rain began to fall with a reckless abandon, soaking everything except the death row captain who waited under a plastic shed that hung over the doorway of the large brick building. The rain splashed against the windows of the van, obstructing my view out of and their view into the van. The minutes seemed to fly by, as did the rain and the wind that slowly rocked the van back and forth. It seemed fitting that a raging storm made my arrival to hell even more ominous. Maybe my spirit was screaming, causing everything around me to erupt with a violent outburst.

Guards in gray uniforms opened the door of the chain bus.

"Inmate! Exit the van!" screamed a guard. I immediately got an attitude. *How in the hell did this jackass expect me to jump out of the van with the shackles on my feet?* The pressure would cause the metal to cut more into my ankles than they already were.

"If you would help me exit this van, being that I am shackled and handcuffed, I would be glad to get out of the van, Officer!"

When they did assist me, I couldn't help but feel like a hockey player with the mask they had on my face in an effort to protect themselves from me. According to the rules, I had to be secured, but putting a mask on my face was a little too much. I understood they felt the tension and that they were fearful of me, but to place a mask over any human being's face seemed like another tactic to break the human spirit. Of course that was exactly what it was. I knew that if I ever allowed these tactics to work, they would win. *Remember who you are.* I thought over and over. *Not what they make you out to be.*

As they escorted me down a long hallway, several guards, the captain and a sergeant stood around me as if to isolate me from the entire world. When we got to the end of the hallway, we made a right turn and entered through a steel door that opened into an office. The death row captain sat behind the desk in his leather chair looking as if he thought he was the god of some lost island. I chuckled to myself as I stared at him. *That damn fool!* I thought. *How the hell could he feel so important when he helps lead the charge in killing people who may or may not be guilty?* Either way, it did not matter. He and those like him would have as much blood on their hands as those they put to death—maybe more. When all the chains and the mask were removed, I was told to sit in a chair to be interviewed by the captain. I welcomed the comfort of the plastic chair.

"Williams, how old are you, Boy?"

"I'm not your boy!" I responded.

"Well, let me put it this way. What is your goddamn age, you smart ass?" The captain attempted to provoke another belligerent response from me, but I ignored him this time. I wasn't from Texas, but I knew that the Texas prison system was split up into prison farms that were nothing more than modern day slave plantations run by slave owners. Prison guards—a great number of people who populated East Texas, and especially the Huntsville area, which is the prison capital of the state—were stereotypically bigots and racists and continued to treat black people as if they were inferior. Most prisoners, both black and white, even in the county jail, addressed the deputies as "Boss Man," a term that has survived since the days of slavery. When I heard them say that, I realized just how programmed they were, and I was determined never to use the term. I realized that those responses came out of fear because law enforcement officers in Texas often believe that "Boss Man" is their rightful title. I've always called these guards "officer," if they were respectful to me, and "pig" if they treated me as anything less than a human being. I would continue to do so.

"Williams, please just answer the questions, and we'll house you in your building as soon as possible," the sergeant said. "Just cooperate and this will be a smooth transition for you."

Although the sergeant behaved in a professional manner, I knew the game they were playing. It was the old standard "good cop, bad cop" routine. This meant that one of them would act like the asshole they both were, and the other would attempt to be civil in order to keep the other bad guy out of your face. The response they expected was that the good guy would get as much information as he could from you while the bad guy looked on in an attempt to pump fear into your heart. I knew the game, and I knew how to deal with that.

"Let's start over," the sergeant said. "Why are you here on death row?"

"If you have any questions concerning my case or my state appeal, I would like my attorney to be present. If you want to know my name, my name is Nanon Williams and I am a black male," I said, continuing to give them the basic information they already knew. The sergeant looked at me and said, "We'll skip the bullshit, Inmate, and I'll ask you a few other questions, fair enough?"

"Go ahead, ask away," I replied with a self-righteous expression.

"Have you ever been involved in a gang?"

If I had been in a gang, it would have been in another state, so I responded, "No. I'm not from a gang and have no intention of being in one." The truth was, I had run with the other teenagers in my neighborhood in Los Angeles, California, and we did get into a lot of trouble, but we didn't consider ourselves a gang. We considered ourselves a big, extended family that looked out for each other. Of course, I was still very young and ignorant then, but I tried to believe I wasn't.

"Here on death row, we have different wings. What we call wings, or cellblocks, are basically different housing assignments," the captain said. "We have a wing for fuck-ups like yourself, and we have wings for other prisoners who don't give us much trouble," he went on explaining the setup of the place.

When he was finished, I realized that I preferred the wing he considered for fuck-ups, because I knew those were the prisoners that stood their ground and didn't allow the system to break them. The other wing, I thought then, was a wing that was filled with kiss-ass prisoners and probably the captain's favorite snitches, and I definitely did not want to be around them. Prison was already a terrible place, and to have other prisoners watching my every move to get in the good graces of the ranking officials wasn't the ideal cellblock for me. But then again, there was no ideal cellblock. Jail was still jail, no matter what they chose to call it.

"Williams, we always send 'new houses' or 'fish,' as the other prisoners will call you, to G-15 or G-13," the sergeant told me. "These are wings that aren't that bad and will allow you to be around prisoners who are less violent, or simply don't want trouble. You'll be going to G-15, Cell 13, on One Row. If you give us problems, I'll personally send you to a wing called J-21, and believe me," he said with a threatening tone, "no one wants to go there."

I want to go home, I thought to myself. I was no badass. I was scared of what death row would be like and deep down, I didn't want to go to the wing called J-21. However, I wouldn't let anyone run over me, whether they were wearing a gray uniform like the prison guards, or white prison garb like the other prisoners wore. I would keep my dignity and stand by my principles, no matter what the consequences, because I didn't have much else. Of course, I had my mother who stood by me unconditionally and believed in me, but she had to go back home to Los Angeles and that was several thousand miles away. I felt so alone in Texas, but being alone in all the darkness would eventually comfort me as nothing else could. It was me, myself and I alone in a new world that was the end of the line for more than a hundred lives taken by execution, and I just wondered if I would join that line sooner, rather than later.

I was escorted to G-15. My eyes widened as we entered the cell through the steel door. Bars were everywhere in sight. There were many, many windows that covered the front wall of all the wings, but the windows had bars crisscrossing them so that there would be no escape.

"No escape, nowhere to hide, and nowhere to run," I said to myself. "Well, this is it." As I got deeper into the wing, I heard noise erupt from everywhere and voices crashed into each other, creating almost a scream of sorts.

"Hey, there's a fish on the wing, y'all!" somebody yelled from Three Row.

"Oh yeah?" another voice called in response. "Is he white or black, or Mexican?"

"I don't know, you fuckhead! I told you, I'm on Three Row," the first voice replied. "Hey Willie, I don't know if he's black or Mexican, but he's a big ole muthafucka!"

"He looks like he lifts weights, so you better shut your ass up before he whips your little bitty ass!" a third voice called jeeringly. "And this guy doesn't look black or Mexican, he looks like he's mixed with a bunch of stuff!"

I knew then, as I listened to their repartee, that this prison, just like any other, thrived on racism. But here in Texas, as all throughout the South, anything with a drop of black blood was called black, and we all lived the same experience.

As I walked down the tier, I saw about eight mirrors stick out from the bars. This was a prisoner's way of seeing who approached along the run. We came to a sudden halt as the guards in front of me stopped abruptly.

"Open Cell 13, Picket Officer!" a little fat guard in front of me yelled. "Well, Williams, here's your new home. I'll be back to give you a mattress, some sheets and a blanket, later on."

This ain't my fuckin' home! I thought. *That fat little bastard has me confused with someone else if he even thinks I'll call this place home!*

I'll never forget just how little that cell looked as the doors opened and those steel bars slammed shut behind me. The cell was about six feet by ten feet, I thought, though I later found out that the cells were nine feet in width by ten feet in length. Everything looked old and rusty and crusted with dirt. In one corner, ants were crawling in and out of a hole on the ceiling. A huge, pregnant cockroach ran for cover as it saw me enter the cell; it ran behind a metal box that was supposed to be a shelf for my property.

Hanging from the wall with steel hooks was a steel slab that was supposed to be a bed. When I sat down on it, I felt the cold run up and down my spine. Right in front of the cell were four or five broken windows, and the wind hit the dingy white walls, only to crash directly into my body full force. Right behind me a yellow light bulb glowed and seemed to produce the only heat in the cell. Needless to say, it could not produce enough heat to do me any good!

Bam! Bam! Bam! I could feel the vibration of the concrete wall. "Hey, man, you new here?"

"Yeah, I guess you could say that," I responded.

"My name is Stumpa. I'm in Cell 14 next door. If you need anything, just holler at me, alright?"

"I appreciate it." His offer was polite and kind. "If you have a towel and some soap, that would be fine."

"M-a-d-i-s-o-n," Stumpa called, "bring your blind, one-eyed ass here so I can speak to you!"

"Yeah, what's up Stumpa?" a short black prisoner who was walking the tier replied as he stopped in front of our cells.

"Say, see if you can go get the guy next door a clean towel so he can clean up that nasty ass cell," Stumpa asked Madison.

"I'll see if I can find one," Madison said, "but next time, you better not call my name so loud, you little muthafucka. You know how these officers around here already watch me like a hawk." He had a deep southern accent like everyone else.

"Fuck you, Madison," Stumpa said. "Just go get the man a towel so he can clean the cell. And if your ass was so worried about those officers, well, yo' black ass shouldn't be workin' for them!"

"Yeah, whatever." Madison shot the finger at Stumpa.

A few minutes later, Madison stopped in front of my cell and said, "Here, Dude. Here's a towel for you, so you can clean your cell. And here's some soap too," his voice rang with sarcasm, "because I know Stumpa didn't give you none!"

"Okay, thank you," I said.

"Hey, man, you don't sound like you're from Texas. Where you from?" Madison asked curiously.

"Nah, I ain't from Texas. I'm from L.A."

"Oh, yeah, what the hell you doin' in Texas?" he smiled. "Never mind, I shouldn't be so nosy. If you need anything, just let me know, okay?"

"Right on," I replied. "I appreciate it, but I don't need anything else."

As I began to clean the cell, I looked at the single piece of property I had, which was the few pictures I had of my mother, little brother and my two sisters. I wondered what they were doing, and if they could move on with their lives without seeing me every day. That worried me. My family was not perfect, but it was perfect for me. We had been through more than most families could ever imagine, but through whatever came, we remained a family and stuck by each other no matter what. Once again, another bad circumstance arrived. But this time, things would be a lot different.

I remembered my mama's last words as I saw her. She said, "Baby boy, I love you. Confess with thy mouth what you wish to happen. Put your faith in God, and know that He is all you need, even when it seems like nothing else will change." She continued to say, "I wish I could have done things differently, but the truth will prevail one day. You'll come back to Mama, Sweetie. Let me know when you get where they're going to send you, and I'll be down to see you as soon as I can. I'll also send you some money," she said tearfully. "I love you, Son."

It hurt so badly. And everyone said it would continue to hurt. Family hurts when you're separated. While I was thinking about my family, I thought about my father. He died when I was ten or eleven years old, under similar circumstances that sent me to death row. He was shot over and over again in a fight over drug territory. Losing him was the hardest thing I ever faced. Until I arrived on death row, nothing else affected me like the last time I laid eyes on my father at his funeral. I don't know if it was the arrival on death row itself, or just the separation from my family that threatened to be permanent that caused me to be so emotional, but I just wanted the pain to go away. I imagined my father lying in his coffin looking pale and yellow with stitched up scars that the mortician tried to correct. He didn't look very presentable with all those scars from bullet wounds, but I loved him and missed him just the same. I couldn't help but wonder if my mama saw me the same way—lying in a coffin, looking pale and yellow. I hoped not, although reality said something different.

Bam! Bam! Bam! The wall vibrated again. "Say, neighbor," Stumpa asked, "where you from?"

I became extremely tired of answering that question, yet I knew it would be asked over and over again.

"I was sent to death row by Harris County, but I'm from Los Angeles."

"So, I guess I'll call you L.A., if that's cool with you?"

"Yeah, that's cool," I answered, not really in the mood to have a conversation with him, although he seemed to be an alright guy.

"Well, L.A., I'll speak to you tomorrow morning at recreation, because I know you'll be up all night scrubbing that cell. If you want a soda or something, ask Madison to bring you some ice."

"I appreciate the offer, but I'm fine for right now," I said. "By the way, is that Madison a trustee or something?"

"Yeah, Madison is on the work capable program, which is a wing that allows death row prisoners to work. Around here, we call them porters, and Madison is a solid dude. So if you ever need anything, ask Madison."

I started to ask Stumpa why exactly they nicknamed him Stumpa, but this was my first day, I didn't want to appear too friendly until I had a chance to scope out the situation, so I just scrubbed the cell and waited for the mattress to arrive. As I was scrubbing the cell, I tried to get used to the fact that I was finally on death row, that there was nowhere else to go, and that I would be at recreation tomorrow with other death row prisoners. I wondered what that would be like and what I should expect. It wasn't as if I would be around regular prisoners. These men would be serial killers, baby killers, rapists, robbers, thieves and every other type of violent criminal one could think of. Under the laws of the state, capital murder was a murder committed during the commission of some other crime, so there was no telling what kind of people I would be surrounded by, but still, what it all boiled down to was that they were all convicted killers—every one of them.

I finished scrubbing the cell, but sleep did not come easily. The little fat guard brought me a mattress and other sleeping necessities, but I still could not put my finger on what exactly bothered me the most. I guess it was a combination of all the pain and the thoughts that bounced back and forth in my mind. I wanted to cry, but I refused to let any weakness creep further into my life. I had to harden myself, strengthen my mind, and my body, just as hard as the steel and concrete that monitored my every movement.

When I awoke the next morning, the wing was extremely quiet, as if I was the only one there. I was mentally exhausted and physically weak from yesterday's beating, but the day was new and how it unfolded would probably be as torturous as the previous one.

A female guard approached my cell, "Turn around and get handcuffed if you want to go to recreation, Inmate! Take off your clothes and place them on the bars."

"Okay, give me a minute."

After placing my clothes on the bars, I stood naked before the female guard, just like the day before. I knew then that this same treatment would occur every day whenever I left my cell.

"Lift up you nuts," she said. And although it was a woman, I still felt degraded because I knew how being nude in front of anyone manipulated the consciousness of one's self and these tactics were often used in war to make the enemies feel weak when they were captured.

"Okay, that's fine," the female guard said after watching me put on my clothes. And when I had them on, she handcuffed me, had my cell opened by the picket officer, and escorted me down the tier to a steel cage. As my clothes hung off me loosely, I realized just how sore I was. While still in thought, a small metal plate slid open in the cage and the handcuffs were removed. And then, as I stood looking on, a metal latch was lifted and the door opened into a dayroom area where other prisoners looked on in my direction.

As I walked out of the dayroom area and exited another open door that led outside, G-15 loomed before me as I looked back into the building from the windows outside. The inside of the building had three long tiers, metal poles that made a walkway, and more steel bars that reminded me of a dungeon. How J-21 could look any worse than the wing I was on was hard to imagine.

I walked around the yard that was no bigger than a basketball court, and there stood many other death row prisoners who stared at me as though sizing me up. I stared back intensely because their gazes felt unkind and disrespectful. I didn't know if the recreation group I was in was filled with gangs or what, but it didn't matter because if anyone stepped toward me in an aggressive manner I would ball my fist up and try to knock their fuckin' head off with all my might. Whether that would be the right decision or not only time would tell, but whatever else it was that I was supposed to expect by being among other convicted killers was a mystery to me.

"L.A.," someone called a few steps behind me. "L.A., it's me, Stumpa, your neighbor," a little short black guy with a bald head said. "Just chill out, man, because you look aggravated as hell!" I didn't respond; I just stared back at him unsure as to how I should take his approach.

"Say man, I don't know what you expect death row to be like, but the other prisoners are alright. Just give everything a chance," Stumpa said.

"I hear what you're saying and all, but I don't know any of you. I've never trusted anybody in my life, so I definitely won't relax if that's what you're trying to get me to do," I said while taking a deep breath.

"Believe me, neighbor, I didn't know you were so damned big when I spoke to you last night; ain't nobody going to fuck with you. To be honest, you look crazier than a muthafucka."

"I appreciate what you're saying," I told him. "But I got a lot on my mind, and I'm sure you understand. How long have you been on death row?"

"I've been locked up a few years, but you've been locked up longer than me. I read on a death row update that you waited three years and one month just to go to trial and that's a long time."

"How in the hell did you find that out?" I was somewhat offended that he knew everything about me—things I didn't tell him.

"Chill out, man! Every time someone is sentenced to death, information about that prisoner circulates everywhere through the court records," Stumpa told me. "In fact, even while you're in trial, information is circulated about you and everyone else, and most of the time it's in the newspaper or on the news as well. Getting the death sentence is big news in Texas."

After listening to his words, I felt somewhat violated that nothing was private anymore. For others to have a chance to judge me by court records of any kind without ever knowing me personally offended me.

"Come on, L.A., let's play some ball or somethin'."

"Not today, alright? Maybe another time." I was still irritated by all he told me. "Say man, my name is Nanon, so you can call me that."

"In prison, people don't call each other by their first name, so I thought I would call you L.A. since you're from Los Angeles. Why does that bother you?"

"It doesn't really bother me. I just see that you seem comfortable calling me that, like you've known me for a few years or something."

"Well, after a while you'll feel that way too. I mean, feeling like you know everybody personally," Stumpa told me. "When you're around people all day long, twenty-four hours a day, you can't help but get to know people well. Just the other day another prisoner, Carl Johnson, was executed. You try to appreciate the time you spend with people here because we know death is right around the corner. After knowing people for a few years, then knowing their exact execution date is hard because you know exactly when their life is going to end, to the exact minute almost." Stumpa's pain could be heard in his voice.

"Hey, what's up Stumpa?" asked a big, tall prisoner. "Why ya'll not playin' no basketball today so I can take your young ass to the hoop?"

"Oh, I was going to show yo fat ass how to play, but I was coming over here to talk to L.A. for a minute, since he got here yesterday. I'll get with you in a minute, ole man."

"My name is Tex," the other prisoner said. "If you ever need any hygiene, food, stamps or anything else until you go to the prison store, just let me know. I'm in eight cell," the other prisoner told me.

"Well, Tex, I appreciate the offer, but I was given some hygiene by the sergeant when I came in."

"I was just asking because the hygiene the state gave you ain't worth shit," Tex said.

"Say, L.A., did they take you to the segregation office and try to give you the third degree about death row, because that's what they always do."

"Yeah, they did take me into some type of office and tell me about J-21. They told me how much of a favor they were doing me by not sending me over there, but jail is jail, you know."

"I hear what you're saying, but you don't wanna go to J-21. A month ago, another prisoner stuck a metal bolt through another prisoner's head and killed him," Tex said. "Then, after the prisoner was dead, this one prisoner dragged his body around the recreation yard until the guards came in with tear gas and restrained him. Death row isn't that bad, but every now and then you have people that flip out and just lash out at anybody. I guess the only thing you should pay attention to is when someone has an execution date, because you never know how they will react days before the execution," Tex advised me. "I have an execution date in two weeks," he finished.

When Tex told me that, I didn't know if he was serious or simply trying to intimidate me, so I told him, "I'm sorry to hear that, but if someone loses his cool, so be it! I can lose my cool just the same!" I replied as though challenging another response.

While I was in the segregation office yesterday being interviewed by the captain and sergeant, I did hear another officer say the Mexican Mafia prison gang stabbed someone the day before, but I thought then they were trying to get me more worried about the environment than I already was.

"Dear God," I said to myself out loud. I knew that when Tex said anyone could go off at any minute, that he spoke the truth. I realized then that I could never be unconscious of where I was, no matter how people treated me. Most men never recover from their first mistake, and I would be damned if I would make a mistake!

I hoped that I wouldn't make any mistakes in the coming years and that I could overcome the obstacles ahead, but only time would tell.

3

FROM DUSK TILL DAWN

THE MONTHS ON DEATH row passed by long and hard. There seemed to be no separation between the nights and days, allowing me no perception of time. I lost track of the days and months as time slowly crept along.

The soft, gentle smile of my mother was fading from my memory. Every time I had a chance to see her, daggers of pain penetrated my heart, making me wish everything would come to an end so the pain would cease. However, the more I thought about my mother, my family, and the few people that cared about me, I realized how blessed I was. So many of the men on death row were alone in the world. They did not have any family at all, and some had no friends, never received a letter and never saw the inside of the visiting room. And yet they still fought for life. They did not necessarily fight to have a life of freedom, but rather to simply experience another day. They fought to hold on to the fairy tale images of life that played out through their minds. I realized that the images prisoners saw in their minds were different for each individual as we each struggled to keep our sanity from slipping away.

For most prisoners, including myself, recreation was the only part of our day we could look forward to, because it was the only thing that was constant. Recreation gave us a chance to go outside and see the gray skies threatened by rain, birds perched on the rusty barbed wire fences, and a chance to play a few games of basketball with each other to break a good sweat. And even when everyone started arguing over who got the ball, or who was cheating, an occasional smile would creep upon our faces, even when sometimes, just sometimes, someone would get pissed off and start a fight. Even those fights were mainly about misplaced frustrations. They never lasted long because someone always interceded.

I realized that G-15 was a wing much different from the other prison wings, because the prisoners on G-15 never protested anything. But I was growing tired of this particular wing and wanted to explore more of death row. I had grown to enjoy the friendships with Stumpa and Tex, but after a few months, I wanted to learn more. I wanted to know the reality of death row, and I realized the images I had of death row weren't necessarily the reality of it. Of course, time would change that.

I learned from a few of the men on G-15 that no matter what we went through, we had to reach deep within ourselves and find something to live for. When I was around Tex and Stumpa, they taught me a few things to do in order to occupy and manage all the time I spent alone in a cell. However, I had one neighbor named James, who was called "Slim" as a nickname. Slim was always up to something constructive, and it amazed me just how much he accomplished. Slim could draw the most imaginative pictures I had ever seen, and with these images he would make cards around Christmastime that he sold in order to make money for his legal defense fund.

Sometimes, late at night, Slim and I stayed up for hours talking about family, school and what we could do in order to make something of ourselves. To me, Slim had already accomplished more than I ever imagined doing myself. His artwork was exhibited in art galleries; he wrote beautiful poetry that was often published; and he found ways to use his talents in order to make money to give to his family. More than anyone else, he was able to achieve the spirit to have a meaningful life where most of our lives held no meaning, except for the suffering and eventual death. Slim's spirit shone from dusk till dawn.

I had never met anyone like Slim. He had the desire to succeed where others failed, even being on death row where it was a challenge just to inhale the air because it reeked of the death that was all around us. What in the hell gave him such courage and the desire to keep accomplishing what he could? He amazed me. His story was one I felt needed to be told and shared to give others the same inspiration that he gave me. He actually changed my life and the way I saw the world.

In trial, prosecutors spoke of the political and moral reasons why the death penalty should be accepted in our society, and I thought about how abolitionists took their stance in the opposite direction. When I thought of the prosecutors and the abolitionists, I thought of Slim and how he dealt with being judged, shunned and persecuted by his peers. If I was to do the same, what would I be but a dumb fool who confessed to seek humanity, philanthropy and progress for the entire human race. Yet, should I deny him companionship and condemn my soul to eternal damnation for not doing what's right toward another human being? I think not.

Since my arrival, I had gradually accepted the darkness of death row. The comfort of giving up was suspended by the torment that lay ahead, but giving up was to admit to being a defeated man. Certainly I had never given up on anything in my life—least of all, on myself. Slim seemed heightened by a new lease on life because he too never once seemed to give up on himself. His torment seemed far greater than my own, so who was I to complain about anything?

"Hey, Slim, you still up over there?" I called quietly, so as not to disturb others.

"Yeah, I'm up over here. I'm just doing a little reading, that's all," came his low response.

"I can't sleep over here, and I guess I just thought about what you said earlier. I want you to know that I admire your courage and your ability to not exact vengeance on the society that punishes you and me. Because of you and your courage, I can't say that I will ever see tomorrow as such a bad thing anymore." I wasn't sure exactly what I meant, I just knew that something had changed within me, and I felt that change coming, and I wanted to share that with him.

"I appreciate that," Slim said. "But whatever you need to get you through the day is already there with you. Whether you choose to make a difference in anyone's life but your own, it is simply your choice to make." My mind registered his words as I felt myself drifting off to sleep.

"I can tell that you're tired, youngster, so take your ass to sleep, and I'll talk to you tomorrow."

The following day Slim was moved to another wing, and Stumpa was on bench warrant back to the county jail for pending appeals. I was lonely without the two people I spent the most time talking with. I read just about everything I could get my hands on. I realized that when most prisoners have no form of education, no family, no hope, or anything else to bind them to this world, death became something to look forward to. In a sense, if a man has nothing, locking him up only tightens the chains that already bind him.

Although I didn't have much education, I had a very loving family, a few friends, my dignity, and my principles, so those were the things that bound me to this world. Whether I chose to enhance any of those things would be up to me. Where I would begin was the question at hand.

One fine morning, the sun radiated the wing with light. I went to recreation to do my normal exercises for the day and to play a little basketball with Tex. While I was outside, I took pleasure in the thoughts that randomly changed my mood in unceasing succession. When recreation was over, I had so much on my mind that I could have been easily provoked by the reality and the future that lay ahead. I began to awaken to the realm of possibility that anything was possible if I just tried to accomplish it.

"Williams, time to rack up!" a guard yelled through the broken window.

As I came toward the steel, revolving door that led to the tier, I was asked to bend down and spread my ass cheeks for inspection. Needless to say, I wasn't going to do that. A decent day quickly turned terrible as the guard entered the dayroom alone, acting big and bad to impress the female guard that stood behind the door.

"I said, bend over and spread 'em!" He placed his hand on my shoulder.

"Punk! You don't put your hands on me!" I slung his hand away. "Bitch! Who do you think I am for you to touch on me?" I said with lethal softness as I walked toward him, and he began backpedaling away from me.

Seeing the fear in the guard's eyes made me realize that I was in trouble because just that quick, the guard scurried out of the dayroom and down the hall. A few minutes later, a new sergeant appeared, one that I had never seen before. He told me he was going to handcuff me and take me down to the ad-seg, or solitary confinement, office to talk to me.

"Turn around, Williams. I'll handcuff you, talk to you for a moment in the office, then bring you back to the wing."

I followed his instructions, not thinking that things would get any worse. He put the handcuffs on me and escorted me off the wing. When we got closer to the office, we suddenly stopped. The steel door we stopped in front of had a wooden plate that read "J-21," and I knew something was wrong.

"What's this?" I asked.

"This is J-21, Inmate. This will be your new home for a while until you straighten up your fuckin' act." He wore a big grin that displayed his pleasure in what he perceived was going to be my suffering. "I'll be on your ass from now on, so see how you like it over here, since you can't comply with regulations." As he spoke, he was shoving me into the entryway of J-21.

4

J-21 THE SIGN OF BLOOD

THE STEEL DOOR ECHOED as it slammed shut. I was on J-21. Voices came from everywhere all at once, and then everything became deathly quiet as the sergeant spoke up. "Quit making all that goddamn noise up in here!" He seemed to believe in the futile thought that everyone would comply.

"Bitch! Fuck you! You don't come up in here running shit!" someone yelled from a cell close to the entrance of the wing.

"Get your punk ass up out of here, or roll my cell open and make me shut up, you muthafuckin' pig!" yelled another voice, then a cluster of voices together hurled threats and insults at the sergeant. After his first command to be quiet, he didn't say anything else.

As we moved deeper in the cellblock, I noticed this wing was definitely a lot different from G-15. There was black, steel, mesh wire covering the bars, enclosing the cells so tightly that no object could be pushed in or out. The tiers seemed very dark because no light could penetrate the windows, yet you could still tell the difference between day and night. There was so much steel, wire and other material blocking off all view, that even the air seemed thin as I took a deep breath to stop my nerves from tingling. I thought G-15 looked like a dungeon, but I was wrong. If there was anything to be called a dungeon, J-21 was definitely that place.

As we went up three flights of metal stairs to Three Row, the other prisoners stood at their cell doors, staring with masked faces, screaming and speaking to one another about me.

"Open Three Row, Two Cell!" the sergeant yelled to the picket officer.

When I was pushed inside, the metal lock on the door slot was opened and the handcuffs were removed. Just as quickly, the slot was closed and locked again. The sergeant appeared to be in a hurry to leave the wing, knowing, I realized, that this wing was going to give him more hell than he cared to deal with or felt he could handle. He knew it was in his own best interest to leave.

I lifted my eyes to gaze around at the new cellblock. A steel bunk hung from the wall and a steel toilet stood in the smallest corner of the cell, reeking with the odor of piss so strong that made me grab my nose. I looked at the dirt colored walls and saw decaying waste splattered on one wall and spoiled food smashed against the other. What happened in this cell was a mystery to me, but I felt sick to my stomach by the smell that invaded my nostrils. When I looked up, a bright light burned with a heat that I found comforting, but the light's reflection made it seem like I wasn't alone in the cell. My shadow followed me back and forth as I paced the small cell, sick to my stomach.

About an hour later my property was brought to me. By this time, I had accumulated quite a few objects that helped occupy my time and make my life somewhat more bearable. I had purchased a typewriter from the prison commissary, a radio, a fan and a few snack items that we were allowed to purchase. I also had quite a few books to read, and I was starting my own personal library of sorts. Whenever my mother sent me money, I spent most of it on writing supplies and books on various subjects to make up for my lack of education. Until the moment of my arrival on J-21, I spent all of my time reading books to understand my environment. Initially, I thought the best way to do that was to study psychology, but I quickly learned that no psychologist could help me understand death row because the environment is unnatural and not within the realm of a psychologist's experience. However, the psychology books did help me to understand myself a little better.

"What's up, my brother?" a voice said below me.

"What did you say?" I asked.

"I said, what's up, my brother? How're you doing?"

"I don't know who you are," I said, immediately defensive, "but I'm not your brother."

"No need to get an attitude. I was just trying to be polite and welcome you to hell. My name is Rogers-el, and I was just introducing myself to you. There's no need to get offended or anything, brother L.A., so chill out." The voice reverberated with sincerity. At that moment, though, I was feeling defensive, and I did not know that the time would come when I would miss the sound of his easygoing voice and the comfort of his friendship.

"How do you know my name, Rogers-el?" I asked.

"I heard about you from a few of the guys I know, and when I saw you pass by my cell, you fit the description. I don't mean to invade your privacy, but why did they move you over to J-21?"

"I don't much feel like talking right now. I have to unpack and try to clean this nasty-ass cell up," I told him. "However, I'll leave it at this, and just say I refused to allow myself to be treated anything less than a human being, so the sergeant decided I should be moved."

"I understand what you mean, but keep your cool, and don't let them get to you. Jail is jail, no matter where you are, so don't let more steel and entrapment make you feel any different than you felt before you came over here."

After all the cleaning and rearranging of my property, I fell asleep and later awoke in complete darkness. The wing had become so dark that I couldn't even see the movement of my own body, but I maneuvered my way around the cell and flicked on the light, grabbing a tablet and pen to write with. With the first stroke of the pen, I wrote my title just as the sun began to rise.

Looking at the Outside, Within

The sun has just risen with bright new rays for another day. On the other hand, it's the walls opening within for a new arrival of the unforgettable.

Can you hear the rooster crow with fresh air breathing through your lungs? On the other hand, can you hear the screams of those who cannot stand the darkness of not knowing what will become of them?

Looking at the outside within is a renewal of the times of joy and love one has shared, only to realize it was all just a fading dream. Instead, looking at the inside is like staring at your own hand, understanding it's never going to change unless something vital happens to it that can tear its structure. And when you stare at it long enough—sometimes a bit too long—you begin to wonder if something does tear its structure, will it heal or ever be the same again, or just continue the same functions? And then you wonder, will every day bring forth the same light until darkness falls again, until death finally brings forth the real light—or those awaiting a final conclusion of life without a beginning? As the cells close, I find myself looking at the outside within again.

When I finished writing, I didn't necessarily understand what I had written, but whatever it was came without thought, guidance or any form of intention. However, whatever it was, it was what I felt like saying at the very moment to whoever would listen, although the only listener was the shadow of my own movement that still reflected from the walls.

"Get ready for recreation!" ordered the same little fat guard who had taken me to G-15 when I first arrived on death row.

"Say, L.A.," Rogers-el called my name for the second time.

"What's on your mind?" I responded.

"Are you going out to recreation this morning, my brother?"

"Yeah, I'm going outside, and I'll speak to you then."

I kept thinking to myself, where does he get this "brother" shit? I wasn't his brother or anyone else's brother in this place, and he was beginning to irritate me a little. So I would definitely tell him at recreation not to call me "brother."

"The only brother I have is not in prison and certainly not on death row, so he better stop with that bullshit!" I whispered softly to myself.

Just before the doors were about to open for recreation someone yelled, "I'm tired! I'm so very tired of this madness, and I'm leaving all you fucking bastards!"

"Shut the fuck up, white boy!" someone else yelled back.

"Ah, you fuckin' nigger! You can kiss my white ass, is what you can do! I'm tired of this shit everyday, and I'm tired of all you charcoal-colored niggers running around here acting like you're all so holier than thou!" the first voice cried out again, and he kept crying out the same words, over and over again, until his screams abruptly halted.

About an hour later, everybody started screaming, "Man down! Man down!" Everyone joined in until the guards came running onto the wing. When they finally came to Three Row, one guard hurried back down the stairs and returned a while later with nurses and a stretcher. The entire wing seemed to be divided with insanity and a cry for attention when a thin line of blood began running down the tier. When the man first began screaming insanely, no guards paid attention to his cries until the sign of blood appeared on the tier. Later on, after an hour or so, guards came and got his seemingly lifeless body and carried him out on a stretcher, in no rush whatsoever to get him to the infirmary.

All morning long the prisoner who had cried out had not been given his psychiatric medication. At last, in insane desperation, he had broken open a shaving razor to cut his wrists. Although the man wasn't dead, as we thought, he passed out because his blood pressure dropped dangerously low. Of course, this would not have happened if guards on duty were doing their job and checked on him when he began screaming.

"Did you see his cell?" the little fat guard laughed as he walked by my cell. "The blood is even on the ceiling and the walls, and it looks like he slung it everywhere, like he enjoyed it. That stupid retard even wrote his name in blood on the wall," the guard spoke excitedly, obviously enjoying the diversion from his usual routine duty shift. I felt as if this sadistic guard must also be in need of psychiatric treatment.

When the guards left, I didn't know what to think. It both saddened and angered me that the guards were so perverted and heartless as to find humor in the morning's tragic events. With conflicting emotions, I allowed that same guard to search me as we went through the usual ritual in order to be let out of our cells for recreation. I stripped, handed the guard my clothing, and then was handcuffed and escorted out of the cell to the recreation yard. With feelings of rage building, I wished like hell I was not handcuffed so I could bust that little fat bastard in his ugly mouth! *Maybe his fat ass would find the sight of his own blood funny, too.*

I left the cell and entered the dayroom of J-21, still uncertain how the rest of the day would unfold. Here I was in the worst place prison had to offer—death row—and the worst wing that the prison claimed they had on death row. To be truthful, I had the feeling that the many months changed me and made me so numb inside that perhaps my own sanity was slipping away. No longer was I the fearful and distraught young boy who was afraid of prison's changing events and moods. I was a young man with so many conflicting emotions bottled up inside me that at any moment I could explode on anyone for the slightest mishap, whether it was a guard or a fellow prisoner. Sometimes I couldn't tell the difference between guards and prisoners because there were so many prisoners snitching on each other that I began to see many in the same light. "Fuck 'em!" I would say. As long as everybody left me alone and stayed out of my face, I didn't anticipate any problems. But I knew then only a foolish man would believe that. I was on death row, not some boys' camp.

As the afternoon progressed, I exited the dayroom and went outside to the recreation yard. This yard looked very different from the yard on G-15. It ran down in a slope, and in the very back were two enclosed structures where two prisoners paced back and forth. They were isolated from the rest of us for reasons unknown to me, but they didn't appear to be paying attention to the rest of us anyway. They were in their own little world.

The rest of the prison yard seemed to fill up with other prisoners and most of them were black, with two Hispanics that stood still with their backs against the wall.

"What's up, young blood?" an older prisoner asked, walking towards me. "My name is Da'Oud."

"My name is L.A.," I replied.

"Okay, young blood, I heard about you. It's good to meet you. We're going to play a little basketball, if you want to join in. Do you want to play?"

"Nah, I'm cool. Thanks for asking though, maybe I'll play tomorrow or something."

"Come on and play, L.A." A little short black man with braided hair approached us. "I know you're new over here and want to sit back and peep the scenery out, but we all cool over here. My name is Rogers-el, the one who spoke to you over the run last night and this morning. Tex told me about you, so you must be a solid dude."

"I don't feel like playing," I frowned. "But I might get down with y'all tomorrow."

"That shit still on your mind that happened this morning, huh?" Rogers-el said quietly.

"Hell, yeah, it's on my mind! It seems like nobody else seems to give a damn!"

"It's not that, my brother," Rogers-el said, "it's just so common around here to see chaos, that we do what we can to not allow it to consume us."

"I told you last night that I'm not yo' damn brother, so quit calling me brother. We're not related!"

"I hear what you sayin,' young blood," Da'Oud said, "but we're both Moors, and it is our belief that we are all brothers under the eyes of God, and as your people, I try to recognize that, as does brother Rogers-el."

"What the fuck is a Moor?" I asked.

"It would take a long time to explain this all to you, but I'll send you a book and let you read up on it, if you want to know," Da'Oud offered.

"I'd like that. Send me the book when we get back inside, if you don't mind."

"You see, my brother," Rogers-el said, "a Moor is someone of African descent, who ruled parts of the Peninsula from the eighth century until 1842 AD. We believe we are descendants of Moors, and another way you can look at it is that we believe in Allah."

"I don't know what no Allah is. What the fuck is Allah?" I asked.

"Allah is the supreme being—God," Da'Oud told me. "When someone has El or Bey attached to their last name, that means they are a Moor. My last name is Adanandus-El, but my other chosen name is Da'Oud. We are like Muslims in many respects."

"I don't mean to disrespect y'all or nothing, but I believe in God not Allah. I believe in Jesus, and I am a Christian. So I don't know if that forbids you from talking to me or not, but keep that shit to yourselves."

Grinning broadly, Da'Oud said, "We respect what you believe in, young blood. We just ask that you do the same and not get offended when we call you brother." Rogers-el started laughing.

"It's cool, L.A., we all need a spiritual side of us, and it's good to know you have one too," Rogers-el added. "Believe it or not, you're the only black Christian on this wing, because most of the brothers on J-21 are Muslims, or just don't believe in God at all."

"And L.A.," Da'Oud said, "don't let your environment manipulate you because you give them more power over you. What happened this morning is nothing new. I've seen men get raped until blood runs down their legs. I've seen men get killed on this very same yard, and I've seen guards that won't help any prisoner for whatever reasons unless they see the sign of blood first. Just continue believing that tomorrow is worth seeing, no matter what comes, and take it one day at a time."

"Now, I'm going to play some basketball," Rogers-el told me. "I'll holler at you tomorrow, L.A."

"Yeah, you be cool, young blood, and I'll send you that book later on," Da'Oud said in parting.

My cell door opened, and once again I entered the tiny cubicle as the door slammed shut, punishing the steel frame.

As time went by, the days seemed all alike. I sat up in my cell reading for hours at a time until I fell asleep with books lying on my chest. They hit the floor whenever I got up.

One of my favorite subjects became philosophy and after reading about such philosophers as Plato, Aristotle, Descartes, Homer, Nostradamus, Marcus Aurelius, Miyamoto Musashi and so many others, it seemed as though my entire reality and how I saw it changed. I guess I began to see reality for what it was, nothing more, and that made me both strive to change it and to further extend my studies to new heights. I learned that reality was sometimes seen through one's imagination, and everyone's imagination is different, as is his perception of reality.

I met many other prisoners on J-21 whom I found had some type of principles and moral values that many of the prisoners on G-15 lacked. I found a few prisoners such as Da'Oud and Rogers-el who became good friends, and each friendship grew to be different and unique in its own way. Rogers-el and I shared books, poetry and discussed a newsletter called *The Williams Report* that I began sending out every sixty days. He gave me advice on subject content that people might be interested in reading about, and I wrote about the reality of death row, particularly the realities of J-21.

My friendship with Da'Oud was unlike any other. In a sense, Da'Oud was like a father figure to me. He was the advice-giver and seemed to always be concerned with what was going on in the other young prisoners' minds. He seemed to pay special attention to me because I was the youngest by far. In fact, the next youngest prisoner was four years older than me. "Don't let them pigs dictate you, young blood," he always told me. And the more he said it, the more I tried not to let the system that confined me dictate what I should or should not do or become. I began to see it was a challenge to accomplish things that I wasn't supposed to or that weren't expected of me.

Sometimes, late at night before I went to sleep, and in the morning when I woke, I would begin my prayers with, "Dear God, thank you for another day and thank you for keeping my family strong as we spend each day separated and each day loving each other no matter what arises. I ask that you continue to keep us strong, and guide us with the grace of God that has kept us what we are today—a family." And when I finished my prayers, I wrote in my journal about the day's events, or sometimes about the special memories that kept me strong.

However, sometimes I sat on my bunk and asked God why I had to come to death row when I didn't belong here. But then, the only response I got was that no one belonged on death row, whether they were guilty or innocent. The death penalty is quite simply a moral wrong, among many other kinds of wrong. It didn't really matter one way or the other, no one should be condemned by the state to die. And sometimes, just sometimes, I actually thought I was in hell. Somewhere along the way, I fucked up and God was punishing me. But then, how could hell be filled with so many men who thrived on a spirit that strengthened us all? That was a wonder to me. "Maybe I have a purpose," I would say to myself. But to find that purpose would take more pain, blood and sorrow and that would make each experience leave a trail of tears too long to dwell upon. But if I didn't dwell upon them, or think about them, I couldn't have written about them. The writing helped soothe the pain of not knowing what would happen next.

4

MY TWENTY-SECOND BIRTHDAY

THE DAY I TURNED twenty-two years old was a Friday. The day was August 2, 1996, and it was a typical, blistering hot summer day on death row in Ellis One Unit prison in Huntsville, Texas. The years I spent on death row consumed me so completely that I couldn't separate who I was from anyone else. I didn't perceive myself simply as another prisoner who didn't give a damn about the system. I saw myself as a prisoner who became obsessed with hating the system. I felt as though the system was controlled by some God-like entity who had no one to answer to for its wrongs. Little did I know that in just a few short weeks, I would be living in solitary confinement wondering if anything would ever again be the same for me.

Having been incarcerated since the age of seventeen, by the time I turned twenty-two I had become prison. The walls, the steel and the razor wire that surrounded me were barriers that restricted my body physically, but the real barriers restricting my mind were the ones I created within myself.

After the first few years, I decided not to continue participating in the regular prison events, instead I chose to make the biggest impression I could within myself in order to show that I was still human and that I was not becoming the beast I was beginning to feel like. By this time, I thought that I had seen it all. I saw men fight to prove their dominance over one another. I saw prisoners kill each other because it made them feel stronger than they really were. I saw men raped savagely because someone sought a momentary thrill to compensate for their lack of manhood. I saw so many acts of violence that I wondered if there really was a hell after death, it must certainly be here, in this prison.

At the time, the worst of death row's cellblocks was J-21. It was considered to be the meanest and most secure cellblock that existed in the entire Texas prison system. Upon entering the doorway, the image is immediately that of a dark dungeon with screams that emanate and echo resoundingly, penetrating the quietest corners of the strongest minds. J-21 is considered the end of the road for anyone who enters. Living in J-21 can be likened to graduating and obtaining the highest degree possible; only the degree you receive in J-21 will either completely destroy who you are, or it will elevate you to a new realm among the state's alleged worst killers. I am not referring to the murderers of human life necessarily, but rather the murderers of hopes and dreams.

Everything in J-21 was steel—chain link fences, mesh wire and steel poles that were not meant to be broken. Every cell was made like three cells within one, for maximum security. Each cell was an individual fortress. When I entered J-21 for the first time, it struck me that this place wasn't my home and never would be.

By the time I entered J-21, I was known throughout the prison because I was so young and because I got into so many altercations with prisoners and guards alike. I was quick-tempered, foolish and just plain didn't give a damn. I didn't consider myself to be an unrighteous person, but I was foolish enough to lay all my cards on the table so that everyone knew where I stood. On J-21, I was the youngest prisoner in the cellblock, and I learned quickly not to let my age bar me from being a convict, as opposed to an inmate. I became everyone's little brother because everyone wanted to give me advice. So I listened, learned and excelled in "prison academics"—those prison life lessons that throw violence in the air like the wave of a wand.

To survive on death row requires an indomitable will. To remain sane in J-21 required monumental inner strength. The more time I spent there, the more I realized that the majority of prisoners around me were allowing their sanity to slip out of control. The living conditions got so bad at one point that prisoners would just scream back and forth at each other, cursing and going outright mad. I sometimes sat back and thought to myself, *What the hell am I doing here? I don't belong here at all!* But then as I questioned myself over and over again, I realized that no human being deserved to be in such a God-forsaken place.

Often, as the steel door slammed behind me, I would just stand there, in a cage, trying to figure out new ways to spend my time constructively in order to escape the chaos. No matter how much I tried, nothing worked. I realized that I had to come to understand the chaos and feel the depths of it in order to remain unscathed and put it behind me. I didn't know if that was possible, but I knew that either I must accept the chaos, understand it and destroy it within myself, or the chaos would destroy me.

By the time I reached my twenty-second birthday, J-21 had stripped away everything from me that I ever possessed, except for my dignity and life principles. Although at times I doubted whether those things were worth salvaging at all, they remained.

Whenever recreation time came around, each row would recreate together, so there were about twelve prisoners on a regular basis who went outside at a time. The ones who did not go out were either too scared, too crazy or just too tired of the same old daily routine. I went out to exercise by doing push-ups, pull-ups, sit-ups and various other exercises to release all the pent-up energy I had. I grew much bigger than I anticipated. As my physical body grew, so did my anger. I was such a bitter young man that I was like a time bomb, waiting to explode. The only fear I had was the fear of what I might become.

On one occasion I was involved in a fight with another prisoner who disrespected me. As a brief verbal confrontation took place, he took a swing at me and I completely lost control of myself as never before. I lost so much control that to this day I can't really remember what happened. All I can remember was steadily punching him over and over again until I forgot what I was doing. All the rage and frustration that built up in me over the years took control so that it scared me. I felt that this system had changed me into someone else. Twenty guards ran into the recreation yard, but not one touched me. One guard who I was acquainted with, begged me to submit to handcuffs, but I just stood there staring at them all. After several long, tense moments, I allowed myself to be handcuffed. As I was escorted down the hallway, I was pushed to the ground and brutally kicked over and over again. The only thing I could do was lie there, looking up at the guards who inflicted this pain on me, and imagine what I would do to them if I got the chance.

After being dragged to solitary, I was left on the floor, still handcuffed and shackled, in a cell for more than forty-eight hours. By this time, the handcuffs became so tight that I could not feel any circulation in my hands. Every time I moved, the cuffs tightened a little more, until I was in such intense pain that I almost lost consciousness. The shackles on my feet were tight and uncomfortable too, but it was my hands and wrist that were so achingly painful.

Lying on my back on the concrete floor, I opened my eyes to see a nurse standing outside the cell door, watching me. She called, "Inmate, are you alright?" I wanted so very much to say, "Bitch, do I look alright?" But I didn't. I just laid there finding it impossible to believe that she could even ask such an obviously stupid question. With all the blood soaking my shirt, it was quite obvious that I was not "alright." When I refused to respond, she simply walked away.

Later that day a sergeant arrived at my cell door and told me to move close enough to the slot in the door to allow him to remove the handcuffs. I saw no way to get to the cell slot without help. "Williams, just crawl over here close to the bars, and I'll take the handcuffs off," he said.

I looked up at him. "No. I'm not crawling over there or anywhere else. Anyway, how do you expect me to move with shackles on my feet and my hands cuffed behind my back?" He then opened the door and removed the shackles and the handcuffs.

After a few months in solitary, I began to realize how many scars I now had on my body. I wondered if there were scars forming on my mind. I thought about what my life was before prison, and I began thinking about my family. If my mother would see me in such a place, I knew how deeply it would hurt her. I never told her what death row was really like. I never told her about the brutality and abuse—mental and physical—that are ordinary, daily occurrences here. I never told her how a simple act of protecting one's dignity and humanity could add up to months in solitary confinement.

Instead, I embraced the solitude and learned from it. I began to read more than ever and to educate myself. I knew I should never have been convicted and sent to death row in the first place, but fighting for physical freedom was a farfetched idea. Instead, I wanted to find a freedom of mind and to try to reach some of the potential I believed that I had. I was always a quick learner; I wanted to learn who I really was. I wanted to devote my time to learning about my strengths and weaknesses, to understand them, and to find out what I could make of myself.

I remained in solitary a very long time before returning to J-21. I cleared my visiting list, further isolating myself from the outside world, gave my property away and obtained as many books as possible. I read everything from fiction to philosophy, metaphysics to astrology and everything else I could get my hands on. The more I read, the more knowledge I gained from my experiences.

DECEMBER 10, 1996 WAS a particularly brutal day on J-21. I had only been back for a short time. That day brought such a raw experience that mere words cannot describe it.

I was scheduled to be reviewed by the Unit Classification Committee. They questioned me about the previous night when several prison guards antagonized and provoked a mentally retarded prisoner. The guards were spitting on the prisoner, calling him "nigger" and physically assaulting him for their own entertainment, simply because they were bored. Two other prisoners and I refused to sit quietly and accept such behavior by the guards, so we yelled and requested that ranking officials remove the guards who were harassing this prisoner on J-21. These were cowardly guards who would not harass a prisoner capable of fighting back, yet they took ungodly pleasure in tormenting and brutalizing the mentally ill prisoners who were incapable of defending themselves. Many other prisoners, tired of such inhumane cruelty, set fires, flooded their cells, screamed and used what means they possessed to protest the abuse.

The following day I sat handcuffed before the Unit Classification Committee. They questioned me about an alleged fight between myself and another prisoner.

This was the ostensible reason that was given to me for bringing me before the committee, but I knew the real reason. No fight took place between me and anyone else; this bogus charge justified my presence before them in order to question me about the incident the previous night.

"Mr. Williams, today is Tuesday, December 10, 1996," said the warden over death row. "You are here regarding an alleged fight with another prisoner. Could you please tell us about this incident?"

Looking confused, I responded, "What alleged fight? I have no knowledge of any fight."

"Well, let's forget about the fight for right now," he said, briskly pushing aside their spurious reasons for bringing me there. "What was your role in last night's disturbance on J-21?"

Again I looked confused. "I have no knowledge of what you're referring to, except of course, the abuse of a prisoner by the guards that took place last night and their assault on another prisoner."

They steadily shot probing questions to me about other prisoners rather than about the guards, so I ignored them completely. After refusing to participate in their little power games, I requested to be taken back to my cell. Before taking me back to the cellblock, another question was hurled at me about an alleged threat by me to inflict harm upon a guard. I refused the question and was harshly rebuked, but I simply smiled at their attempts to provoke me. Since their provocation did not work, I was escorted back to the cellblock.

A few hours later, another guard told me to pack up all my property because I was being escorted to a management cell. A management cell sits at the end of the run and has a solid steel door outside the prison bars that totally encloses the prisoner in the cell, sealing him in and taking away any view and all light. A management cell is often used for prisoners who receive many disciplinary cases, or more often than not, it is a cell used by the prison administration system to exercise power over a prisoner. I had been in this cell more times than I could remember, so this was nothing new. However, this time, I received no disciplinary cases that warranted me being taken to the management cell, and for that reason, I refused to go. When I asked the guard why I was to be taken there, he said he was just doing what he was told, that it was the warden's decision.

Another sergeant appeared in front of my cell and gave me a direct order to exit the cell handcuffed. I then asked him, "Why am I being moved to a management cell? I have no pending disciplinary cases and to do so would be against prison guidelines," he replied, "You'll bring your ass out here, or you can believe I'll drag your ass out!" I replied, "You're too much of a coward to do it yourself, punk!"

By that time, I could see through what they were doing, so I played it smart. I told them that if I had a disciplinary case, or if I was given a reason why I was being moved to a management cell, I would exit the cell peacefully.

A short while later, the warden came to the cellblock. Wardens rarely enter J-21, and so this rare visit rendered the entire cellblock unnaturally still and quiet as everyone waited to hear what the warden had to say.

"You see, Mr. Williams, a mistake has been made." He spoke with an oily smirk on his face. "You are not being taken back to a management cell. You are being taken to solitary, so pack up your shit!"

Before I could respond, a video camera was shoved in my face, and I was told again to exit the cell.

"Is there a reason why I'm being taken to solitary?" I asked. "Because I know I haven't done anything against the rules and regulations."

As I was speaking, the warden sprayed me with pepper spray, directly into my eyes and mouth. I could not breathe or see, so I panicked until I could regain control of my respiration. I withstood the assault as he continued to spray the pepper gas, but then explosive tear gas packets began exploding in my cell, and I lost consciousness. This went on, over and over, for more than an hour. I thought I was going to die as I continued to drift in and out of consciousness. I forgot where I was, but after a while I realized what was happening. I tried to stand but couldn't, and in my efforts to do so, I was sprayed again.

When the cell opened, I made an attempt to exit the gas-filled cell, but an extraction team entered. An extraction team normally consists of five or more guards, each dressed in vest, shield, helmet and boots and carrying a baton. As the extraction team entered, I was hit with vicious blows to my head and abdomen. I fought back as best I could and gave them hell all the way through. I was eventually dragged to the ground and shackled. The guards kept yelling, "Inmate, quit resisting!" But I wasn't resisting anymore because I was being beaten into unconsciousness again.

I awoke with pain searing through the left side of my head from being repeatedly kicked with their heavy boots, while I was still restrained. My head was slammed against the concrete floor, and batons steadily pounded my ribs and back. When I was dragged down the tier by the extraction team, a close friend of mine, Emerson Rudd, known as the Young Lion, dashed the warden with scalding hot water, causing him to scream. I was later told that the warden was still wearing that oily smirk on his face as I was being dragged down the hall, until Rudd wiped it off of his face. I was deeply touched by this act of courage to help a fellow prisoner and by his protest of such inhumane conditions. However, I feared for Rudd's safety as well.

I was dragged to the end of the tier and thrown head first down two flights of stairs (that was standard practice)—a puddle of my blood quickly formed around me. I had cuts everywhere, and it felt as if my head was split open. I was then put onto a stretcher and carted down the hall toward solitary. I felt someone squirting liquid into my eyes so I could see, but soon after blood rushed over my face again, obscuring my vision. Of course, I didn't know all of this at the time, as I drifted in and out of consciousness, I was told later by a sympathetic guard who witnessed the whole act of violence but was not brave enough to intervene and thereby lose his job.

I was rolled into solitary on a stretcher, then pulled to my feet and pushed into the shower to wash off the gas. Scalding hot water was turned on, hitting me directly in the face. I jumped back so quickly that I could feel the shackles tear into my flesh, cutting my ankles. I banged on the bars loudly to indicate to one of the guards that the water was too hot (as if they didn't already know), and they turned it to completely cold water. After the water ran on me for a few minutes, I was taken to the last cell in solitary, and the shackles were removed. Then I had to move toward the slot in the door so they could take off the handcuffs. They told me to remove my wet clothes but I refused, so they took photos of my face. After they left my cell door, I took off the wet clothing.

It was very, very cold. I couldn't see anything at all because there was still pepper gas and tear gas in my eyes. So I was temporarily without sight, freezing, sitting naked on the steel bunk. As I surveyed the parts of my body that I could see, I realized that I had deep cuts around my ankles from the shackles and my left wrist had a cut so deep that it needed stitches. Every time I blinked, blood dripped from my left eye. At first I thought I might have had a cut under it, but I later learned that a few blood vessels were broken in my eye because of the tear gas, and it permanently destroyed much of my vision. I also saw bruises covering my rib cage, and I knew from the terrible pain as I breathed, that some ribs were broken. At that time, I could not say I had ever been battered so badly, but I was alive, and that is what mattered.

Shortly after that, Rudd was brought to solitary. He was also gassed, beaten and placed at the opposite end of the solitary cellblock to keep us separated. He said they kicked my ass bad, and they also tried to smash his ass, but he said he was fine. Just like me, his eyes hurt very badly, but we would survive.

For the next two days, we suffered from the cold. The weather was freezing, and we had no blankets, sheets, towels or anything else to cover our bodies and ward off the cold. We both caught colds and were ill, but our spirits remained strong. The warden decided to further punish us by placing us on food loaf for an extended period of time. Food loaf is a combination of all the leftover foods from the kitchen, blended together and then baked into a loaf. After baking, it is frozen for a few days and then served to us. Of course we did not eat it, but after the seventh day, we were both very, very hungry. Neither of us ate pork, each for our own reasons, but we were finally forced by deep hunger to ask a solitary trusty to sneak us in some sausages. At first, he was too scared to help us, but we finally convinced him to help us with a promise to pay him if he did so. At last we were able to eat. We didn't know how long we would be on food loaf, so we ate sparingly. Eventually, we were served regular trays again. We sometimes had to examine our food very carefully because there was often sedatives placed in our food to make us tired and drowsy—a common practice on Texas death row.

Rudd and I saw each other a week later through the single-man recreation yard, and the first thing he said was, "Damn, your face is fucked up!" He said that the tear gas and pepper spray had peeled a lot of the skin from my face and that my left eye was blood shot. I already knew this, so I promptly let him know that he didn't look much like a movie star either. This wasn't at all funny, of course, but it was our way of shedding a little humor over our terrible ordeal.

After filing grievances and other paperwork, Internal Affairs reviewed the video and found the warden in violation of the use of force policy. They said that they would continue to investigate, but when I had my attorney request to see the video, it was mysteriously missing, although Internal Affairs did acknowledge reviewing the tape before it "disappeared."

In solitary, Rudd and I talked all day and all night long. By sharing experiences with each other, we became close and learned from each other. In a sense, we drew strength from one another, and that was something we both needed. Sometimes we sang all the latest songs loudly over the tier and everyone else in solitary would join in. We learned how to have some fun. In addition to fun, we were learning to enjoy the feeling of solidarity, something that the prison system works constantly to destroy. The warden did not want us experiencing solidarity, and he wanted to separate Rudd and I. They moved Rudd back to J-21 first and I stayed in solitary a while longer.

However, our spirits were more alive than ever before. That's when I realized that I am a survivor. I felt that I had been through some of the worst conditions that death row had to offer, but if I had survived this mentally, not much else could take my spirit away.

Thirty-seven men were executed in 1997, and I experienced many different emotions. For the longest time I was a stranger to myself, but eventually the stranger went away. There is no greater satisfaction than knowing how strong the human spirit can be in spite of the constant knowledge of imminent death. It is hard to exist inside prison and to live amid constant cruelty and degradation. I no longer felt the desperate hunger to *feel* human again; I knew beyond any doubt that I *am* human. Knowing I am human is what allowed me to go in my mind beyond the steel that confined me, into a new world where hope is everything and defeat is simply giving up. I was determined to never give up.

Over time I found a kind of freedom within myself that no one could take away from me. There was so much I didn't know, but I found myself looking forward to learning. I also found myself looking forward to experiencing whatever the future held, and hoping that I would one day find someone to share it with. I shied away from people for so long because of the distrust inherent to the prison system. I wanted to regain all of what was taken away from me, and gain something more as well. I no longer wanted to be a loner, destroyed by circumstances. I wanted to experience the joy of life all over again and everything that comes with it. The pain, the hurt, the sadness, and the love that I've evaded changed me, but these things made me who I am—a survivor.

5

STAND BY ME

O NE DAY I BECAME aware of something that I never knew before, and that something was the stench of death. I knew what it was like to lose someone special because I witnessed my father's violent and brutal death when I was a child, and yet nothing can prepare a person for an on-going life of witnessing the planned death and deliberate demise of hundreds of human beings.

In the blackness of my cell, I thought about the warlike experiences that I and a few of the other prisoners experienced. The experiences of blood, sweat and tears created bonds between us that would link us together forever, throughout our lives, no matter where we lived or died.

There were times when more than eight of us guys held the recreation yard hostage because some guard became obstinate and created a problem with one of us, and in return, we created a problem that would lock down the entire prison.

Things were changing in the prison, and the institution was promoting racism much more boldly and vigorously than they had before. This time they went a little too far.

FOR YEARS EACH WING had been comprised of three recreation groups that were a reasonable mixture of races, but the diversity of recreation changed when the captain of death row decided to separate the prison by racially segregating recreation. On J-Wing there were separate recreation groups that consisted of only Hispanics, only whites and only blacks. Of course, by doing this, it perpetuated any racism that existed within the prisoners and prevented any bonding that might promote cohesion amongst the guys when conflict occurred between the prisoners and guards. Many prisoners were fooled into believing that the separation was a good thing and that it was best to be placed among one's own race. Over the tiers, racial slurs such as "nigger," "wetback" and "white trash" became common words of degradation toward each other, often leading to fights with words among the races becoming a kind of mock warfare. Occasionally someone became so angry they taped metal pieces together and made a spear to stab another prisoner through the fence when he was handcuffed and escorted down the tier. When someone was handcuffed, they were unable to defend themselves and body parts were left wide open for the blow of the spear. Sometimes people would get stuck in the back, neck, arms, head and even their genitals from the blows that left them curled up in a knot while the guards ran away in fear. *Those coward sons-of-a bitches*, I often thought to myself. However, it wasn't only fear that made them run away, they seemed to enjoy deliberately leaving a bound prisoner vulnerable to attack.

The prison was filled with Neo-Nazi prison guards. Most of them were born and bred within a few miles of Huntsville, the prison capital of the state, where racism was rampant and where cross burnings and lynchings were once common practices. Sometimes you could overhear the older guards talking about such things to some of the whites in the recreation groups. Their conversations were rife with racist language, such as "nigger this," and "nigger that," or "wetback this" and "wetback that." Those guards commonly gave the white recreation group extra time and other privileges that blacks and Hispanics did not receive. When the white groups got extra time, the same amount of time was taken from the Hispanics' or blacks' recreation in order to make up the difference.

After weeks of complaining, several Hispanic prisoners attacked a guard on the wing because the guard chose to take away an extra hour of their recreation time. They found a way to get through the locked door when the guard wasn't paying attention. By many accounts, an outsider would look at this scenario and agree that these prisoners were wrong for taking such an action, but I understood it. Forced to stay in a cell twenty-three or more hours a day under terrible conditions, recreation is the only part of the day some prisoners had to look forward to. Simply because a guard chose to take away time to satisfy a cruel streak in himself or herself, and give it to another member of his own race, does not make it right. But that was only the beginning. Shit was about to really hit the fan a few days later.

IT WAS LATE AFTERNOON. The constant noise died down on the cellblock as two white guards kicked a black prisoner with no provocation at all. Through the windows, our recreation group looked on as those guards not only kicked the small black man down the stairs, but continued to kick him and stomp him until blood was smeared all over his white, prison-issued clothing. Such a beating was not an uncommon sight, nor was the degrading racist language. "You dumb-ass nigger!" the guard screamed as he kicked the prisoner over and over. "How does this feel, huh?" He kicked the man swiftly in the groin.

I was across the yard from the windows when this happened. I immediately started tightening my shoestrings on my boots. Knowing that the guys on J-21 wouldn't accept this, I realized that everyone would refuse to go inside again when our time was up. *Fuck that!* I thought. *We'll do whatever today! Whatever it takes to show these pigs we won't continue to accept their abuse!*

"Williams!" the guard yelled as he rolled the revolving door. "It's time to rack up. Recreation is over, so turn around, back up to the bars and be handcuffed!"

"I ain't gonna rack up today. You might want to call *me* a nigger and kick me down three flights of stairs for nothing," I told him, my voice rippling with sarcasm. "Fuck you, pig! If you want me, come and get me!"

"Won't be long now," Rogers-el said. "They'll be back, but ain't none of us racking it up today. They shouldn't have assaulted that young brother and kicked him until he was unconscious. I think he broke his arm when he flew down those stairs."

"You mean, when he was thrown down the flights of stairs," Da'Oud said.

"You know what the hell I mean!" Rogers-el was quivering with fury.

I waited for the gates to open as the guard came back with help, but they didn't say anything. They just stood there waiting for reinforcements. When the captain arrived, he observed the group for a few minutes then spoke. "Okay, who in the fuck is refusing to rack up? Hey you!" he pointed at Rogers-el. "Bring your fuckin' ass over here to be handcuffed right now!"

"My name ain't "Fuckin' ass. My name is Rogers-el," he said. "And I ain't gonna rack up so you can beat my ass too!"

"Put it this way, Inmate, someone better bring his ass up here and get handcuffed right now, or I'll come in there and drag all of you out!"

"Well, Bitch, bring it on muthafucka," another prisoner said, then another and another. "Y'all ain't had no business beating that little guy down like that when he was handcuffed and defenseless."

"Have it your own way, you bunch of dumb-ass nig—" The captain stopped short of completing that ugly racist word. "I'll be back," he said as he turned to leave the wing.

We already knew the racist guards despised black people but enough was enough. It was our time to fight back as a group and not let them punish us individually for retaining our dignity as best we could under the circumstances. As we continued to talk and pump each other up, J-21 loomed through the windows like the iron building would surely collapse on us all for bucking the system.

"Alright," the warden said as he came close to the bars, "if you're coming out, do it now. I'm about to throw so much tear gas on that yard, you'll be lucky to ever breathe again."

The yard was deadly silent. Some of us took off our t-shirts and wrapped them around our faces before the gas was sprayed on us. We all had our fears, of course, but we felt that if we made a stand against them, this would remain in their minds and would let the guards know that we were not going to accept the racism and abuse that was perpetrated against us. Most of us had already been to solitary confinement at least once, some of us more than once, and suffered unimaginable violations of human rights, but this was the only time, and probably would be the last time, that many of us would stand together against the system's brutality. Three of the nine men in this group had execution dates within a few weeks. We were all close to a breaking point.

"First shot firing!" the warden said as a canister flew on to the yard, spraying gas everywhere as it spun in circles.

Before it stopped spinning, one of the men grabbed the canister with his t-shirt and threw it as hard as he could back toward the gate. Although most of the guards had on gas masks, a few didn't, and they began choking and running off the wing. The other prisoners inside were looking out the windows at us; we could hear their laughter, shouts and cheers erupting. Nothing humorous was taking place. Someone would probably die today or get seriously hurt. They cheered and laughed and shouted because the cruel, cowardly guards were on the receiving end of their own actions for a change.

"Fire, fire, fire!" the warden shouted as more canisters flew from three or four places at once. No one tried to grab any canisters this time because gas circled the entire yard now and a fog made us all blind, shortened our breathing, and caused a few of the men to collapse on the concrete. Minutes later, an extraction team of thirty or more guards rushed into the recreation yard with batons raised and began hitting prisoners, even those who were already unconscious and did not require repression.

I laid down in the corner of the yard. Before the first blow struck me, I got up and tackled the guard that rushed toward me. That was a big mistake. More guards began hitting me with batons until I could feel my own mouth fill with blood and a part crease the top of my head. I lost consciousness.

I resumed consciousness later as I lay strapped to a stretcher while a nurse sewed stitches in my head and later escorted most of us to solitary. A few of us were left handcuffed in solitary for more than twenty-four hours. We laid on our stomachs and talked to one another from cell to cell to take our minds off the pain that shot through our bodies. *This is it,* I thought, feeling my wrist go completely numb and the shackles tearing into my ankles, causing small cuts to leak blood. *These damned pigs are going to let us die here.*

"Get your fuckin' ass up and wiggle over here to the bars, so I can remove the handcuffs," said the same little fat guard I had seen off and on since coming to death row was at the cell door.

I started to curse him, but with the pain throbbing through my body, I bit my tongue and just wiggled over to the bars so he could remove the cuffs. When everything was removed, I asked the guard, "You like this, don't you?" He smiled and walked away.

During a long stay in solitary, many of us went through several other horrifying experiences. I was placed in single-man recreation for three years. Single-man recreation is a fifteen-foot cage that separates a person from other prisoners. Being alone meant that I no longer had the chance to talk with Da'Oud or Rogers-el. I often wondered if perhaps isolating and not getting close to others was the safe thing to do.

Most of the time, after I finished doing my push-ups, pull-ups, sit-ups and other exercises, I spent time reading, more time than I ever had before, and eventually I began to write. The only people I showed my writings to were Rogers-el and Da'Oud, but I didn't get to see them very often. By this time, I was forced to live in what is referred to as a management cell, which had steel reinforced sheets completely covering the entirety of the cell. It was sound proof, preventing me from talking to other prisoners over the tier.

At first it was difficult to cope with the solitude, but later—much later—I learned to embrace the solitude and allowed it to explore the depths of my mind. In a sense, it was as though I was studying all I had been through in my life and wondering what I could have done differently to achieve a different outcome to many situations. However, I also could not help but wonder if I was slowing going insane. After all, I watched many of the men talk to themselves for hours at a time, smear feces on their bodies, cut themselves, beat on themselves and some eventually committed suicide. Being on death row was sometimes like being in an insane asylum. On the other hand, it was sometimes a place that could elevate my mind to a new consciousness if I could remain strong enough. Each day I survived became, in itself, a reward. So many men, like Rogers-el, Da'Oud, Slim and Tex, had received so many execution dates that were later abandoned that they could never prepare for tomorrow. They all knew that the end would eventually come, and as each death came, another memory was etched in my mind. I often reflected upon their lives when things got too tough. When one of them died, the burden of living for all of us was the only thing I had left—except for my family.

6

THROUGH HELL AND BACK

M Y GRANDFATHER ONCE TOLD me that death took us to a better place. Since my grandfather's death, I had always tried to believe that was true. When my fellow prisoners died, it was hard to imagine them in heaven, or any of us together, because we had already been through hell and back. But as I grew older, I found myself revisiting my grandfather's statement—"We will all see each other again someday, in a better place."

In 1997, thirty-seven prisoners were executed in Texas. Amongst them were my closest friends. Afterward, the days ahead looked lonely and cold. *I don't need anyone else*, I often thought to myself. I still had me, myself and I. When I first came to prison, I didn't think I would need anybody. I came to realize that we all need someone. No matter who we are or how tough we think we are, no man is truly an island.

When execution dates are serious, most of the time the prisoner is the last one to know. Not many attorneys want to tell their clients that they have an execution date set. When they do, they tell them that the date isn't serious because there are still more appeals to be filed. However, after talking to a few guys who had come within hours of death and hearing about the procedure as though it were common, I would shake my head listening to them because even if it was common, it was not necessarily accepted as part of our reality.

After walking back and forth in the single-man recreation cage I was placed in, I had the opportunity to speak with another death row prisoner who was in the cage beside mine. We spoke about executions and last meals, and he told me something I would never forget.

"Man, do you know I came within two hours of being executed," the Hispanic prisoner said.

"Oh, yeah?" I responded. "What was that like?"

"It's a trip, Holmes, but at least I ate good. I ordered twelve pieces of fried chicken, a couple of biscuits and a bottle of hot sauce. I also ordered a cold coke to wash it down, and at first I almost didn't get my order. It made me mad, Holmes."

"Why you calling me Holmes?" I asked. "My name isn't no damned Holmes. You can call me L.A. That's what everybody calls me."

"Okay, L.A., I meant no disrespect. Holmes is just another slang word for brother, dude, guy, homeboy or whatever. You know what I mean?"

"Yeah, I know what you mean. Go ahead and finish what your were saying."

"Well, anyway, I thought I wasn't going to be able to get my fried chicken, and I was pissed off, Holmes. I've been locked up almost fifteen years, and I had been looking forward to my fried chicken for a long time."

"I would ask you what happened, but obviously you didn't get executed, and that's why you didn't get your chicken." I couldn't help but wonder if he really would rather have had that fried chicken than his own life.

"You got it wrong, Holmes," he said. "I got my chicken and ate that shit up. In fact, I got so full that when they told me I had gotten a stay of execution, I laughed like a motherfucker. I got a free meal, Holmes! And you never get nothin' for free from the system." He nearly doubled over laughing.

Later that day as I sat in my cell thinking about what he said, I couldn't help but feel sorry for him that his whole life had been reduced to something so simple as looking forward to a meal of his choice. That made me think about a lot of things I didn't care to think about. I doubted very seriously if I would be reduced to such a state, but I was only human too, just like he was, wasn't I?

I always believed that you could learn something from anybody, even if all you learned was not do to what his dumb ass did. However, sometimes I was that fool, and I only hoped others would learn not to do the dumb ass things that I did at times.

One day the prison chaplain came into the wing looking for Rogers-el, and we all knew what that meant. Since Rogers-el was a Moor (Muslim), we knew he didn't want to talk to a Christian chaplain, especially the one that came on the wing. No one really liked this chaplain because he only came around when someone had an execution date, and he didn't really care about the men on death row. In fact, this chaplain had the other chaplain transferred, the one who did care about the men, because he complained to the warden that the caring chaplain was spending too much time with us. So, from the get-go, the majority of the death row population did not accept the new chaplain. Every time anyone saw him they would yell out, "Here comes the Grim Reaper!" Because he was like a sign of death to us all, since he only came around when someone had an execution date.

"Whose cell is he at?" I could hear some of the men asking. Word was passed down that he was at Rogers-el's cell. This meant that he had an execution date.

With only a week left for Rogers-el to live, I began thinking about all the times he and I got into trouble for standing up for ourselves and those experiences turned into memories. It's funny that when bad things happens to us we call those things "experiences," but when anything good happens to us, we call them "memories." Rogers-el and I had a little of both.

I wasn't able to see him because of my security status, so I wrote Rogers-el a letter telling him I would miss him and that he would have breath as long as I had breath. I let him know that I would write about him and the other men that I had known, but no matter what, we always promised to live through each other when one of us died. He would always say, "Little big brother, we can ride through hell and back, as long as we have each other." And I knew he meant that. He always called me "little big brother" because I was much bigger than him, but he was older than me. I would miss seeing him running around playing basketball and pissing me off by cheating all the time. No matter what, he always told me he could beat me in basketball, because cheaters always win, then he would burst out laughing until I playfully wrestled him to the ground. I would miss the moments we had together, whether it was on the basketball court, in solitary or just talking back and forth from cell to cell.

The day before his execution, I received a letter from him. It was passed down by other prisoners and this letter touched me so deeply that I often find myself thinking of him and reading it over and over again. In sharing this letter, he can live at least for a moment as he lived in my life.

My Dear Brother Nanon, (Yeah, I used your first name. Smile.)

I received your letter today, along with the love and concern for me. I truly don't know where this letter will take us, but for sure it's all out of love for you. Though I do not know what tomorrow will bring, I fear it not! I know what getting to know you has brought me in my life and death can never take that away.

My little big brother, you have taught me so much that these written words can never capture it all. You see, I have little brothers myself, and I see them in you every single day. Even when you think I don't see you, I see you through the window pacing in that single-man recreation yard, frustrated and angry. I often see a young man with deep thoughts, and more consciousness than a man your age should have. I see a young African warrior (even though you look like a Cuban, *smile*). Seriously, I see a young brother that tries to strive for something more than what death row has to offer, and it inspired me long ago when we used to sit up in solitary talking for hours at a time. Even when I would hear you sing in your cell at night, I knew you had a passion for life many do not have. (I bet you didn't know that I heard you, huh? I heard you very well, and it didn't sound bad.)

I never thought about how others looked at me; I only wished to live up to what I proclaimed to be and that is a Moor. I know we do not have the same religious beliefs but that didn't stop us from becoming friends. Early this morning, before I wrote my family final letters that said my goodbyes, I wrote a poem for every brother I knew over the years, and I had you in mind when I wrote it. The poem was called *Love in the Form of a Poem*, and hopefully you will see it in print one day. Whenever I write poetry, I always tried to write about the truth, as I see it. When I read your writings, they inspired me to push myself, because you were pushing yourself every day. I had always attempted to lead by example, but often I found myself following young warriors like yourself. No, I didn't mind, for I knew we were headed in the right direction, even when pain seared through my body causing me to suffer. It didn't matter though; we suffered together and never gave up!

Ego, I didn't possess. I humbled myself, for rare is it that any young man with a consciousness and a will to stand up for others appeared. I consider myself to be blessed to have been around you and a few more brothers like you. I truly miss you already as I sit in this deathwatch cell writing. My thoughts stay focused on my family, on you, and the rest of the brothers and their families. I know that your case got affirmed, but I somehow believe that you will be free one day. Don't ask me why. I know your family will still go through pain until that time comes. I think of my family going through that turmoil, and it hurts like anything anyone could imagine, but I know my little big brother understands. (smile).

L.A., you made my life here meaningful, for we have been able to grow as people, as men and as fellow human beings. When one was hurting, we felt the pain. We have all been able to inspire each other to achieve things we normally would not have attempted! So you must understand this, my young brother, I respect you and by my respecting you, it turned into love. But you made it easy for me to love you, my brother, because you respected yourself!

Me and the other brothers often speak of you, and they all respect you, so don't push yourself away from them when you are deep in your studies. They need your strength too, just like we all need each other's. If these people kill me tomorrow, I will tell the other brothers in heaven that you said hello, and I'll be watching over you. You have to stay strong for me and not do anything stupid when they execute me. I have done many wrongs in my life, but you helped me make them right by giving something back. You made me want to give something back.

I'm not ashamed to admit it, but I'm crying like a baby now as tears fall on this very same paper. I've always planned not to grow this close to anyone, but as time went on, nature took its course, and I grew close to many of you. L.A., don't be afraid to allow others in your life because you have so much to give, but knowing the way you are, you will continue to seclude yourself from the world. You can write some wonderful stories, so if you ever write about me and you, please share this letter with others as I wrote it. Promise me?

Yesterday, I gave an interview with DateLine, and I cried two times when I spoke of all of you. When the tears hit the floor, I wasn't even embarrassed, and I was on national television! But they were tears of reflection because I knew I would be leaving you all behind to battle the system without me. My tears were also tears of laughter that we shared, tears of pride in knowing some individuals true to themselves, and tears of joy for God blessing me to know you all. So yeah, I cried, cried, cried and will cry some more tonight, but I'm not ashamed because it doesn't make me any less of a man.

You know I also smashed America and their justice system, but most of them act like a bunch of Klansmen anyway. They also want to put a foot in the door in everyone else's business but can't get their own shit straight. I talked so bad about them all that I know they will edit the interview because they're scared of the truth!

I had a visit with my Queen Mother last week, and I call her Queen because that's what she is to me. Remember that woman that came to say hello to you while you were visiting your mother? Well, whether you knew it or not, that was my mother. I told her that you be trying to beat me up! And she asked me why? And I said because I beat you in basketball all the time! So then my mother said, so when he finally beats you in a game of basketball will you beat him up? And I said, "Mama, you know I'm non-violent," and she just looked at me and shook her head laughing.

You know my mother and auntie loved my bad ass no matter what, and when I see them tomorrow for the last time, I know it will be very hard. I wish you could be out there with me, but who knows, maybe you will be.

Man, I love you forever and always know that, okay? I want you to stay strong and keep up all the writing because we need a voice to tell people how it is, not how the system tells them it is. I'll be watching over you, little big brother, and send my love to all the rest of the brothers. I'll miss y'all.

Peace & Love,
Patrick Rogers-El

June 2, 1997, Rogers-el was executed. How I felt at that moment, I don't want to even attempt to describe. Words cannot do justice to that grief. I was taken to solitary again because the guards thought it would be best for security reasons to send a few of us prisoners to a more secure area, as if a steel cage with wire fence and steel sheets was insufficient to cage our grief. During the year of 1997, Da'Oud was also executed, as were so many other prisoners I was accustomed to seeing every day. By the year 1999, I had bore witness to the execution of more than ninety men.

The more executions I witnessed, the more purposeful my writing became. Writing became a mechanism for me to help us all experience life when we saw nothing but death all around us. I felt compelled to help my friends achieve life through the written word. Death row is a horrible place to live, but it is still life.

When many of the men on death row saw death drawing nearer, their visions tore aside the veil of ordinary reality. I tried to write the visions as intensely as reality brought them to me. Perhaps my greatest challenge was to find opportunities for mental and psychological growth and to listen to my spirit and trust that life was truly worth living. I've learned that although words can be manipulated with fantasy and an imaginative thought or two, life is by far all the fantasies we need, if we learn to see it as we see our dreams. All we need is within us.

None of the men I knew on death row confessed to being choirboys. In fact, many of the prisoners I knew committed the most sickening crimes the human mind can conceive of, but they are still a part of the human race, and people can and do change. Through the years of chaos, death, pain and confusion, some of the men went through many obstacles, only to find out that the love that brought them into this world was still there. There is a love that exists within us all. This love is in everything and everyone. If we choose to ignore it, the pain of separating from it makes us realize what we are missing.

In writing this book, I wanted to create a poignant account of what death row is like—the intense and prolonged suffering. My goal was not to garner sympathy but rather understanding. I lived so many years in dark isolation on death row. Sometimes I felt like I was alone in the world. But feelings are a choice, and they are self-inflicted. Sometimes I closed my eyes and attempted to bury the pain. But like the child I once was, and even like the boy that came to prison, I had to reach down and find my own ignorance and foolishness to laugh at with the sole intent of uplifting my spirit when it failed.

Violence is like a disease that needs its own special doctor to prevent the spreading of it to others. Death row captures violence and stores it for future generations to come. Yet, the cycle of hatred is still being broken down against all odds.

Life's events will be allowed to speak for themselves and reveal a story so polemical that it will always be questioned as to how things can be changed, but things will change if we allow humility and a willingness to let our hearts make a difference in our own human condition that challenges us to become the best people we can possibly be. So if we learn to cherish all the wisdom our lives have to offer, and we can keep growing even in our ignorance, then the door of hope will forever stay ajar and invite change and a better tomorrow everywhere.

8

THE SHADOW OF DEATH

I GREW UP IN prison amidst the concrete cells, the piss-colored stained walls and the fortified steel bars that make everything look like a giant dungeon. I learned to fight, I educated myself, and I learned to survive as best I could. The shadow of death presided over death row like a dark ominous cloud.

In the mornings, I often sat crouched in the back of my cell, half naked and cold as the sun rose, bringing forth daybreak and dispelling the shadows of the night that roamed the empty corridors and darkened the vacated cells. It was as though the naked eye could see those shadows claw and scratch their way to the darkest corners of the cellblock, staying safely hidden from any and all light.

Sometimes, I closed my eyes and listened to my own heartbeat, thumping and pounding as if it fed off the thoughts and emotions that sprung forth, uninvited. A decade after my arrival on death row, I still did this. I often felt drunk afterwards, as though I sipped some forbidden wine, and just like a drunkard amidst silence, I immediately became sober when the cellblock awoke with the groaning and deep sighs of the other prisoners. Every morning each person awoke engulfed by the nightmarish reality that was death row.

A GUY IN THE cell next to mine was given an execution date. His name was Billy Joe, but for short, everyone called him B.J. Most prisoners eventually adopt some kind of nickname, as if calling someone by their given name is an invasion of the little privacy we were afforded. In a sense, calling someone by his first name did invade that person's privacy because for the most part, being on death row was a whole new life. The pain of incarceration could be so overwhelming that seeking a new identity of sorts allowed many of us to build walls around ourselves and to block out our old life and the outside world completely. Everyone on death row called me L.A. because I am from Los Angeles. The memory of the outside world and my family was the only thing that kept me going. I can't say that many other prisoners felt the same, because they didn't. Reality was perceived differently by each prisoner and most struggled to believe whatever reality helped them get through the day.

Ole Man B.J., as I called him, knew that he had a couple of days at best, maybe even less, until he would be executed. Neither of us kept up with the days, but we knew the month. B.J. was well over fifty years old and was incarcerated most of his life. He honestly didn't give a shit about being on death row. He would often say to me, with an accent that never failed to make me grin from ear to ear, "Young'un, or L.A. as you wish to be called, this ain't nothin' but t'ree meals a day and a nice bunk to lays ma'head." I would always laugh because, without fail, he said "t'ree" instead of "three." I had discovered that all Southern accents are not exactly the same. Since I was from Los Angeles, most Texans thought those from the West Coast sounded quite proper and that those from the East Coast sounded like they were foreigners.

"Hey, Ole Man B.J., you up over there?" I called out one morning.

"Yep. I'm a jus' makin' me a shot of coffee and waitin' fo da porter to get on the cellblock so's I can buy me a smoke. Sum-bitches about five years ago quit lettin' us smoke in prison, and ever since then, them goddamn porters charge me's an arm an'a leg jus'ta buy a cigarette to get ma nerves right." (Porters are prisoners who work on the lockdown cellblocks.)

"I hear you, Ole Man, but that shit ain't no good for your ass anyway."

"Well, it ain't like I'm a tryin' out fo the O-lympics! Hell, L.A., you know I'm a be executed any day now. If I can get me a whole pack of smokes, I'll make this muthafucka look like a smoke house," he chuckled.

"I know you have an execution date," I said, "but I was hoping when you saw your sister the other day, you might have a chance of getting a stay of execution."

"Young'un, that ain't no damn sisa a mine. That's ma po' sweet Mumma. She's the only reason why I'se put up wit this shit for twenty-somethin' years. When the state execute me, ma Mumma can move on wit' her own life, and all this pain and sufferin' is goin' to come to an end." For the first time, I heard uncertainty in B.J.'s voice.

"S-s-say, B.J., y-y-you gonna be alright?" little Junebug asked from the tier below. "I-I knows the Fifth Circuit C-C-Court of Appeals turned ya'll down."

"What's your stuttering ass doing up this early in the morning, Junebug?" I asked. "I can see you down there eavesdropping on me and B.J.'s conversation."

"N-nah, I was just a layin' here, and I-I just overheard ya'll, is all."

"Just anotha' day, Junebug," B.J. said. "You normally asleep this time a day, so I'se, I mean, we's just surprised yo' snaggletoof ass is up, is all." B.J. burst out laughing so hard that others tried to quiet him down.

"I got up early this morning, the door k-kept slammin' shut as I was t-takin' a leak. But I was too much in a h-h-hurry to get back to sleep, so I didn't pay it much mind at first," Junebug said, as though alarmed. "The door kept a s-slammin' and slammin', and since sleep failed me, I kinda just listened to the two a you."

"Why do you think the door kept slamming, Junebug?" I asked. "I'm surprised me and the Ole Man didn't hear it, but being way up here in the corner, well, we can't hear shit except what's below us, and B.J. said that means listening to your snaggletoof ass." We all laughed then.

"F-fuck you, L.A.," Junebug said. "You ain't f-funny, you young-ass dude! You still good peoples, though, even if when I look at you, I can't tell if you're black, Cuban, Samoan or Italian!"

"Don't worry about what I am, Junebug," I said. "I'm going to be that muthafucka whippin' your ass since you trying to be funny." I could hear B.J. snickering to himself.

"Junebug got a point, L.A. You could pass for a bunch of stuff, so what is ya?"

"I don't pass for nothin'. I'm a mixture of black, French, Native American and English," I said. "I guess you could call me Creole, since my Mama is from New Orleans."

"Goddamn, young'un, you really is mixed with the whole planet, huh?" B.J. asked. "Since you got a little Caucasian in yo blood too, can I call you brotha?"

"Fuck you too, ole man! I'm not your brother, but when I get hold of you, I'll make you look like a Junebug, snaggletoof and all," I said. "Now seriously, it's good to see you always laughing, B.J., no matter what circumstances arise. I don't want to get sentimental on you, but I'll miss having someone to share a laugh with. I sure hope you get a stay of execution. They already executed thirty somethin' people this year, including Da'Oud and Rogers-el. I really miss them, you know."

"I-I miss them too," Junebug said. "I've been here sixteen years myself, and it's a cryin' shame it becomes c-c-common p-p-place for any man to be a constant witness to death. I know this gonna s-s-sound strange, but I-I's ready to go, myself."

"What you mean you ready to go, Junebug? You thinking about committing suicide by dropping your appeals, or are you thinking about killing yourself outright?"

"To tell you the truth, I've thought about both," he replied without a stutter in his voice and sounding clearer than I had ever heard him speak before.

"Man, I hear you, but I ain't never thought about killing myself. But, I guess in one form or another, the thought eventually crosses our minds, us being in here and all. I don't know if you're religious or not, but for me, I pray each and every day that I find the strength to keep going, and more often than not, I find that strength when I think of my family and the few friends I have. Mama always tells me, 'Baby, be born of the Holy Spirit and let it fill you up.' And sometimes I do feel it, especially when I'm with Mama."

"I know what ya mean," B.J. said. "I kinda feel the same way. Like I said a few minutes ago, without my Mumma being around, I wouldn't deal with this shit! Hell nah, this here is just too much!"

As we were talking, a guard approached B.J.'s cell and told him to pack up his property. He was being moved to a deathwatch cell. A deathwatch cell is normally the first cell on each block where prisoners are placed a few days before their execution so they can be monitored every hour on the hour to prevent any attempts at suicide.

"The time is near, L.A.," B.J. said, trying to be strong, but I could hear his voice crack. "Yep, the time is near," he repeated softly, as if he was speaking to himself now instead of me.

"I don't know what to say, Ole Man, except keep your head up and know I'll be thinking of you." I really didn't know what to say, and normally when we don't know what to say, all we can do is say a prayer or two. "I'm not going to get sentimental on you yet, because there's still hope you might get a stay, right on?"

"Billy Joe, you about ready to go?" asked a tall, lanky guard.

"Hell nah, I ain't ready to go! You just tole me a ta pack up ma shit a few minutes ago. Give me some fuckin' time!"

"Yeah, g-give the man some time, you punk-ass pig!" Junebug yelled over the tier.

The guard hastily walked away from the cell, realizing that on most days he could get away with saying something smart, but not today. The atmosphere suddenly changed as other prisoners began to wake and call out to B.J.

"You going to death watch, Billy Joe?" one voice asked.

Then another voice, "You keep your head up, old timer. I'll be thinking about you."

"Stay strong. Walk out the way you walked in."

The chants of encouragement went on and on.

Thirty minutes later the big-nosed guard came back, while at the end of the tier, more guards gathered like a flock of vultures, silently waiting for Billy Joe to exit his cell.

"Young'un, you hang on and stay focused on what's important to ya. Ya hear me, L.A.?"

I cut him off before he finished. "I hear you, Billy Joe. Be strong for your mother and—" my words were cut off as his cell door opened with a loud creak and slammed against the steel post.

Bang, Bang! The door crashed twice as they slammed it shut. When the chants started again, B.J. saluted everyone for the final time, because deep down we all knew this was it for him. We hoped that B.J. would be placed in a deathwatch cell on our cellblock, but since there was such a strong emotional attachment among the prisoners on J-21, we knew they would place him on a different cellblock.

"Hey, L.A.!" Junebug yelled.

"What's on your mind?" My response was rather cold because I was no longer in a mood to talk with anyone.

"N-nothin.' I-I was just checkin' up on ya. You sure got quiet up there."

"I'm cool," I said. "I'll rap to you later on, dig?" I knew Junebug did not intend to disturb me, and the truth is, well, I liked Junebug a whole lot, but his nosiness and choosing to strike up a conversation at the wrong time were bad habits that he possessed.

"Okay, L.A. I know there's a-a lot on yo' mind right now. It's a l-lot on my mind too, but I feel uncomfortable when it's this quiet. I can't stand it when I can hear my own breath, is all."

Two days later, Billy Joe was executed. As usual, the media gave a one-sided report as we listened to the television out on the run or to our radios. "Death row prisoner, such and such ..." the news reported, "... executed for the mass slayings of twenty people, thirty people, kidnapped and raped two girls, robbed a convenience store, etc." These reports always included rehashing of the alleged crime committed by the prisoner and inaccuracies were common. Billy Joe had been no angel, none of us were, but he accepted his own fate. To continue to make society hate him in the aftermath of his death has no justification at all. What good could come of it? They accomplished their goal of killing him. "Sons-of-bitches!" I said to myself. The media are a bunch of buzzards that continue to harass the weak and the dead— and for what? To boost their ratings. They either televise disaster, killings, pain or suffering and anything else that encourage onlookers to watch their news shows and to make them feel better about themselves. Even me, I've watched television and said to myself, "Damn, I'm glad that wasn't me!" And sure enough, a sick, twisted feeling takes over that makes me feel appreciative of what little I do have.

When it came to Billy Joe, well, nothing the media said made me feel any different about him. He was just an old white man in the eyes of the system, but to me, he was a friend and someone who gave life to the explosive and hard atmosphere of death row.

AS ANOTHER YEAR SLIPPED away unnoticed, more prisoners were executed, including Junebug who sung a song as the lethal poison flowed through his veins. I never knew Junebug's real name until I read it in the newspaper. Knowing a prisoner's real name didn't ease the pain, it just brought back memories that either made me laugh, cry silently inside, and at times, even created an unbridled anger inside that replaced the pain for a while.

In my early years on death row, I wrote as a way to lessen the pain and to use words to keep some of the men alive. The Bible teaches us in the Book of Wisdom, "Even our name will be forgotten in time, and no one will recall our deeds. So our life will pass away like the traces of a cloud and will be dispersed like mist, pursued by the sun's rays." In a sense, I like to believe that I am giving each man immortality through my writing, because these writings will outlive most of us, whether we die ten days from now or a hundred years from now. My dream is that these words will exist somewhere, someplace, in someone's hands who can still feel life flowing through their veins. In these words, I am alive; we are all alive.

I learned that the ability to use language can create something very beautiful. The written words can take everything to a new realm. Just the same, words create many feelings that come to the forefront of our being—if and only if, ordinary words could be filled with enough passion and imagination that could be transformed to come alive. Words, unlike anything else, can tear away the veil of reality and create an illusive state that forces us to explore ourselves, our minds and hearts, and the world around us. The more information we receive from words, the more clearly we see the ways of the world that we don't understand, and that gives us a vision more intense than we care to possess. In order to share our lives on death row and to become a better writer, I became a voracious reader. The more I read, the more knowledge I gained. The primitive knowledge of life was never to be buried. Knowledge was nothing more than a way we could classify the analyses we picked up along the way that gave us character, wisdom and a spirit within ourselves that would lead us down many paths. But honestly, with death constantly looming around every corner, sometimes my newly found knowledge made me doubt my own sanity. In fact, the more I continued to read, to learn and to explore, the more distant I became from others while I was also struggling to become so very close. I was in a double frame of mind.

I began reading philosophy. My appetite for books grew, until I could never seem to remain focused on one book long enough to grasp complete theories. Soon, my own theories formed and my interest would dive somewhere else. I even tried to understand Sigmund Freud's theories on the Id, Ego and the Oedipus complex. I grasped the Id and Ego very will, and in fact, it not only made me understand my environment more, but men altogether. But when I thought of the Oedipus complex, I was confused and once again, I began studying it. Sleep failed me altogether, and I plunged into other studies to learn who Laius and Jocasta were in order to grasp the Oedipus theory completely. I learned the theory was a libidinous feeling toward the parent of the opposite sex and is often found to be normal in young children. I thought, *Mr. Freud, go on and get me all fucked up, will ya? Because I don't have any sexual thoughts about my Mama, and if that's what you call normal, then I'm glad as hell I'm not normal!*

Some theories I found to be farfetched, and they interested me unlike anything else. I went on to read Dante, Jean-Jacques Rousseau, Descartes, Machiavelli, Chu His and more than forty other philosophy books that caused me to question everything, which confused me more than ever. I began to realize that the more I knew, the less I knew, all of which left me in an analytical state, especially when it came to understanding other prisoners.

9

SERGEANT NONE OF YOUR BUSINESS AND SOLITARY CONFINEMENT

A PRISONER, WHOM WE called Silo, was one of the strangest people I have ever met. At the same time, he was one of the few prisoners who played a lot on my mind. Everyone called him "Silo" because he was in an asylum for a few years before he came to prison. I suppose "Silo" was short for asylum, but I don't know the whole story of why the name was given to him.

Although not often, Silo sometimes ran onto the basketball court and interrupted our game because he saw something and would quickly go after it. If the game was intense, normally someone from the losing side would usher him off the court, or just outright give him a swift kick in the ass, and push him off the court. The recreation yard was no more than thirty feet long, so outside of playing basketball, or doing push ups, there wasn't really much to do. One day out on the yard, instead of playing basketball, I was just kinda kicked back, watching Silo. Suddenly he became alarmed. He turned his back to me and ran to the furthest corner of the recreation yard, his eyes fixated on some object the rest of us could not see. He reached down and picked up the object. It must have been a small rock, or a twig, or something really small, that the guards had not noticed when they searched the yard.

I did not say anything to Silo, but I edged my way toward him. He became alarmed and shouted, "Get back! Stay where you are! I mean it, don't mo—"

"You ain't the muthafuckin' police, so quit saying all that 'don't move' shit! What's your crazy ass doing back here, man?" I said, cutting him off in mid-sentence. "You okay? Cause you trippin'!"

Silo ignored me, turned his back again, and continued staring at the object in his hand. He was of average height, his back was slightly hunched, and he was very dark skinned. His hair and beard were extremely long, and he never combed his hair. Nor did he take a shower unless he was forced by the guards. When guards passed out laundry, Silo often tore his clothes into strips and tied his socks around his ankles. He looked like some village shaman, or perhaps he could have been mistaken for an old hippie. Silo was now my neighbor. I'd had so many different neighbors by that time that I couldn't remember them all unless someone was executed and I read about him in the newspaper. However, twice Silo had been my neighbor. I am one of the few people Silo talked to. He was selective with who he chose to communicate with, and so it seemed like a privilege when he did speak to a person.

As I continued watching him, he acted as though he didn't know what the object was or how it had gotten there. He held the object very, very cautiously in his hand, as if it was sacred and meant for his eyes alone.

I wasn't the only one watching Silo. Everyone on the yard watched curiously. However, I was closest to him and was only a few feet away. Normally, he would sit next to me and talk, but not today. It was easy to see that many thoughts were running through his mind. He acted as if he was the protector of this small object, as if he was the chosen one. He was mesmerized by it, and he put it in his pocket. His desire for the object was blatant. His eyes glistened because he knew, I mean, he *really knew*, that this was his secret, one to be kept from the rest of us.

"Hey, Silo, what you got?" another prisoner called, trying to reach into Silo's pocket and take the object. Suddenly, without warning, Silo slashed the other prisoner across the arm. The other prisoner stood in shock, staring at the blood that trickled down his arm.

"You bastard! You cut me!" the prisoner screamed and began hitting Silo with a fury of fists. Silo dropped the object, closed his eyes and swung back blindly. A rule among prisoners: no one is allowed to interfere in a fight, so the two of them fought until they both fell to the ground exhausted, neither one yielding to the other.

One of the guards noticed the fighting, and shortly thereafter twenty or more guards raided the recreation yard, wielding batons at those prisoners who were not lying spread-eagle on the ground. A fat, pimpled-faced little guard noticed a razor, covered in blood, shining in the rays of sunlight. Needless to say, this was the object Silo had so mysteriously held in his hands and coveted.

Moments later, a guard shoved me against the brick wall and ordered me to lie on the ground.

"Pig, get your hands off me," I said with such rigid control that he immediately signaled for the other guards to surround me. I shuffled my feet to the side, and it was on. When the guard missed, I flattened him with a stiff right blow and then all I could feel was the hard rain of batons as I was knocked unconscious.

I awoke still on the yard, handcuffed and shackled, as were all the other prisoners—except Silo. He had climbed the fence that hung over the recreation yard. For a while, Silo ignored the orders of several ranking officials to climb down. They were filming him with a video camera before taking any further steps to bring him down. Prison rules stipulate that whenever an incident takes place, a video camera must be brought to the scene. However, one of the unwritten rules of the Texas prison system is to videotape the prisoner in question first, turn the camera off and *then* brutalize him.

I stared at Silo after the physical confrontation. This wasn't his or my first physical confrontation with guards, nor would it be the last. They looked upon us as animals and treated us accordingly. Silo eventually climbed down, and they followed their own unwritten rule and beat the shit out of him once the video camera was turned off.

Once again, I was headed back to solitary confinement, as was Silo. A few years back, I wrote a story while in solitary about the experiences of surviving in the hellhole called prison and the strength of the human spirit to remain strong. *Would I remain strong this time, or would I end up like Silo?* I wondered. I guessed that time would tell, and time would do just that.

Darkness descended upon me as I entered solitary. The white concrete-draped walls stood out like columns as I looked out from behind the steel bars, and the wind blew through the cracked windows, creating a chill that caused the prisoners to shiver as though in fright. No matter how much any of us blamed the shaking due to the cold, solitary was a place to be fearful of for many reasons. Prisoners have quite often been found dead hanging from a blood-stained sheet, and of course it was ruled a suicide, but then, what was the explanation for all the bruises?

After one of the guards who took me to solitary removed the handcuffs, I had to slither across the floor on my stomach, then lie on my back in order to place my feet close to a small slot at the bottom of the door so the shackles could be removed from my ankles. It disgusted me to be shackled like an animal, but the battle I faced was to not respond to the way I was treated. In anger, I sat down on the most uncomfortable steel bunk I had ever sat on. The lower part of the bunk hung to the floor and as I sat on it, I slid up and down, like a seesaw at a park. Of course, I wasn't a kid anymore and this was certainly no park. Maybe if I had just gone outright mad I may have believed it to be so. I wondered if this would be my last time in solitary? I frowned, knowing damned well that this wouldn't be my last time unless I gave up on possessing any dignity. If I had nothing else, I mean *nothing* else, I always had my dignity because it was the only thing they could not take from me—unless I surrendered it. And I knew that if I surrendered my dignity, I might just as well give up my appeals and surrender my life.

"Williams," a commanding voice called my name.

I stared at a white guard who was as thin as a piece of straw and wore an extra uniform to make himself look bigger than he actually was. He had blond hair, red-rimmed blue eyes, and a bald spot in the middle of his head, with thin strings of hair combed over it in an ineffectual effort to conceal it. His jaw line was strong and square, but it was faintly bruised as though someone had slapped him. He just stood there staring at me with a hard gaze, sizing me up. His eyes belied the tough appearance he was striving for, and his gaze dropped to the ground when I returned his gaze. He kind of stepped back from the cell door as though he had touched fire.

"Nanon Williams, is that you, bwah?" he said with a thick southern drawl.

"My name is Nanon Williams, but if you see a boy anywhere around you, open the cell door and slap his ass, pig!" I said, sickened by the sight of him and the sound of his voice. Most guards look at any person of color as a "boy" to make themselves feel as if they are better than us, but he had another thing coming if he continued to disrespect me. I didn't invite problems, but if I just accepted ill treatment, it would never end.

"You have a disciplinary case for assaulting several officers, and here is a paper I want you to use to write down what happened, bwah!" I started to respond to that "boy" shit again, but I didn't. He handed me a blank piece of paper and an eraserless pencil so that if I wrote anything down, I couldn't erase it.

"Who does the disciplinary case say I assaulted, boy?" His face turned red with anger when I addressed him in the same manner he had addressed me. "How am I supposed to write a statement without knowing who said I assaulted them?"

"That is none of your fucking business, just write the statement!" He spat the words at me in fury. "And I am not a 'bwah'! Address me as Sergeant!"

Rather than argue with him, I snatched the piece of paper from his hand and wrote in big letters, "I WAS PHYSICALLY ASSAULTED BY SEVERAL GUARDS AND NOW I AM BEING THREATENED BY A SERGEANT ..."

"Um, what did you say your name was?" I asked.

"None of your business," he snapped furiously.

So I continued writing the statement: "BY SERGEANT NONE OF YOUR BUSINESS. I AWOKE FROM UNCONSCIOUSNESS, HANDCUFFED AND WAS ESCORTED TO SOLITARY." I normally don't write a statement, but when I did, it was similar to this. After all, it was the truth. I wrote something so that when they tried to railroad me in their mock disciplinary court, they couldn't say that I didn't cooperate when I pled "not guilty."

"What the fuck is this shit?" The sergeant read the statement. "Nobody assaulted you! Change this goddamn statement!"

"Man, if you don't get your pencil-built ass away from this cell, you'll be giving me another disciplinary case!" I said, standing at the bars and towering over him. "Take that statement and get the fuck on, pig!"

He scampered away, but I knew that he would throw the statement away and tell his superiors I refused to give one. I was no new boot to these petty procedures that were not designed to be fair to prisoners. It was a silent joke for them to pretend to investigate any matter anyway.

Somewhere in the building, I could hear voices rising. My mood seemed to drastically change as the air vent thudded with a loud sound. *Tha-voom!* The vent blew hard. Solitary had a smell unlike any place else in prison. It smelled of something sickly like dried urine, shit and soured milk. While the air vent blew, it only made the smell hit you dead center in the nostrils, then just as quickly, the smell would disappear as if it consumed you and you became a part of it.

"L.A.! L.A.!" a voice called.

"That you up there, Young Lion?"

"Yeah, it's me. Why you back here in solitary again?" he laughed. "You come to keep me company?"

"Yeah, that's it! I came down here to keep your crazy ass company. I knew you was sad and lonely." I felt immediately better, glad to hear his voice.

Young Lion was my best friend. He had a dark brown complexion, and at that time he wore his hair in a big Afro. He was of medium build with finely-toned muscles. When you stared at him, his eyes always seemed fixated on you, quickly analyzing, as though contemplating the best possible way to deal with you if a problem arose. His name was Emerson Rudd, but we called him simply Rudd or Y.L., which is short for Young Lion. He and I went through hell and back together. We were sprayed with tear gas, pepper sprayed, beaten by guards, and fought back against the system together. Everyone called Rudd the Young Lion because he was fierce, intelligent and courageous. He had been on death row for eleven years, since he was only eighteen years old, and he had overcome many things. He was well respected by other prisoners because he believed with feeling in what he did, and he was a man of his word. I guess that's why we became such good friends—because we both were men of our word and stood our ground, no matter the consequences.

"So, why are you here, Bro? You bumped heads with one of them pigs again?"

"You know how it goes, Y.L. Our egos get the best of us sometimes, and since bowing down to the oppressor is out of the question, one thing led to another and BAM! Now I'm keeping you company in this hellhole." I then explained to him what happened.

I knew we were put in solitary to suffer. In another lifetime, I wouldn't ever have been on death row in the first place. I would have had a beautiful wife, a houseful of children, a place to call home, and the very same friend I had in Y.L.

In solitary, I wasn't only worried about myself. I was worried about everyone, including Silo, because he was somewhere down here too, very quietly licking his wounds.

"Say, Y.L.?"

"Yo, what's up?"

"You remember the last time we were in solitary?" I said laughing.

"L.A., we done been in solitary so many times, you act like it was along time ago. It was just a few months ago. I even remember in 1996, when them white folks gassed your ass with tear gas and yo' big ass head looked bigger than usual."

"Yeah, right! It wasn't like you was lookin' like Mr. Casanova yourself! After them folks gassed me, you were next in line, and it looked like you went fifteen rounds with Mike Tyson afterwards."

"Yep. I guess we both looked pretty bad, but we stood together, didn't we? And we looked bad together with pride and dignity, right on?"

"Right on," I said. "We surely did, we surely did—just like so many other times. Remember last time we had everybody in solitary singing oldies and all the latest songs?"

"I remember. We were strong in spirit and were having so much fun that they even separated us. You know them folks hate to see two black men stay strong against everything they throw at us," Y.L. said thoughtfully. "Our forefathers would be proud. Frederick Douglas said, 'If there is no struggle, there is no progress.' And I believe that."

"I believe it, too, Y.L., but in your mind, how much have we progressed?"

"I can't rightly put it all in words, but through constant struggle, we learn from each other, we've grown with and from each other, and, even more so, we live the life of freedom through our mind and transcend the walls of this prison in spirit. An African proverb describes it as, 'Kir duka a kita mbwa wa.' It is something to remember."

"What does that mean, Y.L.?"

"It means one head cannot lift the roof, but the phrase is deeper than that. In so many words, it implies that in unity we stand against the odds of anything, but in victory we stand in constant struggle."

"I dig that," I said. "I know a phrase that says, 'Uwagh sen tswen hule.' Do you know what that means?"

"Nah, but break it down to me, Bro." Y.L. asked because amongst all of the other prisoners I knew, he had a lust for knowledge. He liked to be the teacher, as well as the student—just as we all should. He taught me long ago that the only way to gain knowledge was to learn from others and let wisdom come as it may.

"In English the proverb means, 'The stream descends alone and bends.' It teaches us a deeper meaning as well, but we must think about it. It is meant to teach us that when someone tries something difficult to learn, it is wise to learn from those who have taken the path in order to correct mistakes." I went on to say, "The reason I mention this phrase is because, like you, most of my life experiences have been in prison. We both came to prison as teenagers. You have taught me many things since I have known you, but I have only recognized the mistakes after I've taken the path myself. I guess we call that just plain ignorance."

"I think it's fair to say that most do that. It's a part of growing up," Y.L. said. "We always do what others warn us not to do, but when we repeat the same mistake twice is when we become a fool."

"You're definitely right on that account, Y.L." Thoughts began to cross my mind. "I'll holler at you tomorrow, Bro. I'm going to lay back for a minute, dig?"

"Right on," Y.L. said. "I know it's been a long day for you."

Talking to Y.L. provoked many thoughts. As I laid back on the bunk, hanging from the side, sliding towards the floor, I gathered my thoughts. I made it a habit to understand them rather than just allow them to pass by me.

I could picture the guard's face as I fell semi-conscious in the day's prior events. Even as I turned from side to side, I could feel the bruises on my ribs. The bruises were a reminder that I was human and no matter how much I tried to ignore both the physical and the mental abuse, it sometimes wrapped me in comfort to know I was still a soldier on the battlefield, and that I was alive.

The vision wouldn't leave. It was twisted in both fear and rage as I continued to picture the guard's face. The image in my mind was that of glory. *Yes*, I thought, *he was glorifying himself, and he enjoyed participating in my suffering.* He felt the position of power it placed him in, he definitely was on a power trip, but that was the nature of man. Most men who have ever obtained a sense of power did it by glorifying themselves in death and in the pain they inflicted on others, or even those under their command. Although men surely understand pain, they don't understand pain like women do. As I explored my thoughts further, I asked myself, *Why? Why is that so?*

In prison, men seek to be respected so that they can feel safe among the prison populace. Initially that respect is sought because of fear. I felt that very same fear when I was a young teenager, engulfed by the prison atmosphere. Reputations among men were formed through physical combat, as each attempted to become the victor of a duel—if there was a fight in prison, whoever inflicted the most pain upon the other prisoner was looked upon in admiration and fear. Some would say, "Man, that such-and-such guy is a bad dude! He almost beat that other guy to death." Word would spread throughout the prison and the tale of the "duels," as I called them, caught bigger and bigger. And eventually, the process repeated itself.

I suspected the prison guard who assaulted me with his posse thought that if he could inflict pain upon me or anyone else, then his fellow guards would look upon him with admiration.

Few women glorify themselves in others' pain. Women understand the power of life and death because as childbearing people, they have the capability to bare life. They then become very protective of their children. When women look at other people, they often relate to that person as someone's child. One could also say that they give birth to humanity, because their love often runs much deeper. When women obtain power, they tend to turn that power into devotion and love. That is why history has produced some of the most remembered rulers that we call "queens." People often love their queens and will lay down their lives for her, but they only defend their king and bail out on him if the kingdom seems near to collapse. That guard would have known what I meant had his little surrounding support collapsed, and I beat his ass.

If a mother saw her child teetering towards a cliff, she would run blindly off that cliff in an attempt to save her child, whereas a father may stop to think before plunging off the cliff and lose the chance to save the child. Women, I believe, are the glue that holds society together and that is probably one of the reasons why men try to dominate women.

CLANK! CLANK! CLANK! THE shift changed and a guard was banging a cup against the bars. "Chow time! Everybody up if you want'a eat!"

The wind had picked up outside and a bolder draft penetrated solitary as I awoke, bundled in a knot on the steel bunk with no mattress, no sheets and no blanket.

"Williams! What are you doing back here again?" Mrs. Milly asked as she handed me a tray.

Mrs. Milly was a short black woman with a charming smile and a heart made of gold. She was a guard, and as much as most of us disliked guards, everybody respected and liked her. She treated all of us with respect. She did her eight hours of work and went home. She never harassed any prisoner, and I can't recall any prisoner ever disrespecting her. In fact, she was a sort of a grandmother figure to everyone because she seemed to truly care about how we were treated. She often went out of her way to make sure we had everything coming to us that the state was required to provide for us.

I looked up at Mrs. Milly and said, "Them folks came on the yard trying to beat a brother down. I could tell you the whole story, but you know how it goes." I stood up and looked at a tray with one hard biscuit, one blue, half-cooked egg and something that looked similar to oatmeal.

Mrs. Milly smiled. "Yeah, I know how it goes, and I can see someone beat poor Silo up pretty bad, too, but I didn't know you came to solitary with him. Has the nurse been down here to give y'all an examination?"

"No! You know them folks ain't escorted the nurse down here. And besides, she won't do anything."

"Don't worry. I'll go get her because that's her job to check on y'all. And Baby, you mean to tell me they didn't bring you a mattress and clothing? And look at that bunk, it's hanging down on one end to the floor." Mrs. Milly looked around at my cell, hands on her flared hips, an expression of genuine concern in her friendly brown eyes.

"You don't see any sheets and stuff, huh?" I said, smiling, "I yelled for some last night, but I didn't see any guards until you came this morning." As she was walked slowly away, I said, "Before you finish passing out trays, Mrs. Milly, tell me where they put Silo?"

"You sho' do need to see the nurse if you don't know where Silo is," she said. "He's right next door to you in fifteen cell, laying on the floor by his toilet. That poor child sho' need some help, and he ain't got no reason being here with his mental state and all." She shook her head sorrowfully.

"I hear you, Mrs. Milly," I said, thinking how nobody should be on death row. Some prisoners do deserve life sentences because of the horrible crimes they committed, but they don't deserve to be slaughtered like cattle.

"Let me go before these trays get cold. I'll be back." She stared up the stairs to the second tier and yelled, "Chow time, Two Row!" *Clank! Clank! Clank!* The cup banged on the bars. "Chow time! Everybody up if you want'a eat."

Mrs. Milly once told me that she regretted becoming a prison guard and wished she could have taken another direction with her life, but after years of struggling for a job that could pay the bills, she became like a slave to the system, living from paycheck to paycheck, with no other experience to help her get other work. Eventually the job became more than a paycheck for Mrs. Milly, and as the years went by, well, it was fair to say that Mrs. Milly became attached to many death row prisoners and mourned when someone was executed. Not as deeply as we did, but she did mourn. She would occasionally mention a few of the men that were executed, and she never had anything bad to say. She reflected upon something funny or profound that person did or said. The things she said often made my eyes twinkle with kindness toward her.

To be honest, it is not common practice for any prisoner to acknowledge a prison guard for who he or she is as a person outside of the prison atmosphere and the hated gray uniform. Individuality was not something that I or many other prisoners recognized in the guards. We perceived them as we did the government, as the well-oiled parts of a killing machine. But when it came to Mrs. Milly, we often felt gentleness emanating from her, and she made us feel like respected human beings. Every person responds to kindness; so why wouldn't we?

"Well, I found you some sheets and a blanket." Mrs. Milly returned and handed the things to me through the small slot at the bottom of the door. "And here is a towel and a bar of soap to scrub the cell, because it's filthy!"

"I appreciate it, Mrs. Milly. If you wouldn't have brought the sheets and stuff, I don't know who would have. Thank you."

"That's my job, Baby. I'm suppose to make sure you get these things. I just hate to see you young men be any worse treated than you already are, and secretly, I admire the courage some of you brothers show in standing up for yourselves when you know they're going to bear down on you afterwards. You all walk with your head high above all else, and this is something to witness," she said. "Yeah, that is something to witness."

"You alright, you know that, Mrs. Milly?"

"I sho' hope so," she said, walking away from the cell, mumbling to herself.

I looked at the ragged towel that she gave me and went straight to the sink to turn on the water. As the water sprayed with force from the rusted fount, I placed the soap and towel together, trying to create as many soap suds as I could. I drenched the towel with more water, wrestled with my courage, and attacked the cell with blind force. Back and forth I went with the towel against the walls, the floor, the bars, and the steel bunk I had already slept on. I then repeated the process over again. After cleaning up the cell as best I could, I then faced the hardest part of cleaning any new cell—the toilet.

As I looked in the steel-rimmed bowl, the toilet water looked like a swamp. It seemed to be saying to me, "Trespasser beware. Keep out." So I flushed and flushed, hoping to flush as much gunk as possible. Let's be realistic here, that wasn't just some mysterious gunk rimming the toilet, it was shit. I dreaded the task.

"Hey, L.A.," Y.L. yelled over the tier.

"What's up?"

"Good morning to you Bro. I'm just hollering at you. Have you been up a while?"

"I've been up for a little while. Since breakfast, or whatever you call that meal."

"I've been up doing a little reading. What you doing?"

How was I supposed to tell him that I was getting ready to stick my hands in the toilet and wash some shit out of it before I even had a chance to wash my face and brush my teeth? I didn't have a toothbrush, and I was scared to wipe my face with the towel because I wasn't even sure Mrs. Milly gave me a clean towel before I started to clean the cell. I then looked over at the toilet, and it seemed to be saying the same thing ... "Beware. Keep out." So I yelled up at Y.L. and said, "Oh, ugh, I've been down here cleaning the cell."

And right on cue he responded, failing to stifle his laughter, "So what you're trying to tell me is that you've been cleaning that shitty ass toilet?"

"That's what I've been doing." Then I lied to try to lessen his laughter. "Well, uh, the cell wasn't actually that dirty. It just needed a little light cleaning."

"You in sixteen cell, right?"

"That's right."

"Then you is a goddamn liar! That cell ain't clean," he continued laughing. "I've been in that cell before, probably twice. That's the cell with the bunk sliding towards the floor, and besides, Monty just left that cell and you know his ass don't ever take a shower or nothing else."

What could I say? He had been in solitary not only more than me, but he knew who left the cell just before I was thrown into it. He caught me in my little lie, but he knew how nasty it was to clean a new cell. I yelled up to him, "Okay, you got me. I'm down here cleaning this shitty ass toilet, and that's one hell of a way to start a morning, ain't it?"

"It sure is, and that's why I told Mrs. Milly to make sure she brings you a soap and towel."

"So now I see why she brought the towel along with my sheets and stuff. Right on." We always used the term "right on" in acknowledging each other, as a way of saying thanks or saying you understand something.

I continued to clean the cell and the toilet but afterwards I was exhausted. I knew that showers would be run shortly, just as they normally were this time of day, so I decided to do a few exercises to make the time pass quickly. I probably smelled really foul after yesterday's confrontation, and now after this morning's scrubbing, I needed a scrubbing myself. I wish I had my property so I could read a book, but of course I hadn't received my property yet.

When Mrs. Milly passed by the cell, I quit doing push-ups and called out to her. "Mrs. Milly. Hey, Mrs. Milly, hold up a second and let me holler at you?"

"Whatcha need, now, cause I sho' am tired?" she replied.

"I was just wondering when you was going to run showers. I didn't get a chance to shower yesterday because of what went down, and I know I don't smell too good."

She peeked into the cell and said, "It looks a whole lot better in there, and it smells better, too. That Monty sho' is a mess. I can't figure out why that boy won't take a shower for the life of me."

"Yeah, Rudd told me he was in this cell before me. It was really nasty."

"I'll shower you in about thirty minutes or so. I have to bring Rudd these bags to pack his property in because the captain don't want you two down here together."

"Oh yeah?"

"That's right, he said alone, you both are a handful, but together y'all give him too many problems."

"Hey, Y.L.!" I yelled. "Hey Rudd, you hear me calling you?"

"Yo! What's up?" he answered.

"They fixing to move you, and Mrs. Milly is on her way up there to bring you some property bags."

"They fixing to what?"

"You heard me right. They fixing to move you to another building."

After Mrs. Milly told him he was moving, we talked a while longer, and I must admit that I wished he could stay down there with me in solitary a while longer. It was always better having a friend nearby to talk to, although I was used to the solitude. Sometimes the solitude even became my friend and allowed me to dive further into the books I read undisturbed. That is, if I got my property, or at least some of it.

"Say, L.A.!" Y.L. shouted.

"What's up?"

"I'm heading out the door, so keep your head up down here. Mrs. Milly said I'm being moved back to J-21 and be sure that I'll give the brothers your regards, right on!"

"You keep your head up, and I'll see you whenever the captain's punk ass lets me out of here," I called back to him. "And Y.L.?"

"Yeah?"

"Make sure you get a towel and clean that toilet in your cell," I said, glancing back at mine. It shone now and did not have a "Beware!" sign on it anymore.

"Alright, Bro. You got me back with that one. You be cool."

"Right on." I didn't know how long it would be until I would see him again. It was an empty feeling.

The days turned into weeks and weeks into months. Silo and I were still in solitary.

Occasionally, we talked to each other. When Silo really got into the mood, he would tell me what he saw, or I should say, how he saw reality and his strange visions spooked me. Who knows? Maybe he wasn't really so crazy, after all. Maybe I was.

10

AX MAN

EARLY ONE MORNING, SILO began banging on the bars back and forth, screaming loudly, "They are trying to get me! HELP, somebody, PLEASE!" The bars rattled as he kicked them with unrestrained force. *Bang! Cling! Clank! Bam!* The steel doorframe rattled off a series of sounds.

After listening to Silo for more than an hour, I was filled with frustration and banged on the bars with him. I yelled too. He needed help, and I certainly wished they would hurry and give him some. Even though loud outbursts were a part of every day in prison, I was really on edge with all the additional noise. All day every day, we listened as guards and prisoners alike banged on the metal bars and doors. One prisoner described it best when he said, "It is like sitting in an empty, metal dumpster and someone walks by once every hour and slams a baseball bat against the metal." The loud metal on metal slamming was a regular and hourly occurrence everywhere on death row. But this particular morning, a storm was brewing inside and outside solitary confinement.

Lightning struck and thunder crashed with a loud echoing that added to the sound of the voices. I moved swiftly to the door and tried to look out the windows above the staircase. I could not see outwards, but even though the caked mud sealed some of the broken cracks in the windows, I could see the light disappear and watch the clouds turn dark and grow, silhouetting the structure, as rain pummeled the building and the grounds, while steady, sure drops poured through the cracks of the window, hitting the white column a few feet away from my cell door, creating a puddle that grew bigger and bigger.

"Shhhhh! Everybody be real quiet and they might come," Silo said.

"Go to hell, punk!" a voice from the cell that used to be occupied by Y.L. said. Some prisoners cursed Silo because he would do the same to others, but this morning Silo was really tripping. Some prisoners acted wild among the prison population, but then, Silo was something else. I wouldn't say he was the wildest, but he had my vote to easily be in the top ten.

I stood back from the bars and suddenly the lights started flickering off and on, then everything went completely black. The emergency generator attempted to kick in and keep the lights on, but it failed. Another lightning flash burned with a glow across the sky, and then figures appeared from a dark shadow with a flood of small lights following, as two guards walked by.

"The security is fine down here," one of them said as they walked up the stairs.

Guards did not ordinarily remain in solitary for any length of time, so if a prisoner had a heart attack, a seizure, or began throwing fits like Silo was now doing, all of that fell upon deaf ears. What made solitary so dangerous was that anything could happen down there, and more times than not, anything did. Deaths occurred, savage beatings, a string of insanities, rapes, if one prisoner gained access to another, and probably many other things that I wasn't even aware of. The Ellis Unit is old, built in the early 1960s, and solitary was one of the oldest places within the prison, if not the absolute oldest. I had heard many stories about the Ellis Unit, particularly about solitary.

"Hey, L.A., let's talk, man. I'm worried over here." As the lights finally lit up for the umpteenth time, Silo spoke in a low, deadly serious tone.

"What's up, Silo?" I answered immediately. "Why are you worried?"

"I'm worried about eternal punishment, and I think death is calling me. Damn it! Somebody's calling me! I can hear him now, whispering sweet nothings to me ever so gently, and it's driving me crazy!"

"Man, what the fuck are you talking about? Did that nutty psychiatrist bring you your medication?" I was perplexed as to how to respond to him in a way that would help him.

Silo's crazed laughter seemed almost desperate, but it seemed to have a soothing effect on his mind. Silo and I had many conversations during our time in solitary, but I didn't know if participating in his bouts of insanity was wise. I could tell his thoughts were wickedly disturbed. It was as if he had two minds, and one was torturing the other, while just a piece of him—a small piece—tried to battle against the raging war inside him. Sadly, he was losing the battle. Defeat seemed around every corner as his mind searched to set him free.

"There is a horror in here too terrible to explain without sounding like I'm a crazy man," Silo said, just as another streak of lightning hit and the lights flickered out once again.

"I-I d-don't understand." Now I was stuttering like Junebug.

"I believe there is a mad soul dwelling around this place, right now, at this very moment. I've seen it occasionally over the years. I call it "Sleeper" because it often comes while everybody is asleep. Have you seen it?" he asked slowly.

"Silo! You're not making any sense. What mad soul are you talking about? Do you mean yours?"

"No! No, no, no, no. I don't mean mine. I have my soul still in my flesh. I'm talking about Sleeper. He's a ghost or something. I've seen his face." For some unknown reason, Silo kept stamping his feet as he spoke.

"A ghost?" I asked. "Get out of here with that bullshit. I don't believe in ghosts." Maybe I did believe in ghosts a little, I wasn't sure. Or maybe I was just fearful of talking about something that pertained to the netherworld. Heaven, paradise, purgatory, hell or whatever name people use to describe a place where our souls go, left me uneasy. In a way, I wanted to believe in heaven, because I wished to see my father and grandfather there, but I didn't want to talk about it with others. Most death row prisoners had these thoughts though. After all, death was right around the corner and most of us would not escape. However, talking about this ghost shit seemed taboo. I had may own battles to keep sane, so I didn't need Silo to give me anymore.

"Do you remember James Gunter?" Silo asked.

"Yeah. I remember him very well. He was the young white guy who hung himself with a dirty sheet about nine months ago?" I mused softly.

"Do you remember how quiet it was afterwards when everyone awoke the following morning and that Mexican guard ran down the tier screaming?" Silo asked.

"Yeah, I remember clearly. I've been producing a newsletter for a couple of years, and I wrote a poem about that day. I placed it in my newsletter. Do you want to read it?"

"I can't read, but if you read it to me, I will listen to you," Silo said.

I was stunned because I would never have thought that Silo of all people, would want to listen to a poem. I really didn't feel like reading the poem to him, I had just hoped to hush him up for a while, but it was too late now. I had most of my property back, so I dug out the poem. "Can you hear me, Silo?"

"Yes sir, I can hear you."

"The title is *Lost Hope*, and I named the poem that because he didn't seem to have any hope left. It goes like this:

A young man decided to kill himself last night,
And so he is dead,
Hanging by a dirty white sheet

In the stillness of the night.

His frustrations became so high,
They collapsed on him
Like a great wave
Slamming into a mountain of rocks.

Feeling crushed
He hopelessly surrendered
To his guilt
Ashamed to face another day.

And so his lifeless body hung
As we sat in silence,
Affected and drained
Because his death lingered on.

Minutes became hours,
Day became night,
And tomorrow turned
Into yesterday.

But eventually, the silence broke,
Shouts rang out,
And people calmed their fears
About succumbing to the same fate.

"Well, that's it Silo," I said. "What do you think?"

I could hear him suddenly stamping his feet again and then he spoke. "I heard you, but I don't like poetry. Crazy people write poetry, and that's why you see most of them ridiculed throughout history as being insane," he said, continuing to stamp his feet.

"Why did you have me read it if you didn't want to hear it?" I was pissed off at his attitude about the poem. After all, he had asked to hear it; I hadn't particularly wanted to read it to him.

"Because you asked, and it's rude to say no."

"You crazy muthafucka! I've heard you say 'no' to people a million and one times."

"That's different. I talk to you, not to many others, so they have no business asking me anything," he said, continuing to stamp his feet.

"Silo!"

"What?"

"Why do you keep stamping your feet?" I was thoroughly agitated by now. "I can hear them quite clear over here."

"Don't worry about it! That's my business; so don't ever ask me that again. Ask the ghost if you must know. Now, do you want me to finish telling you what I wanted you to know before you started reading that poem or whatever you call it?"

Although Silo had a way of getting under my skin and making me want to give him that swift kick in the ass he was so used to, I did want to hear what he had to say. At first I hadn't wanted to, but since I couldn't read with the lights constantly flickering on and off, I thought I might as well listen to him. Even as I read the poem, I had to strain my eyes to do so because it was dark, but the sun gave a little light. "Go ahead, Silo," I said. "Finish what you were saying."

"Just listen, okay?"

"Alright, man. I'm listening. Go ahead."

"They say people like James roam the halls of the Ellis Unit. Both you and I have seen close to a hundred prisoners get executed, but how many prisoners have we seen die in their sleep, beaten to death by guards or other prisoners, or have gotten tired and just committed suicide like James did?"

I thought about the number for a moment, then said, "I don't know the exact number, Silo, but there have been quite a few."

"Exactly my point! All of those have become suspended souls, still earthbound. Some of those souls are roaming around the Ellis Unit, especially down here in solitary. Remember, this part of the building sinks into the ground."

"That's bullshit," I told Silo. "Ain't no lost souls roaming around here." Although, if I was to be truthful with him, the thought was now crossing my mind. I do believe most people have souls, but to admit to the idea that souls or ghosts were somewhere around us just didn't fit into normal conversation.

"Have you ever heard of the Walls Unit, L.A.?"

"Why are you asking me a silly question like that, Silo? The Walls Unit is where the execution chamber is, so they can kill us. What death row prisoner doesn't know about it?"

"I know that you know that much," Silo said impatiently, "but what do you really know of the Walls Unit?"

"Not much besides that. No, not much at all."

"The Walls Unit was the first prison built in Texas."

"So, what's your point?"

"This is the last time, L.A. Don't interrupt me!"

Silo was much older than me, but he was getting on my nerves. He acted as if I was in some king's court, and he was the king. "Go ahead, man. I won't interrupt you anymore. I'm just going to sit back and listen."

"Okay. The oldest part of the Walls Unit is called East Wing. There have been stories about that place for decades. Some people claim they have seen the ghosts of old convicts roaming the prison and this is not just some tale. If you ever ask any of the old convicts or guards around here, they'll tell you."

I began laughing, trying to take away some of the stir-crazed feeling the story gave me because the lights started flickering out of control and here was Silo telling me some ghost story.

"Quit laughing! Do you think I'm playing or something, L.A.? This is no joke."

"Nah, I hear you loud and clear," I said, tired of his constant badgering, as if he was some great authoritative figure, and I should consider it as a privilege to hear his fabled words.

"The East Wing was built in the mid 1800s and has rarely changed over the years. I was once in that prison, about fourteen years ago. East Wing actually looks very much like this here solitary confinement and that's why I hate it down here. Both the Walls Unit and Ellis Unit are notoriously known across the state because it has been a common sight to see prisoners commit suicide there and here or for the prison guards to kill someone blatantly for all to witness. Many people claim to have seen prisoners who died there over at East Wing walking around in chains with no heads. And there have also been rumors that prisoners and guards have been found shivering in a corner crying and refusing to tell anyone what they've seen. Not just a few, but many guards that used to work over there have quit their jobs."

The story Silo was telling me was better than most fiction novels I had read, but I wondered if what he was saying held any truth? Just a little bit? After all, Silo was crazy himself, so what would that make me if I believed him?

"L.A., they've even run newspaper articles talking about East Wing and one newspaper said there is a ghost there they call, 'Ax Man.' The newspaper said that Ax Man was thought to be the ghost of a convicted murderer who decapitated his victims and people say he walks around with some of those heads clutched in his hands."

"Silo! You tell one hell of a story, I give you that much!" I said, turning around quickly, thinking that I heard something. I went to the back of the cell and heard a piece of metal "Cling" and wondered whether Silo's story was getting the best of me and my mind was playing tricks on me! "Silo?" I whispered quietly.

"What? I have to finish telling you the story."

"Hold on a minute with that story. Did you hear something in the back of the cell?" I know I sounded a little spooked, but with all the lightning and thunder I guess maybe I was.

"Man, you ole scaredy youngster, that's maintenance in the pipe chase fixing one of the generators."

"Oh yeah, I know, I was just wondering if you heard it," I said. *Maybe my mind wandered off, too deep into Silo's story*, I thought.

Silo started stamping his damned feet again and spoke. "I've seen a few ghosts here, and they all look angry, so that's why I call them mad souls. The one that bothers me the most is the one that doesn't belong here."

"Which one is that, Silo?"

"It's a little boy in a diaper that I always see crying. He runs around with a dark face, convulsed in pain, and he has empty eye sockets. I think he is the victim of somebody on death row."

My first thought was that it must have been Silo's victim in his nightmare, but I no longer wanted to hear his story. "Silo, man, I'm done listening to that bullshit. You need to take that medication them folks give you, or quit taking it, one or the other."

"Now nigga, listen to me." Silo's voice pleaded with me now, no longer imperious and commanding.

"I'm not a nigga, and don't say that ever again! And I don't want to hear anymore of your crazy stories." Silo ignored me after that and kept talking, whether I wanted to listen to him or not. He was determined to finish what he had to say.

"Sometimes at night when the prison is asleep, souls from the prison graveyard roam the prisons around the state," He said. "They say that when it becomes foggy or when lightning strikes, they are at their strongest, and that's when they come to claim other souls, because they are lonely."

"I told you I didn't want to hear anymore," I said angrily. "You are going to make me put my foot in your ass when I catch you!" I continued sputtering curse words at him because he wouldn't stop. I felt as if he was trying to drive me insane.

"L.A., don't be mad at me," Silo said. "I'm just trying to get somebody to listen to me."

I wasn't really mad at Silo, as I knew more than most how the frustrations of incarceration can build up and how we all had to search for outlets to release all the pent-up anger, but Silo was bugging me. I thought he needed to talk to someone to clear his mind, but I wasn't the man for the job. However, if I treated him like he was crazy, he would act that way because it was expected of him. Maybe he wasn't crazy. People had the right to believe whatever they wanted to believe. Who was I to say they were wrong, no matter how farfetched their stories seemed?

"Silo?"

"What, L.A.?"

"I ain't mad at you. You alright with me, and if you want to finish telling me the story, well, go ahead," I told him reluctantly.

"Nah, I don't want to talk about it anymore. They are going to take me to Jester Four later today, and I'll tell the psychiatrist."

"I didn't mean what I said. I'll listen to you, man. However, when you go to the Jester Four, I wouldn't tell the psychiatrist nothing, because they will only shoot you up with a lot of drugs, huh?"

Jester Four is one of the state's psychiatric wards where they take prisoners who are mentally ill or refuse to take their medication. I've heard some strange stories about that place. I know many prisoners who often go there and some actually like it. Others, well, they beg and plead to never be taken there again, but those pleas don't amount to anything.

"Hey, L.A.?" Silo called.

"What's on your mind?"

"Nobody was in the pipe chase making any noise when you asked me. There is no generator back there either, only pipes. The main generator is on the other side of the building, and besides, maintenance don't work on Sundays."

"So, what you're saying is you didn't hear anything?"

He hesitated for a brief moment, then said, "No! I didn't hear any noise at all. I just wanted you to be quiet so I could finish telling you my story, as you call it, but it's not just a story, it's a reality that you just don't see."

"You got that right. I damn sure don't see that reality," I said. I realized then that Silo was trying to play with my mind. And he was right, there couldn't possibly have been a generator in the back of the cell where the pipe chase was because there was nothing but pipes in the back that was a direct link to our toilets and sinks. I asked myself again, was I going crazy, or was Ax Man roaming around here?

"Hey, Silo?" I called his name. "Hey man, you hear me calling you?"

"What do you want?"

"You said you were going to Jester Four, and I want to know ... is it better over there than over here?"

"Hell, no! I hate it over there, but I do like this one woman psychiatrist. After they strap me to a bunk for a day or so, she'll then come spend a nice piece of time with me. I mean really, she is something to look at, and she has these small hips and—"

"Silo!" I cut him off. "What do you mean they strap you to a bunk?"

"For the first couple of days they may strap you to a bunk with your hands and legs spread apart in a prone position," he said, growing excited. "The psychiatrist has the most beautiful—"

"Why do they do that?" I cut him off again.

He was silent for a few moments, then he said, "I think that's a way to read peoples' emotions, to see how they will respond. They want to know if you'll panic, if you'll get depressed, or if you'll get angry and act violent."

"No shit! I can't imagine myself being treated like that. How do you respond, Silo?"

"Uh, well, sometimes I just start screaming real loud so they will come talk to me, but they don't. The nurse just looks through the slot in the window at me. Other times I just lay there and sing."

"But what if you have to use the restroom or something? You know, when you have to take a piss?"

"Oh, that depends on how you respond. If you act aggressive, the nurse and trusty will put you in something similar to a diaper in case you urinate or shit on yourself. If you're not aggressive, they come around and do what they call 'head calls' and will unstrap you. I piss on myself so this nurse named Ms. Jackson will come clean me up. She's real nice."

The way Silo said it made me realize that he liked that part, but regardless, if they treat them like that, it is very dehumanizing. In fact, Junebug had been to Jester Four before, but he never liked to talk about it. He had said if they ever tried to take him back again, they had to beat his ass and kill him. He told B.J. about it once, but B.J. never talked about it either.

I knew that if I ever went to Jester Four, I would fight back just like Junebug said he would. And when I lost the struggle, as I know I eventually would, I wouldn't say anything at all but would cling to my secrets for dear life because my sanity would depend on it. After thinking about what Silo had said, I wrapped my blanket around me and just listened to the continuous thunder. The cell was very dark, and the sun was hidden behind the clouds, but I could still see the rise of my chest moving up and down very slowly as I drifted to sleep. I thought about the world around me, full of beautiful and exotic images, pleasant to the eye. I clung to hope, but I was still faced with the living hell around me and all its varied realities. I said to myself before my eyelids fluttered and closed, "Stay away from me, you sadistic bastards, stay away from me." I thought about the psychiatrists who did not help men like Silo, but only tortured him.

I rolled over on my side and slept, wishing like hell that the many years that have passed was only a nightmare I would awake from to find peace. But if it wasn't, then I just wanted to disappear from this mortal world and never confront anymore nightmares or the dark shadow that mimicked life.

11

WELCOME BACK

WELCOME BACK TO J-21. The sign of blood still seemed to be everywhere as I entered the cellblock after so many months in solitary confinement. Silo was taken to Jester Four, and it felt as if he had been kidnapped without a trace late one night. "Perhaps Ax Man got him," I said to myself, laughing. I kind of missed ole crazy Silo.

"Open Three Row, Ten Cell," the escort guard yelled to the picket officer.

I entered the cell, and a few seconds later bags containing my property were thrown on the cell floor. The door rolled shut as I maneuvered my way toward the small metal slot to have the handcuffs removed. I looked around the cell. It was much cleaner than the cell in solitary was, and the bunk bed wasn't hanging toward the floor at one end. I would certainly have to clean it up though. *Not again!* I thought, staring at the toilet and shaking my head.

At the back of the cell was a life-sized poster of a nude woman, her head flung back, her legs spread wide and her finger inside her vagina. I stared for a moment, feeling a hard-on growing, but I quickly tore the poster down before more thoughts invaded my mind and captured my attention. Being sexually deprived was hell as it was, so I tried to erase the thoughts as fast as they came. However, I often failed.

Bam! Bam! Bam! Someone next door in eleven cell banged loudly on the wall.

"What!" I shouted.

"What's goin' on Bro?" a familiar voice asked.

"Is that you, Tee?"

"Yeah, youngster, this is me. The one and only. I was just letting you know I'm next door to you. It's been a long time since I saw you last, hasn't it?"

"Sure has, Tee. It's been way too long," I said, trying to figure out when I had seen him last. Then I remembered. He had been on the yard with Y.L., Rogers-El, Silo, Da'Oud and me when we all got sprayed with tear gas a few years back. That one experience had bonded us for life, so it seemed, and the only people left from that who hadn't been executed and were still alive were myself, Tee, Y.L. and Silo.

Tee was much older than me. In fact, he had by this time been on death row for twenty-two years. He was a short black man with a large, round Afro, and he wore spectacles that were similar to those that Malcolm X had worn. He was very soft spoken and was by far the most informed and intelligent person I knew when it came to black history. Tee prided himself on knowing his history, and he read books like most people ate, constantly. I often found myself learning things from him that had never before crossed my mind before. When I thought of Tee, he reminded me of the many philosophers I had read about. I pictured his face with the large spot of gray hair that came from all the years of hardship.

"L.A., I'm glad they moved you next door so we can rap about books and shit, but I'll talk to you later on when you get situated over there."

"Alright, cool. I'll rap to you shortly."

I walked over to the doorway of the cell and yelled out, "Young Lion, where you at? Hey, Y.L.?"

"Yo, what's up?" he finally answered.

"You can't speak, or what?"

"Ah, man, that you up there, L.A.?" he asked.

"Yeah, I just got back over here a few minutes ago."

"Right on. I can't hear you that well because I'm down here in management cell on One Row, but I'll talk to you outside at recreation. You need to go ahead and clean that toilet and the rest of the cell. You know how it is, huh?" somebody said in a husky voice. "Tee and Y.L., the only two people you know over here?"

"Who's that talking?" I asked.

"This is me in nine cell, fool. It's me Li'l Dez."

"Hey man, what's happening?" I said. "I was wondering who was on the other side of me. I can see they gave me two good neighbors, but we all will talk later on. Man, you know I have to unpack and shit."

"I know that. I was just letting you know who existed around this camp. You act like you couldn't holler at nobody else."

"Don't be like that, Li'l Dez," I said. "I didn't even know you was over there."

"I'm just messing with you. Man, it's good to see you too. The last time I saw you is when all you brothers got gassed on the yard when them pigs threw me down the stairs handcuffed and broke my arm."

"I remember, Li'l Dez, and yeah, it's good to hear your voice, too."

Shortly after, many of the guys I knew hollered up at me, and I said my hellos and went to work. I tore an old t-shirt into pieces and wiped the walls down, scrubbed the floor, and stuck my hands in another nasty-ass toilet to clean it. I hated that part. However, it had to be done.

"Hey, Williams!" a guard yelled up. "You got a visit, so get ready and I'll be up in fifteen minutes to get you."

I was astonished to learn I was getting a visit because I wasn't expecting anyone. I didn't know who it could possibly be and the guards do not tell you. I was caught at an awkward time, and I probably smelled funky after cleaning the cell, but a visit was a visit and I didn't want to miss that.

"I see you already back into the swing of things, L.A.," Tee said.

"I guess so. It's been a long time since I had a visitor. I don't even know who it is."

"Well, enjoy yourself, whoever it is, and we'll talk when you get back."

Then Li'l Dez spoke up. "Maybe somebody will surprise me, too, but everybody ain't special like you," he laughed. "Have a good one, Bro."

"Right on."

I opened one of the property bags and threw all the contents on the mattress, looking for a comb and some grease. Once I had found it, I hurriedly put some grease in my curly hair and combed it straight. I hadn't had enough time to shave, so I tried to look as decent as I could. I knew my skin probably looked sickly yellow because I hadn't had any sunlight for many months. *Oh well*, I thought.

"You ready to go, boy?" It was the same toothpick-thin sergeant who had asked me to make a statement while I was in solitary. I wanted to tell him, "Bitch! I told you before I ain't yo muthafuckin' boy!" But I had to put my pride in check, or he would find a way to cancel my visit. Knowing he could get away with his little word games at the moment certainly made his day. He took even more liberty as we proceeded with the usual movements.

"You were told to be ready in fifteen minutes. Why aren't you ready?" the sergeant shouted.

"Man, three minutes haven't even passed since the other guard hollered up here, but yes, I'm ready," I said, trying to swallow the feeling of disgust this pig aroused in me.

"Turn around and be handcuffed then, boy!"

I turned around and got handcuffed as he clenched the cuffs hard around my wrists and the metal bit into my flesh. I sealed my lips with a rage boiling inside, but I wouldn't give him the satisfaction of provoking me further. Some Southern whites continuously used the term "boy" when referring to black men, as another means of calling us slaves, or nigger, spook, monkey and a few other names used to make themselves feel superior to us. Race didn't mean anything to me because I was taught to recognize the heart had no color, that love had no color, but sometimes I just couldn't help but recognize a racist, and this fucking sergeant was racist to the bone.

As I was escorted down the hall, I felt the sergeant kick the back of my heel and then say, "Oh, excuse me." And when I turned around, he said, "Make sure you keep facing ahead." I knew he was trying to provoke an incident, but I held on to my cool. I gritted my teeth and held on.

In the visiting room I was placed in a cage with a steel frame and mesh wire folded around me. I had to squat down to be un-cuffed through another metal slot. I then sat on the stool and stared through the plexiglass window in front of me, until I spotted my visitor walking toward me.

"Hey, Mama!" I said with a brilliant smile stretching my face. And when my mother smiled, all the anger that I felt towards the guard disappeared instantly.

"I surprised you, huh? I bet you had no idea I was flying to Texas to come see you?" She was so excited to be here with me.

I didn't want to tell her that if I had still been in solitary, the surprise would have been hers—the terrible sorrow of not being able to see me. "No, Mama," I said, "I didn't have any idea you were coming, and I'm so happy to see you. I miss you so very much."

I was from Los Angeles, as was most of my family, so whenever I saw my mother, it was only when she could afford to buy a plane ticket and fly to Texas to see me for a couple of days.

"Your sisters and little brother told me to tell you they love you, and they hope to come see you when they can," Mama said. "And why haven't you written me lately? I came down here without really making any plans because I was so worried about you."

I didn't ever want to tell her I had been in solitary because it would only cause her to worry, so I lied shamefully. "Well, uh, I didn't have any money on my account to buy stamps," I told her. I did have money that she sent me a couple of months before, but I couldn't spend it due to all the restrictions I was placed on.

"Baby, whenever you need anything, you make sure you tell me, okay?" She was frowning. "I will do whatever I can, and besides, it would have been a whole lot cheaper to send you some money rather than rushing with plans to come down here to see you. I was so worried." Sadness haunted her beautiful face.

"I'm sorry, Mama. I just ..." Not really knowing what to say, I quickly changed the subject. "How is everybody?" I asked.

"Everyone is doing fine. Your sister Angie is working real hard and taking care of her little baby, Lauryn. Your little sister, Darra is now in college, and she can't sit still for one minute without ripping and running them streets, but she's doing good. And your little brother Darryl, is growing up so fast I don't even think you'd recognize him. He now goes to the same high school that you went to, and he's playing football and everything."

"That's good, Mama," I said as I thought about the ever-so-clear memories I had of all of them. I wished they would all be as I remembered them, but they wouldn't be. Everyone had to eventually grow up and move on with their lives. I had no choice but to accept that.

"One of the main reasons I came down here was to tell you that there's been some new development concerning your case. Your attorney said that you've been granted a very important hearing and that you may be transferred back to the Harris County jail within the week. I don't want to tell you everything here, because they have ways of taping everything we say, so I'll let your attorney tell you," she said, then waited for my response.

The news kind of hit me hard because I wasn't expecting any good news to come concerning my appeal—ever. It didn't matter if I proclaimed to be innocent or not. Who didn't claim to be innocent in the face of death? No one wanted to die.

"Say something, Nanon."

"Oh, uh, well, I just don't know what to say." The words stumbled out of my mouth.

My mother sat there with her mouth open. "What's wrong, Baby? Something is bothering you, and I sure wish you'd tell me what it is?" Tears were welling in her eyes.

"Ah, it ain't nothing, Mama. I'm just a little shocked that there are any new developments in my appeal. Who knows? Maybe I'll be home soon."

"I always pray to God you will come home, and even your little brother and sisters pray too," Mama said. "I'm going to take you shopping, but you a car, enroll you in college ..."

"Okay, okay," I said, not really wanting to cut her off. Seeing her excitement felt good, but entertaining any ideas of freedom seemed dangerous, although I desperately wanted to believe it. I did believe it in a sense. It just existed in a quiet place in my heart, somewhere. I just tried not to acknowledge it. "So, how long will you be here this time?" I asked.

"I can only visit this one day. I want to go to your grandparents' house because your grandmother is sick, and then I have to fly back home. I don't have any days off, and they need me in the hospital. But I called in sick to come and see you."

"I'm sorry that you go through so much trouble to come see me."

"Don't say that! I love you, son, and I'll go to the end of the Earth to see you if I have to. I gave you life, and you better believe I'm going to fight for your life!"

"I hear you," I smiled. My mother had a way of making any day special, and her presence made most people feel that way. She had been through a lot during her lifetime, but she never gave up. *Nor would I,* I thought. *Nor would I.*

"So, tell me what you've been doing the past year?"

"Well, I've actually been working on a book. I sometimes don't know what to write about, so I find myself writing about the days, the months and the years that pass by. I try to write about my reality, as it is; the language, the experiences and my thoughts—no more, no less. I guess you could say I write as a form of therapy to force myself to remember everything, rather than succumb to the illusions that insanity seems to bring."

"What do you mean, insanity? Tell me, is it that tough here? Because your face seems creased with anger. Don't let anger destroy you, son. It's an irrational emotion."

"I know, Mama. It's not that bad here. There are a lot of good people around here. I just write to keep some of the men alive, so they won't be forgotten. Do you remember two prisoners named Rogers-El and Da'Oud that you met out here a few years ago?"

"No, I can't say I do. But I'm sure I'll remember them when I see them."

I didn't want to tell Mama that Rogers-El and Da'Oud had already been executed, nor did I want to tell her about the conflicts we often had with the guards. I knew Mama would understand if I told her, I knew that, as my mother, she probably blamed herself for everything that happened to me because most parents believe they failed when their children get caught up in life's circumstances. Yet that's what it was—just life itself that created so many different paths we traveled.

"Whenever they come and get you to take you to the Harris County jail, you be sure to call me every single day, okay? Promise me?" Mama said as she waved her finger close to the plexiglass.

"I promise. I'll call you a lot."

"And why don't you ever call me from here?"

"Because we can only use the phone once every six months here, for only five minutes, so I actually never bother to call," I said, as I knew she would want me to call anyway.

"Please call anyway, okay?"

"Okay."

My mother and I talked about many things, and although I was her son, we sometimes talked and laughed as if we were the very best of friends. We talked about relationships, among other things, and she told me a little something about the guys she dated.

"So, who are you dating?" I asked.

"Oh, just some doctor that works in the hospital with me."

I continued my investigation. "How old is he?"

Now it was my mother who was stuttering. "Oh, uh, he's in ... ah, he's in his thirties."

My mother was very close to fifty, so I said, "What! He's in his thirties? You got you a little young something, huh?" I wore a serious inquisitive expression on my face as befitting a son who was lovingly teasing his mother.

"Nanon, you need to quit! You are not my Mama. I'm yours, so quit asking me all these questions like I need your approval!" She was laughing so hard, and it was so good to hear her laughter. "And quit looking at me all crazy!"

I grinned and said, "It's cool. I'm just asking, woman. Give me a break."

It was good to see her laughing, but I didn't like the idea of any man dating my mother. I have no problem with the age difference or someone's race because people fall in love for a million and one reasons, but I felt no man could treat my mother with the respect and love she deserved, so I really didn't want to hear anymore.

"Boy! Say something before I come through this window," she said, still laughing, and her ebony eyes were sparkling. When she said "boy," I immediately thought about the toothpick-thin sergeant who was approaching the visiting cage.

"You got five minutes left," he said.

"Well, get on, and let me get 'em," I told him. My visit was over now, so if he wanted a problem I would surely oblige him!

"What did you tell him?" my mother asked.

"Oh nothing. He just said we have five minutes left."

"The time went by so quickly. Well, you know I love you, and know that God loves you too. In the meantime, I'm doing the best I can right now. I'll write you when I get home." Tears suddenly trickled from her ebony eyes down her beautiful face.

"I love you, Mama," I said, trying to be strong and hold back my tears. "You tell my siblings I love them too, and you cling to the faith you've always had, okay?"

"You better cling to it too, Nanon." We both put our hands on the plexiglass that separated us, and we just stared at each other.

"Time's up!" the sergeant said. He could see the deep emotions between Mama and I and was wallowing in his authority to break up the visit.

"Be safe and don't look back when you leave," I told her.

"I will. Call me when you get to the Harris County jail." She blew me a kiss and walked with her head held high like she always did.

"I love you," I whispered as the sergeant flipped the steel plate open so he could handcuff me. I knew that he had cut the visit short, but I never wanted to make a scene for my mother to see, nor for any other visitor to see.

When we get to the back of the visiting room, we are supposed to be strip-searched to see if we have any contraband and that meant the handcuffs had to be taken off. I stopped when we got to the back.

"Aren't you going to strip-search me and take the handcuffs off, Sarge?" I said in a mocking tone that even in his stupidity he could not fail to understand.

"No! Just keep moving so I can take you back to your cellblock!"

"Okay then, boy! Let's go," I told him. If he had taken off the handcuffs, I wouldn't have assaulted him, but I wanted to give us both the opportunity to provoke each other and deal with each other. However, I knew the pain of seeing my mother leave was turning into anger, and I recalled what she had said, that anger is an irrational emotion. So I walked down the hallway toward the cellblock, trying to get away from the jerk.

We moved swiftly down the hallway and entered the corridor of J-21. As we ascended the steps, I walked a little too fast and stumbled back and fell against the railing.

"What are you trying to do, Williams?" The sergeant sounded alarmed.

"I just tripped," I told him. "I ain't trying to do nothing!" I felt somewhat embarrassed, although it did feel strange ascending the steep stairs with handcuffs behind my back.

I stood still for a moment, staring at him. He wasn't quite my height, so I towered over him, looking at the same bald spot he tried to cover up before, only this time it looked even thinner.

"Don't try anything," the sergeant said in a dismantled voice tinged with fear and uncertainty.

He stood back a few feet for the time being, but I turned my back and went up the steps. I don't recall what was going through my mind. It seemed as if all my senses went dead, and I couldn't hear the ruckus of normal life on J-21. I was debating something. What, I wasn't sure.

"Roll Three Row, Ten cell!" the sergeant yelled. He was smiling as he shoved me into the cell, and the door slammed shut.

I didn't even respond. I just stood there waiting for the handcuffs to be removed, and then the sergeant slapped his thigh, and said, "You are an asshole, Williams, and the first time you get out of line with me, you'll regret it."

"Pig! March yo ass down the tier," I heard Li'l Dez say. "L.A., chill out, man, you know they want to take you back to solitary."

After the handcuffs were removed, the sergeant stormed down the tier hurling insults at Li'l Dez, but I just looked at my property that I had earlier thrown on the bunk and finished cleaning up the cell. Once I had finished, I thought about my visit and felt good all over again. "Fuck that sergeant!" I said quietly to myself. I wasn't going to let him ruin the visit I'd had with my beloved mother.

"Say, Bro," Tee called from his cell next door. "How was your visit with whoever?"

"It was great! My mother flew down from Los Angeles and as you know, I wasn't expecting her. I didn't even know I was getting out of solitary until they came to get me today, so we're lucky we got to have a visit at all."

"I know it must have felt good," Li'l Dez said from the cell on the other side of me. "I know seeing my people makes my day special, but what was you and that sergeant trippin' on?"

"I don't know what that sergeant's problem is, but that pig kept calling me 'boy' on the way to visitation, and he even kicked me in the back of my heel when we were walking down there, to try to provoke an incident."

"For real?" Tee asked. "That's the same sergeant that ended my visit early one day when I was visiting my woman."

"Oh, yeah, he ended my visit early too, but I didn't want to create a problem in front of my Mama, or other prisoners visiting, out of respect. But I did try to provoke him a little when we were coming back. I also tripped on the steps when I was coming up, and I guess he thought I was up to something when I stumbled backwards."

"What happened?" Tee asked. "Your big-ass Jupiter head got too heavy and weighed you down?"

"Ha, ha," I said. "Tee, you are forever the comedian, huh?" I laughed along with Li'l Dez clapping his hands.

"Your head is real big though, L.A," Li'l Dez said.

"Since you think that's so funny, Li'l Dez, I'm going to tell you who I was really visiting. Me and your woman have had a little something going on for months now, and she came to see me in a blue dress with no panties on," I started laughing. "Now, what do you think about that?"

"Man, that shit ain't funny, but I tell you what! Next time I see you in the visiting room, I'm going to tell her what you said and send her down to you."

"You better not do that shit, Li'l Dez," Tee said with a gurgle of laughter, "She might like the thought."

"Shut up, Tee," Li'l Dez and I both said in rapid succession. Tee was still beside himself laughing, but we always cracked jokes on each other.

But then Tee spoke up, "Fuck both of y'all, and your little woman too." And then we all laughed together. We did everything in good humor, but if someone overheard us, they would have thought we were serious. It felt good laughing with the fellas after so long a drought, and laughter always felt good.

"I got some legal work to do," Li'l Dez said, "I'll rap to y'all later."

"Me too," Tee said.

And the day just passed on by.

12

REVOLUTIONARY EDUCATION

A FEW DAYS LATER, after catching up with many of the guys that I had not seen in a while, I was placed back in a group recreation with all the other prisoners on Three Row. A classification committee that consisted of two wardens, a captain and that same skinny-ass sergeant who obviously hated me, decided that I could participate in group recreation. Of course, the one vote against me was from the skinny-ass sergeant.

It was still early morning, and I looked forward to going outside in the sun and maybe playing a few games of basketball with a few of the prisoners who liked to play. When I was finally outside on the small recreation yard, Tee was already waiting.

"What's up, Bro?" I said, smiling.

"Glad you're out here," Tee said, rubbing his eyes. "I don't like coming out this early."

"Didn't get much sleep, huh?"

He walked past me and sat down on the bench. "Hell nah! I stayed up reading a book about Huey P. Newton and the Black Panther Party. The book was so insightful and full of struggle that I couldn't put it down," Tee said, yawning. "I wasn't going to come outside today, but I wanted to see you in person instead of talking to you between the bars, I also think Li'l Dez is bringing his dominoes out, too, so I can show you youngsters how to get down. I'm what you call a dominologist'"

"Oh yeah, we'll see who's the best as soon as he comes out," I responded, laughing at his made up word.

As we both looked toward the doorway, Li'l Dez was being un-handcuffed and came toward us with a frown on his face. "What is it, home boy?" he said.

"Ah, nothing much," Tee told him, "why didn't you bring the dominoes out here so we could play?'

"Shit. I didn't even think about bringing them out today. I was just coming out here to get some fresh air," Li'l Dez said wearily, looking up at the sky. "What's up, L.A.?"

"Nothing. I'm just looking at Tee looking tired like he hasn't slept in a week, and I'm just observing you looking at the sky like something is going to fall out of it."

"Maybe something will," he said. "Maybe something is going to come snatch me out of this hellhole."

"The sky is beautiful, ain't it?" Tee looked up at the blue sky with white clouds drifting lazily.

"It sure is," I said. I could smell the fields and feel the warmth as the sun came up full force, blinding us all and preventing us from looking directly at it.

"Let's move to the back of the yard," Tee said as other prisoners came outside and started shooting the basketball. "I just feel like chatting today. I don't much have the energy to shoot some ball."

"Man, we can chat and all that shit in the cell," I said. "I came out here to get my hoop on!"

"I don't feel like playing," Li'l Dez said. "Look who came outside today? Them fools can't play anyway, and they foul too fuckin' much. Fuck that shit." Li'l Dez walked alongside Tee and leaned against the back fence when they got to the end of the recreation yard.

I walked behind them, not without arguing and pleading with them to play anyway. "Y'all come on and play. You know I haven't had any exercise since I've been in solitary. Bring yo' ole ass on, Tee."

"Come on, have a seat, just today, Bro. We'll play tomorrow." Tee looked serious. "Let's just sit back and chill."

I squatted by the fence, surrendering myself to mere chatter and any knowledge he had to give. It didn't surprise me to discover that Tee wanted to spend the few hours we had wanting to enlighten us.

"Struggle is inevitable," Tee said. "Every day is a struggle, but we gotta keep trying to progress, you know?"

I stood back up lazily, brushed the dirt off my prison jumpsuit and took notice that both Tee and Li'l Dez had something on their minds. I am not telepathic, so I couldn't scan their minds and figure out what was up with them today.

"It's another execution tonight," Tee said, casually propped on his side, getting comfortable.

"Who?"

"Joe," Li'l Dez said. "He'll be one of the first prisoners executed that has been on death row since he was a juvenile. Everybody thought he would get a stay of execution from the governor, but time is ticking away."

I leaned back up against the fence, shaking my head. "Is there no hope left for him?"

"No, that's quite clear now. The Fifth Circuit turned him down yesterday, and a clemency hearing didn't do any good." Tee was making hand motions as he spoke, showing his frustration.

"If them bitch-ass muthafuckas ever talk about executing me, I'm going to fight them with everything I got!" Li'l Dez said. "They won't shed my blood in a peaceful manner. I'm going to fight for my life! You understand what I'm sayin'?"

"I've been here for twenty-three years, and nobody has ever actually fought back the day of their execution. Not to say that you won't," Tee stressed, "but some people want to go out with their head held high and others try to make peace with God and the victim's family."

"I feel what you're saying, Tee," Li'l Dez nodded understandingly. "I'm just not one of those people. I have my peace with my God, but God gave me life too, and I'm fighting for it with every breath I have, physically, when my time is up. I'm no angel, but I'm not the monster they say I am, and I don't belong on death row!"

"Li'l Dez, don't get so riled up," I said as the basketball rolled over in our direction. Li'l Dez then picked it up and kicked it as hard as he could toward the three men who were playing.

"They will try to take me by force, but I'm filled with spirit, and I'm going to let it loose!"

"I agree with you, Li'l Dez. Although I have always liked to believe I'll someday go home, especially with the recent news my mom told me at visitation, but if they ever come to execute me, well, I'm going to fight their ass too," I said, envisioning such a scene. "Just think about it. If no one comes to claim your body, what will they do with it? They say it's placed in an unmarked grave at the prison cemetery, but who is to say they don't take it and run experiments and shit? Man, they might be putting us to sleep and taking us to a lab to do all kinds of stuff if nobody actually comes to claim us."

"You got a point there, L.A.," Tee said. "In Germany, Hitler experimented with humans like lab rats, and this place is certainly not much different than Auschwitz."

"What is Oshwitz?" Li'l Dez asked.

"It's pronounced oush-vitz, and it was the site of one of the biggest death camps Adolph Hitler had in Poland during World War II. They slaughtered millions of Jews at the death camps."

The way Tee spoke about Auschwitz made it sound like a curse to even speak about it. Tee was normally a very gentle and humble brother, but sometimes he got real riled up.

"You see, Huey P. Newton recognized long ago that America has run concentration camps all over the world. Instead of outright killing people like Hitler, they use capitalism as a way to exploit people through slave wages. And when the wages aren't enough, what happens?"

"You create hustlers," I said. "Those that work outside the system of economics to survive. In a sense, they create their own economy."

Li'l Dez looked at Tee and said, "So this is why we have so many pimps, ho's, drug dealers, burglars and many other types of individuals who basically make up the prison system?"

Tee smiled. "Right on, you got it! But look a little deeper than that. A capitalist is someone who invests capital (money) in various business enterprises. In order for someone to successfully reap benefits out of those investments, someone had to be manipulated and used in order for them to gain profit. Prison is big business and this entire community of Huntsville thrives off the prison system. Not only do prisons create profit through free slave labor (prisoners), but those prisoners also create profit for the system because they become a bigger instrument for other creative ways to make profits. Those who create all this are the real criminals. They thrive off the 'dog eat dog' theory."

"Go on, Preach," I said to Tee. "Can we get an Amen?" I joked.

"Why don't yo big-ass head listen to what he's saying, L.A.?" Li'l Dez told me.

"Anyway," Tee went on, "do y'all remember when they executed Karla Faye Tucker?"

"Of course, we remember," I said, "it was all over the news because it was like a huge event for America."

"It was even a popular execution in Europe," Li'l Dez said.

"Right! The community of Huntsville profited off her death. How?

Li'l Dez and I looked at each other, and although we both had our own ideas, we preferred to listen to Tee because he had a knack for teaching others. The brother actually had a passion to give others knowledge and to gain it as well.

"How did the community profit?" Li'l Dez looked a little perplexed.

"The Ellis Unit is in Huntsville, as is the Walls Unit where they execute us, and about four or five other prison units too. When all the people who come to protest the executions and media circuits around the world came to interview Karla and talk to the wardens and other prison officials, how did the community make money?"

I looked at Li'l Dez and spoke up. "I figure that whoever owns hotels and sleeping lodges make money because they have to stay somewhere to sleep, right?"

"That is my point," Tee said. "Not only did those who owned hotels prosper, but the whole community prospered because the city of Huntsville became a tourist attraction. The store owners of all kinds profited from people buying clothes, food, gas and other things people need daily."

"I understand what you mean," Li'l Dez said, "They made profit through someone's death. Do you got some books on this?"

"Yeah, I do. I'm going to send you a book on Marxism. It's the theories of Karl Marx and Friedrich Engels that show us various doctrines on class struggle and manipulation by the capitalist structure. Or, I can send you the book I'm reading by Huey P. Newton. He was a member of the Black Panther Party who tried to uplift the poor black and Latino communities through organizing. He believed in uplifting and raising the spirits of the poor and oppressed in order to better our living conditions. He too studied Marxism, so that's why I mention these books to you."

"Wait! I know who he is," Li'l Dez said, "but yea, send me a book on something I can relate to. Karl Marx sounds interesting, but I can relate to Huey and the Black Panther Party. I know they fought against the system through takin' up arms if necessary, yet they did it all legally."

"Well, y'all, it looks like our time is up," I said. "We can finish talking about this when we go in and maybe we could do a little reading to each other."

"That'll be cool," Tee said, "me and Y.L. read to each other all the time. I was thinking that maybe one day a week we could have a study session out here and talk about all kinds of things. If we control our thoughts, we can consciously direct ourselves and regulate our reactions in all that we do, if we educate each other. Right on."

"Right on," Li'l Dez and I said in unison.

"Recreation is over!" Mrs. Milly yelled through the window. As everyone stared to flock in like sheep, we shook hands and embraced each other as we normally do. "You all come in at the back!" she yelled again, pointing directly at us.

"Man, you didn't want to see me out here on this court anyway," Tee said as he strolled on the basketball court and grabbed the ball. "Michael Jordan can't touch me, fool! Watch this shot!" He shot the basketball, and sent it smooth and straight into the basketball goal.

"Man, that shit was luck!" Li'l Dez said. "Bet fifty push-ups you can't make that same shot again."

Realizing the odds of Tee making that shot again from the same distance, I spoke up too. "Yeah, I betcha fifty push-ups, too, Tee."

"I'm not going to bet both of you youngsters fifty push-ups a piece, but I tell you what," Tee said. "Y'all put up fifty push-ups between the two of you, and if I lose, I'll do twenty-five. Is that a bet that I'll make a goal?"

"Yeah, it's a bet," we quickly agreed.

"Okay, now here I go," Tee said. He didn't shoot the ball from where he was, but instead he just walked under the goal, and shot it directly in. "There it is. I made the shot. Now, do my push-ups," he said with a smug grin.

"You didn't shoot from where you shot from last time!" Li'l Dez complained. "Fuck that shit! I ain't doing nothing!"

"Me either!" I added my complaint. "You cheatin' ass ain't getting away with that."

"I didn't cheat either of you," he said. "I quote, 'is that a bet I'll make a goal?' and the both of you said, 'yeah.' Listen to what people say to you instead of immediately responding."

He's right, L.A.," Li'l Dez said. "He said he would make a goal, not shoot the ball from where he was standing."

"You a good slick-ass muthafucka, Tee. I'll listen carefully to your exact words next time," I said. We all laughed good-naturedly.

As I was doing the push-ups, Tee, being ever the comedian, put the basketball close by my head and asked Li'l Dez, "Hey, be truthful, L.A.'s head is as big as this basketball, huh?" Then he and Li'l Dez ran inside the doorway, laughing at me as I playfully chased them down.

"Man, fuck y'all!" I said, wondering if my head was really that big. I knew I had a big head and all, but I was tired of them always cracking jokes on my behalf about it. I just smiled to myself as I watched the two of them continuing to have their fun with me.

"Williams, come on and rack up so I can take my break," Mrs. Milly said. I went inside, feeling pretty good about the time we spent at recreation, but I knew our laughing was just a way for us to lift each others' spirits, knowing that there would be an execution at six o'clock that evening.

13

POPE JOAN AND LI'L DEZ

L I'L DEZ AND TEE had been asleep for hours. The other prisoners were quiet as well, so I spent the rest of the day reading until night came. I could hear Tee snoring and then suddenly plunge back into his dreams because of the utter silence, but Li'l Dez had just wakened. I heard the creaks of his bunk break the monotony of the day, just as the sun disappeared under the cloak of darkness. The main lights of the cellblock went out, and the sight of a sheeted figure appeared off the reflection of the window when Li'l Dez turned on his light.

Bam! Bam! Bam! Li'l Dez banged on my wall.

"Man, people are asleep! Quit banging on my wall so hard," I admonished him.

"I was just seeing if you were up, L.A. The rest of these fools will be up in a minute, watch and see."

I wasn't really tired, so I figured I might as well chill with Li'l Dez for a while. "About time you got your ass up, Li'l Dez."

"Yeah, I know. After staying up late last night and then getting up early this morning, I was tired."

"Tee has been asleep too," I told him, wondering if he was going to be getting up soon as well.

"You mean you ain't been to sleep?"

"Nah, I ain't tired. I've been up doing a little bit of reading."

"What were you reading?" Li'l Dez asked.

"I finished a book that my friend Andrea from Switzerland sent me. I reflected upon the book for a moment. The character reminded me of her. I have never read anything like it.

"L.A., I didn't ask you who sent the book. I asked you *what* you were reading. Damn! Can't you hear, or what?" he said jokingly.

"I just finished reading a book called *Pope Joan*. It was a fiction story based on the legendary tale of a woman who disguised herself as a man and became Pope."

"I'm not Catholic, of course, but I thought there never has been a woman Pope. Not that I give a good goddamn, but am I wrong?"

"I'm not a historian, so I can't tell you if you're wrong. But according to this book, there once lived a woman who disguised herself as a man and ascended to the throne of Christianity and reigned for two years, more than a thousand years ago."

Before he could reply, a guard stopped in front of his cell and asked his name and number.

"Desmond Jennings. 999161," he replied tersely.

"Name and number?" The young Hispanic guard stepped in front of my cell and asked me the same question.

"Nanon Williams," I said.

"Number please."

"999163." I hated having to identify myself with a number, as if I was less than a human being. The guard continued on down the tier.

"L.A.! L.A.!" Li'l Dez tried to get my attention.

"Yeah, what?"

"Finish telling me about Pope Joan. Why did you stop?"

"Oh man, I was just trippin' on always having to recite a fuckin' number like that's all we are. I get tired of saying my number is 9-9-9-…"

"I feel the same way, but can you finish telling me about the book?"

"Anyway," I said, the book is a novel, and it goes on to tell about the extraordinary life of a very independent and intelligent search for knowledge by Joan."

"That's all, L.A.?" He wanted to know more. I could not help but admire his seeming thirst for knowledge. "Exactly how did she become Pope?"

"Well, Joan wasn't trying to become Pope, nor did she want the responsibility. As you well know from extensive reading, women have always been considered inferior to men, especially in the western hemisphere."

"And what's your point?"

"If you let me finish, you'll know," I said, stalling in order to gather my thoughts on the book. "In the ninth century it was practically against the law for a woman to become educated. Back then an educated woman was considered dangerous."

"Why?" Li'l Dez asked.

"I don't rightly know, but you can ask Tee when he wakes up. Of course he can probably tell you more than I can. Anyway, women in the ninth century were not allowed to go to school or even read books."

"So, what you're saying is, women were treated like slaves here in America were treated? As you well know, white people didn't allow slaves to read, or to learn how to write in order to keep them in ignorance."

"Well, yes, something like that," I said. Li'l Dez knew a great deal about slavery because he loved history, and he compared the differences between how black Americans were treated now as compared to a couple of decades ago.

"I won't get into that, Bro," he said. "We'll talk about that next. Please continue."

"Joan's father was an Englishman who raised his two sons to be scholars in the hope of them studying at a special school for gifted young boys from respected families. I won't say Joan's family was respected, because they weren't."

"Why?" Li'l Dez asked.

"Well, although Joan's father was an Englishman, he married a heathen, and he was looked down upon."

"What do you mean, a heathen?"

"Back then, Saxons were considered heathens. In fact, those were the white people who predominately had white blond hair and blue eyes."

"No shit? So when we're talking about Hitler today, it wasn't always blond hair and blue eyes that was the ideal image in the west?"

"Like I said, I'm no historian, but I guess at one time or another, most races were treated ill. Slavery has a way of repeating itself throughout history." This was something that I had begun to realize as I read more and more. "By Joan's father marrying a heathen, he wasn't well respected, and their entire family became outcast although they were free."

"What is freedom then, if you are still an outcast?"

"That is another story. But the belief of MAAT, which are teachings from our African ancestors, can give you the founding beliefs that we can talk about with Tee one day."

"Right on," Li'l Dez said enthusiastically.

"Being a scholar in the ninth century meant studying under the belief of Christianity. A scholarly language was considered Latin and maybe Greek as well. Joan's brother, Matthew, taught Joan how to read when she was a child. By the age of nine years old, Joan could read and write and that was uncommon for anyone that age back then, especially a girl."

"Okay, move on. Don't tell me the whole book. Just get to the main point."

"Alright, damn. To make a long story short, Joan was summoned by a bishop and was the first girl selected to enter one of the few privileged schools. Needless to say, she excelled much faster than the boys and everyone thought her unnatural. She was even accused by some of being designed by Satan."

"Why?"

"When Joan first entered the school, the bishop who selected her, quizzed her for show at the court. This was a test that was both forbidden and dangerous for her to answer as she did. She responded to the bishop's court to a question asked about the superiority of men over women. Her response was, "Women should be considered superior over men because Eve ate of the apple for love of knowledge and learning, but Adam ate the apple simply because she asked him to." So, can you imagine how the bishop's court took this response by a young girl no more than nine or ten years old?"

"No man would want to be made a fool of by a little girl, of course," Li'l Dez said, obviously contemplating how to respond. "Who wrote the book?"

"A woman named Donna Woolfolk Cross."

"I should have known it was a woman who wrote the book," he said smugly. "She made an arguable point, didn't she, L.A.?"

"Yeah, she did. Now you can see why I brought it up."

"Tell me more."

"Joan's brother died—the one who was supposed to go to a Benedictine monastery. And, in the book, Joan took his identity. Her father had often beat her, so she wasn't a pretty girl at all. Therefore, her sex was never questioned because monks dressed in thick robes that completely covered their bodies."

"Man, people should be able to recognize a woman."

"I would like to believe I could recognize a woman, too, but anyway, the book doesn't really describe Joan as being God-fearing. She was a little bit, but she chose to live the life of a man for quite a few reasons. Men had more freedom, and as a monk, the knowledge contained in books was open to her. Even more so, it was easier to live as a man in a monastery. After all, monks lived a life of chastity."

Our conversation died out for a while. At last Li'l Dez spoke again, with more questions.

"Why would you say she wasn't very religious?"

"Because the book describes Joan as being a woman of reason. Faith is believing in the unseen, and faith wasn't something Joan really felt. She believed in reason because the threads of understanding life could often be found in the evidence. For instance, she created all types of medicines that healed people. In the ninth century, especially in Rome, faith was considered all the evidence needed to heal anyone who was sick. Joan proved otherwise by using herbs and chemicals to heal people. Many considered medicines as a form of witchcraft because they didn't understand how to use them."

"Yeah!" Li'l Dez said excitedly. "Even some African cultures taught about reason, and creating medicines for healing the people from the mother earth. I can dig that part of the story."

"To end this shit about the book," I said, "the Catholic Church doesn't recognize Joan's papacy because they obviously took it as an embarrassment."

"In a sense, yes. History can be manipulated as time passes. I believe Pope Joan is not just a legend, but even if she is, the story is meant to show that men and women are both capable of achieving the same things in life, that gender doesn't matter. So yes, Pope Joan did exist, if only in spirit."

A thought occurred to Li'l Dez, and he spoke up. "You know what, L.A.?"

"What?"

"Our lives are much like Pope Joan's life."

"Why is that?"

"Like women in the ninth century, we too aren't encouraged to be educated. The state of Texas wants to keep us in ignorance so they can kill us quicker. They don't want us to be able to raise our consciousness, so they stifle our voices."

That was so true. I sat down, slumped on my bunk, as Li'l Dez turned off his light. "Hey, Li'l Dez?" I called over to him.

"What's up?"

"The newspaper not only writes us off as monsters, but they destroy our legacy through lies and propaganda without reason. Decades or even a century from now, how do you think history will remember us?"

Li'l Dez took a moment to answer. "I don't know, Bro. I don't know. Perhaps society will perceive us as a mistake in a primitive government, or just as dead men. One thing's for sure though, we'll never know all of our own history. Maybe we'll know of each other's, but we'll never truly know how history will see us and treat us. We can only hope for the gentle stroke of the pen to write about us."

"Do you want me to send you the book?" I asked.

"Hell, no. I got enough on my mind as it is."

"Well, if you change your mind, let me know."

"I'll let you know. But I prefer to read stuff from revolutionaries. I need something that shows spirit in the trenches of struggle."

"I feel where you're coming from, and I'll dig through my property and see what I can come up with."
Each night about ten o'clock, Li'l Dez and I held conversations like this, and sometimes, though not often, those conversations turned into outright arguments. We even pretended to be mad at each other at times because of some argument, but Tee always seemed to find a way to make us realize what initially started our arguments. Afterwards we felt foolish because we debated with the intention of teaching each other.

The weeks passed. September's sun lit up the cellblock for once, burning away the dark shadows that crept into the corners of my cell. I waited to go back to the Harris County jail for some hearing I was having, but no news came. I grew somewhat impatient.

The nightmarish thoughts of what would happen at the hearing were gone. The time was finally near. Suddenly the death row captain blocked the rays of sunlight that filtered through my cell.

"Pack!"

I looked up at him. "Pack what?"

"Pack up your property. There are some sheriff's deputies waiting to take you outta here. Just grab what you need, and put your other things in a bag."

"Alright," I said, "I'll be ready in a few minutes."

The captain nodded. He eyed me carefully as I shoved most of my things into the sacks I had. He looked down the tier, regarded me thoughtfully, and without handcuffing me, he yelled, "Roll it!"

I came out of the cell with my hygiene and legal envelopes and followed him down the tier.

As we walked along, I called out to everyone, "Tee, Li'l Dez! Y.L.! Sticky Boy! Capone!" and many other prisoners. I was leaving J-21, hoping perhaps, just maybe, I was seeing it all for the last time.

14

BENCH WARRANT

THE HEAVY METAL DOORS slammed behind me as lock after lock prevented entry or escape. I continued following the captain, amazed at not being handcuffed. It felt good to walk freely, not to be shackled or handcuffed, but I was still on my toes, very cautious, very wary, because if I ever let my guard down, more pain could embrace me at any given moment. Not that I wasn't feeling pain, but then, I realized long ago that my pain was something that crept up on me, unnoticed.

Nearing the end of a long, spacious hallway with steel shutters covering every window, two black female sheriffs stood waiting.

"Here's your inmate, Ma'am." The captain beamed with delight at seeing these two women in long-sleeved shirts and tight tan slacks that fit one of the women like a second skin. Even I gave a second look at one of the deputies whose skin tone resembled caramel. Her eyes were green with specks of ebony, and her long kinky hair draped curls around her shoulders. I thought to myself, *Damn, I've been locked up too long.* But the thoughts vanished as quickly as they came when I saw various chains that hung in the other woman's hand.

"What's your name?" the green-eyed woman asked.

"I looked at her, legs spread apart, and I responded while the other deputy looked at me with a menacing scowl, "My name is Williams, Nanon Williams." I refused to volunteer a state identification number.

"He's our man," the deputy with the menacing scowl said. Then quickly, "Strip!"

"Strip what?" I responded.

"Strip out of everything," the green-eyed deputy commanded. "We can take over from here, Captain."

The captain said goodbye, backing away but still smiling at the two deputies. He was in his late fifties with solid white hair, and I was smiling inwardly, thinking of what his white wife would think of him lusting after these two black women.

"Strip! Come on!" the deputy with the menacing scowl barked.

I hesitantly stripped, feeling uncomfortable as their gazes crawled slowly over me like an army of red ants. I took off the white prison jumpsuit, my t-shirt, and socks, down to my boxer shorts.

"Come out of those too!" they said in unison.

Embarrassed, I stepped out of my boxer shorts and stood before them naked as a jaybird.

"Okay, grab your nuts and lift them! Turn around! Lift your left foot! Now turn around and face me!" The green-eyed deputy snapped orders at me like a drill sergeant. I reached for my boxers, but she spoke again. "Hold it!" I assumed that she was going to ask me to bend over and spread my ass cheeks too, and if so, well a problem was brewing. "Okay, open your mouth for me." I complied with her order. The deputies smiled at each other as I finally pulled on my boxer shorts.

"Why are you two smiling?" I asked, feeling uncomfortable.

"It's just a shame all you young black men are in prison," the scowling deputy said.

Her scowl turning into a smile as she came closer to me. "Please sit on the bench so I can shackle you."

I sat on the bench, not knowing whether to feel flattered or violated by their little whispered comments to each other about me. First she shackled me with a two-inch thick chain that looked ancient, and then handcuffed me while keeping a third chain around my waist. Seconds later the green-eyed deputy opened a bag, pulled out a black metal box, and positioned it on my wrist, making my hands turn to the side so as to keep separated. Lastly, the chain around my waist was looped through the box, and now I was full standing, wrapped in chains like a blanket.

"Okay, now he's secure. Let's get him processed out and hit the road," Green-eyes said.

I was taken to the front office, shuffling my feet as each of the deputies held on to one of my arms. A photo was taken, papers were signed, and along with an entourage of guards, I was escorted out of the office to a white van with metal screening across the windows. When I was placed in the back of the van, Green-eyes disappeared and about fifteen minutes later she came back with two pistols and a shotgun. She handed one pistol to her partner, strapped the other to her side, and began loading the shotgun. The menacing scowl reappeared on the other deputy's face as she slammed the back of the van shut and got into the driver's seat. Green-eyes walked with the entourage of guards to a tower. The van's engine ignited, and we moved slowly under the tower as the van was checked from the outside.

We drove outside the gate slowly, then stopped. Green-eyes trotted out of the tower and got in. The van accelerated down the back dirt road exiting the Ellis Unit. As I looked out the back window, the prison loomed behind me. *Why do I feel sad leaving?* I thought. It had been years since I had ridden in a vehicle, and the speed at which we were moving scared me, perhaps because I wasn't in control.

Out on the highway, my eyes were hungry. I devoured everything in sight, although the screens stretched across the windows and restricted my view. At that time, my hair was long, and it hung around my face, irritating me, but I couldn't brush it aside. All I could do was shake my head constantly, because I didn't want to miss anything. The free world had become foreign to me. The sight of cows and horses, of old beat up cars and houses, everything this rural atmosphere contained, was beautiful to me. A truck was driving behind the van and a little girl who rode in a truck behind the van could see me. She waved continuously to me, telling me hello. I desperately wanted to wave back, but I couldn't. The chains, handcuffs and the black box that crossed my hands prevented that. *Would the little girl have waved if she had known I was a death row prisoner?* I wondered. I doubt it, because when people thought of death row, they immediately assumed that they were serial killers, rapists or, for lack of a better description, monsters.

As the van moved on, I didn't tire of seeing so many colors. Purple, blue, yellow, iris and many others, exploded all around me as I stared at billboards, gardens, people jogging. I longed to be free. In prison all I saw were red brick walls, gray concrete slabs, rusted steel bars and white. Everything was white—white walls, white prison jumpsuit, white shoes, white paper, white sheets, white this and white that.

Truly, the world outside the prison walls made knots form in my stomach. I wanted to be free, damn it. For a split second I just wanted to scream, but suddenly Green-eyes turned around, "You alright back there?"

It was probably very obvious to her that I wasn't. I couldn't imagine how my facial expression must have looked. "Ah, yeah, I guess I am." My words dripped with uncertainty.

We should be in Houston any minute now, hold tight," she said.

Green-eyes didn't seem so bad, but what the hell did she mean 'hold tight'? It wasn't as if I had a choice, I was tight alright. All the chains wrapped around me felt like a giant Anaconda was squeezing the life out of me.

I mean, what if the van crashed and flames were to erupt? I was secured so tightly that I would be like a hot dog roasting in a barbecue pit. Damn, no wonder Silo went to Jester Four. The mind has a way of conjuring up all types of possibilities that in turn created anxieties.

I looked out of the windows, scanning the scenery. As we entered Houston I could see large buildings, people everywhere and cars backed up in traffic; so many different scenes. I realized I had been holding my breath, and I inhaled deeply, filling my lungs with air. I tried to shuffle closer to the back door so I could get a better view. The chains rattled noisily. I saw big signs—Liquor, Food Mart, K-Mart. People were everywhere, rushing in and out of these stores. We stopped at a red light beside a strip bar called The Pussy Cat, and it seemed as though every man entering or leaving had on a long trench coat. Perhaps they were trying to conceal their identity. I wished like hell I could go into the bar myself to see a nude woman. I had been locked up so long.

When I looked back at the deputies, Green-eyes was watching me intently. "Caution!" her eyes seemed to read. She may have thought that my being so close to the back door meant that I was going to try to escape. She had the shotgun between her legs, and her warning was clear, "Try something, and I'll bust some caps in that ass of yours!"

At last, the van made a sharp left turn, skidded to a halt and the rubber burned as the van accelerated up a large ramp and stopped. The deputy with the menacing scowl hopped out of the van, slipped her gun out of her holster and pressed a button set in the wall. Suddenly a large screen in front of the van lifted, and she jumped back in and drove the van inside. When the screen closed, she hopped out without taking her gun out of the holster. Green-eyes hopped out next, shotgun in hand, and they made their move to the back of the van.

I sat very still. I didn't really have a choice. Both doors of the van flew open. "Jump down, Williams!" Ms. Menacing Scowl barked the order, and Green-eyes took up her spread-eagled stance with a tight grip on the shotgun.

I moved very slowly, then jumped out, hoping like hell I wouldn't fall forward. Green-eyes backed up, finger on the trigger, and the other deputy grabbed my arm, smiling. "Tough ride?" she inquired sarcastically.

"Nah, I'm cool," I said, totally perplexed by these two women. They were nice at certain moments then they played the role of tough gals. I guess they were trying to be professional. These two were not so bad, but I couldn't say that about most of the Harris County deputies.

"Oh, it is a gorgeous day, isn't it?" Ms. Menacing Scowl said.

I looked ahead, remembering the many experiences I had suffered in the Harris County jail, and as I was being escorted into the building, my feet shuffling in small movements, I whispered sadly, "It was a good day."

I knew Green-eyes was staring at me, and I felt uncomfortable under her gaze. When I stared back at her, she said, "Um, well, Williams, this is it for us. I hope you believe this, but I honestly wish you well."

She caught me off guard with that sentiment, and I acknowledged her and smiled to show I appreciated her good wishes. When she turned to leave, I called, "Hey, sheriff lady!"

"What is it?" Green-eyes asked while Ms. Menacing Scowl made her exit.

"Take care, and thanks for wishing me well. Be sure not to shoot anybody."

"I'll try not to," she laughed and caught up with her partner. Green-eyes was actually a beautiful woman, and I could not help but wonder why she became a deputy sheriff.

"Follow me, Williams," a large Hispanic deputy led me to a small holding tank deep in the building next to several processing booths where new arrivals to the Harris County jail entered. "I'll have your paperwork processed, and we'll get you a housing assignment."

I looked at the shackles around my feet. "Say, what's up with these chains? Aren't you going to take them off?"

"Oh, yeah, sure. I'll take off a few." He removed the handcuffs, the black metal box and the chain around my waist, but he left the shackles in place. "There you go," he said.

"What about the shackles?"

"I said a few. I can't remove much else until I process your paperwork and see your security level. You are a state prisoner, right?"

"Yeah. So?"

"I have to follow certain procedures. I'll be back, or someone else will." With that, he slammed the door shut, leaving me alone.

I stood in the tank waiting impatiently, watching prisoners go through processing. They gave their names, addresses, ages, occupations and were drilled with a series of other personal questions. The men and women were brought in small groups and kept separated. Most of the prisoners who came through did not realize it yet, but that's what they had become—prisoners.

"Who are you talking to like that, bitch?" one of the women prisoners who was being processed screamed, standing with her hands planted firmly on her hips. "I'm not a fuckin' kid! I'm treating you with respect, so treat me with some will ya!" There were deputies standing behind the prisoners being processed. I watched in silence as several deputies shoved the woman up against the wall and smashed her face against it.

A petite blond female deputy came out of the booth with a baton in her hand and walked over to the deputies who had the woman pinned to the wall. She stood before the prisoner with her baton held threateningly. "Now who are you calling a bitch?"

"No one, ma'am." The prisoner was obviously frightened now.

"Turn her around," the blond deputy commanded. Two male deputies spun the prisoner around. "Now who's the bitch?"

"No one, ma'am."

"No one, huh? I don't think I agree with you. Now, repeat after me—I'm a bitch."

"I will not." The prisoner struggled to maintain some dignity.

"You won't huh? You prostitutes come in here reeking of coitus, and you try and give *me* some attitude?"

The prisoner raised her head. "I am not a prostitute. I am here because I have overdue traffic tickets and—"

"What do you want to do with her?" One of the other deputies, a fat man with slicked back, black hair, cut her off in mid-sentence and turned to await the orders of the hateful blond deputy.

"Maybe we should strip search her and make sure she doesn't have any contraband?"

I stood at the door staring, feeling sorry for the woman prisoner. This was obviously her first time going to jail, and she was not a criminal. She did not know what to expect or how to behave or how to respond to such demeaning and cruel treatment. "Okay now," the blond deputy said with an arrogant toss of her head, "take off your blouse and your skirt."

"Why?" the woman asked, stunned.

"Because I said to." The deputy reached with her baton to lift the woman's chin. "Now take it off!" she shouted, and I could see spittle fly from her mouth, showering the prisoner's face.

The prisoner slowly unbuttoned her blouse as tears steamed down her cheeks. She tried to wipe them away but only succeeded in smearing her makeup so that black streaks ran down her face. A moment later she stood in the hallway in her panties and bra while the other women prisoners huddled together, whispering among themselves.

"All of you! Face the wall!" the little fat deputy shouted to the other. "And the next sound I hear will result in a strip search. Now shut the fuck up!"

I shook my head, wanting to go to the woman's aid, but I was in no position to play hero. "Now, how about a cavity search?" the blond deputy said with sweet sarcasm.

"But there are men here," the prisoner said. "Let me call my attorney."

At the mention of her attorney, all the deputies backed off somewhat. The woman was well dressed and wore a diamond ring, suggesting that she could indeed afford a decent attorney.

"Okay, that's enough, guys," the sadistic blond deputy dismissed the male deputies. "I got it from here on."

The two men went on harassing the other women prisoners. The woman who had been strip searched, got dressed again, still crying. She was led away to another holding tank. I was quite familiar with the tactics they were using on her. To strip people of their clothing and leave them standing naked with no privacy was a tactic used in the concentration camps during World War II and other wars, and it is a primary tool used in prisons. The purpose is to degrade and humiliate people so that their thoughts are no longer focused on resistance. It is a tactic used to break the spirit and to dehumanize people.

I squatted down in the holding tank because the shackles were biting into my ankles. The stench of the holdover tank was horrible, and I could not wait to be moved out of it. The holding tanks have an odor of unwashed bodies, urine, feces and vomit. New prisoners at the county jail, or "fish," as they are called, are often drunkards, drug users or homeless people. Most of these fish have waited in other small, outlying county jail facilities for days before being transferred to the main jail. At the small facilities, they are not allowed to shower, nor are they given any type of medical treatment or medication for illness.

I was very tired and sleepy, and I began to drift off to sleep. Just at that moment, an older deputy who had bars on his collar awakened me. I got back to my feet, furious. My feet were numb, and I was in misery.

"Hey, guy, I'm going to take you upstairs to the sixth floor in a little while. They would have done it this morning, but nobody wanted to deal with you because you're level three security. You're a death row prisoner aren't you? Nanon Williams?"

No one could ever pronounce my first name correctly, so I just nodded my head, acknowledging that he was correct.

"I'll be back in an hour, bud," he said.

I wasn't his "bud," or anything else. I just wanted these shackles to be taken off. I shuffled my feet back and forth to regain some of the feeling in them. By now, I probably smelled just like the holding tank, and that meant I smelled foul. There was nothing else to do, so I just stood back at the door watching the fish being processed in. I couldn't help but notice most of the fish were either black, Hispanic or listed as "other." More than seventy percent of prisoners across the United States are African-American or Hispanic, even though seventy percent of the general population is actually Caucasian. Justice certainly isn't color blind.

Staring out the door, I watched as one deputy lined up a few fish against the wall. He was conducting roll call and having the prisoners identify themselves. When he called out a name, that prisoner stepped forward in order to have an identification band placed on his wrist. It came to mind that this was similar to cattle branding. I also recalled that many slaves were branded by their owners before emancipation.

"Gonzales, step forward!" the deputy barked loudly.

Deputies, neither male nor female, ever speak in an ordinary voice. They bark, shout and scream, even when it is not necessary. It was partly a control tactic, and, I suspect, partly an ego booster.

"A. Gonzales, step forward!" I noticed that the ranking deputy who spoke to me earlier stood behind the other deputy, his arms folded menacingly.

No one stepped forward, and the deputy asked each individual his name. At last he came to a small Mexican man, about five feet four-inches tall and weighing no more than one hundred-forty pounds. Out of the entire group, there were only two Mexicans. The others totaled five blacks, three whites and one Asian. "What's your name?" the big deputy barked brusquely, but the small Mexican man only smiled. The deputy poked his finger into the man's chest and asked again, "What is your name?" Once again, the prisoner only smiled. It did not take a genius to realize that the man did not understand English.

"I'll handle it," the ranking officer said. "Como te llamas?"

"Mi nombre es Gonzales," he responded.

"He's your man."

Poking the prisoner in the chest again with his finger, the deputy said, "A. Gonzales, step your greaser-ass forward, pronto!" A. Gonzales only stood there smiling, waiting for the older officer who spoke Spanish to speak to him again. No response came from the deputy who spoke Spanish. At that moment, the big deputy walked over to him and slapped him on the back of the head.

"Now, step forward, you fuckin' wetback!" The big deputy loomed threateningly over the small man with his fists clenched, and the older deputy was now the one smiling, as if to encourage cruelty form the younger, larger deputy.

"No comprende," the Mexican prisoner said softly.

"Look, you imbecile, get your ass over here!" As he spat the words, he punched the small Mexican man in the stomach. The prisoner doubled over in pain.

It was more than I could bear, and I began banging on the door. *Bang, Bang, Bang, Bang!* I continued to hit the door with all my strength. "Bring your coward ass over here, punk and quit hitting that little guy!"

Suddenly, without warning, the small Mexican man squatted and grabbed the big deputy around the knees, lifting him off the floor, and driving him into the ground.

"Fight! Fight!" the older deputy yelled in alarm, but he did not move to help the other deputy. Other deputies came running to the scene and converged upon the small Mexican man, beating him with tremendous force.

"No mas!" he cried out, but his pleas fell on deaf ears. Moments later he was lying on the floor, handcuffed, with blood spurting from his head. Several of his teeth lay on the floor near him. They dragged him away, leaving a trail of blood on the floor.

I had stopped banging on the door, but my rage was boiling over. These deputies in the Harris County jail beat more prisoners than prison guards on the units ever do. Beatings such as this were no longer new to me. I had seen so many that it should not have even fazed me, yet it did. I felt every blow as if it was being rained on my head instead of the little Mexican man's.

For whatever reason the small man was in prison, he had just gotten himself another five or ten years for assault. The only way they could justify all the stitches that poor man would require was to say that he assaulted a deputy, and this meant giving him an additional charge.

Not long after that, the big deputy appeared at the door of the holding tank. He stared at me through the door, his gaze roaming slowly up and down, taking in my six feet one-inch tall, two hundred fifty-two pounds, and the muscles I had built with constant exercise. The expression on his face told me that he was considering whether to open the door. The older deputy came to his side.

"Don't open the door," he told the big deputy. "He's a death row prisoner, so he has nothing to lose. Go ahead and finish processing the other prisoners and get a trusty to mop up the blood."

I stared with fury blazing in my dark eyes at the older deputy who casually slung orders because to him, this was a typical day on the job. In my head, I could still hear the small Mexican man crying out, "No mas! No mas!"

"I'll be back to get you in a minute, bud," the older deputy said to me. "We had another little problem with one of these wetbacks."

I was still outraged, and his familiarity toward me, along with his derogatory references to the little Mexican man, further fueled my fury. "I'm not your 'bud', and your racist ass will either come get me or not, but get the fuck out of my face!" He smiled, walked away and left me there. I don't know how long I stayed in the holding tank, but it was much more than twenty-four hours, and the deputies had, by this time, changed shifts several times.

I took a deep breath. I was trying to be patient, trying not to get angry, but I was failing miserably, and besides, I knew anger would not help the situation, and it would not help me. I was hungry, but food was not what I wanted most at that time. The hearing still overshadowed everything, and I wasn't sure exactly when it was going to take place.

"Hey, is your name Nanon Williams?" a tall white deputy with red hair called to me through the door.

"Yeah," I said. "How many times are people going to ask me my name and then walk off without doing anything?"

"What are you talking about?"

"I'm talking about not getting processed through this hellhole and not getting a housing assignment. I don't even know now how long I've been down here!"

"Oh. Well, I'm not working down here. When I walked by and looked in the window, I remembered your face. You don't remember me?" he asked. "My name is Daniels. I used to be a jailer here before I became a deputy."

"No! I don't remember you. Are you sure your memory isn't playing tricks on you?" I really did not remember his face, and I was trying very hard to.

"Maybe four or five years ago, I watched you get stunned with a taser gun for refusing to bend over and do a proper strip search. You fought like hell, and I had to help put restraints on you while you were unconscious."

"I remember that day well, too well, in fact. I have scars on my body that remind me of it every day of my life," I told him. "Yes, I remember that day like it was only yesterday."

"You're much bigger now. I felt kind of bad the way they kicked you afterwards because you were just a young foolish boy."

"Do you call keeping your dignity foolish?" I asked.

"When you're in a no-win situation, I do," he replied. "Why are you back here after so many years? Didn't you get the death penalty?"

"I did. I'm back on bench warrant now for a hearing. Can you help get me processed and moved, or what?"

"Maybe," he said. "Give me a minute, and let me see what I can do." On that note, he left.

I knew the routine. Tell them what they want to hear and burn out. I didn't want to create a problem, but the shackles had rubbed the back of my ankles raw, and I could see some blood at the back of my socks.

"Okay, Williams," Daniels said when he returned a few minutes later. "Guess what?"

"I'm too tired to do any guessing, but what?"

"You are going to sixth floor, it's an open death row tank, and that's the floor I'm assigned to. You've been down here twenty-nine hours, and I believe your paperwork got mixed up."

I seriously doubted my paperwork got mixed up, but I kept quiet about it. Daniels fingerprinted me, inventoried my little bag of hygiene and legal work, took a picture and then gave me a couple of sack lunches with cookies and peanut butter and jelly sandwiches.

"Thanks. I appreciate it."

"No problem," he said. "Let me take those shackles off too. You won't be handcuffed or shackled on the sixth floor."

As he took off the shackles, he looked at the blood on my socks and shook his head. "Damn! We might need to take you to the clinic and put something on those cuts."

"Nah, just get me a few Band-Aids if you can. This is nothing new." My feet were still so numb that I could not feel them.

"Good then. Let's get out of here and go upstairs before I get into trouble for not being on my assigned floor. The captain and the sergeant on the sixth floor can be real assholes, you know what I mean?"

"Yeah," I said. "I do know what you mean."

We got on an elevator and stopped at the sixth floor. Daniels got me a roll with a blanket, sheets and a pair of shower shoes.

"Here we go, Williams," he said, rolling open the mechanical door to the tank. "If you need anything, I mean anything, you just have someone get me on the floor. I normally work on this floor a few days a week."

"Once again, thanks." He stuck out his hand, offering a handshake. I thought about it for a second because he was still a pig to me, and his uniform reminded me of that, but I shook his hand. Everybody responded to kindness, so why shouldn't I?

"Take care, Williams."

"You too."

I put my things on the dayroom table and looked around. Coming out of an open cell was a guy I knew named Duck. He was of medium height, a few years older than me, and he wore a haircut called a "fade," that was popular among blacks.

"What's up, L.A.?"

"Nothing, man. I'm just tired. I'm going to take a shower and crash."

"I dig that. I'm sho glad I got some company! You can put your stuff in three cell; it's clean and stuff."

"Right on." I picked up my stuff and went straight to three cell. The door remained open and led into a small dayroom that had a shower, a television and a few board games. I hurriedly took a shower, put on my hygiene, then Duck and I talked for a while. Not long after, I went to sleep in three cell. I slept and slept and slept.

15

REFLECTIONS ON THE AMERI**KKK**AN NIGHTMARE

"OH HELL, NO! THAT'S domino! Game's over. Now break off them push-ups you owe me." Duck had just beat me at a game of dominoes for the umpteenth time. I shook my head. "That's all, Duck. Give a brother action one more time," I laughed. "Double or nothing?"

"You said that shit two games ago. Man, go on and break off all those push-ups you owe me. I'm tired of beating you."

Duck and I had been playing dominoes all day. I was well rested and for the past few days I had a chance to talk on the telephone, watch television and had even received a few visits. While I was doing the push-ups I owed Duck, I was called to the bars by a deputy.

"Williams, you've got a visit."

Of course, I immediately ceased doing push-ups and hurried to my cell, threw some water on my hair and combed it back.

"Come on, Williams!" the deputy yelled.

It felt good not to be handcuffed and escorted to visitation. I was just given a pass, and I strolled on to the visiting room for my fifteen-minute visit. Visits at the Harris County jail are allowed daily, but they only last fifteen minutes, and you are allowed only one per day. When Daniels worked on the sixth floor, I could probably hustle him out of some extra time, but I just hurried on to the visiting room because I was excited about seeing my grandparents.

When I got into the visiting room, I saw my grandparents sitting at one of the visitation windows. Grandma and Papa. Papa had been a mechanic for fifty years or so. He could fix almost anything with an engine, but cars were his specialty. I believe working on cars gave Papa a sense of peace. Some people pray and meditate. Papa worked on cars. Grandma, throughout her life, took on all types of odd jobs. She had been a cook, a maid, a janitor, a construction worker and almost any task that would earn an honest living. Grandma wasn't picky about working, but whatever she did, she held her head high like the queen she was.

"Hi, Grandma, Papa," I greeted them.

"We've been out here a long time," Grandma said with a frown that slowly creased into a beaming smile. "We wanted to come down here to make sure you was alright, Nanon."

"So, what's up with you, Papa?" I said, smiling. "You can't say hello or something?"

"I don't need to say nothing, Meathead." He slapped his thigh. "I just came to see your face. You'll be in court tomorrow, and your attorney said things look real good."

"Oh, I haven't spoken to her yet, but I probably will before court starts tomorrow. She wrote me a letter and basically told me what was happening. But you can't write about legal matters too much because they often read our mail at the Ellis Unit, even though they are not suppose to."

Papa smiled again and said, "You just make sure you be good in here, and don't let these sheriffs provoke you. They scared of you young black men, so don't be giving them any reason to justify doing something worse to you. Do you understand what

I'm telling you, Nanon?"

"I hear you, Papa," I said, trying to keep a smile on my face. "So far I really haven't had any problems. I'm just rolling with the days as they come."

"Well," Grandma said, "you better not make me unroll my belt. You might have grown up, but I'll still put this belt to your butt if you don't listen to me and your Papa."

"I'm listening to you, Grandma," I said again and repeated myself. Grandma always had a way of making me smile, but she meant every word she said. That much I definitely knew. I can remember many butt-whippings, but she also always hugged me and pointed out my mistakes as well. Grandma always said a hard head made a soft ass.

"We'll be in court tomorrow, Nanon," Papa said. "Son, I want you to come home, but still, I've never stopped being proud of you. I read that newsletter that you do, and you keep doing positive things."

"I will, Papa. I will."

"If you need some money, you let us know," Papa told me. "I just want you to have everything you need."

"I'm fine, but if I do, I'll call."

"You call home now that you can use the phone everyday," Grandma said. "As long as I can hear your voice, me and your Papa won't have to drive all this way," she said, smiling up at Papa. After all these years, they still looked so in love.

"Time's up, Williams!" a deputy told us.

"That's it?" Grandma asked quizzically.

"That's it," the deputy responded. "Sorry, ma'am, but I'm just following the rules."

"Well, we love you, Nanon," Papa said. "We'll see you tomorrow in court."

"Okay. I love both of you. Drive safe, and hopefully something good will happen."

I watched them leave, still smiling. It felt so good to see my grandparents, but as always when visits with loved ones end, there was that tinge of sadness that gripped my heart.

AS A CHILD, I was practically raised by my grandparents. Out of all their grandchildren, I always had a room in their house. Sooner or later they always expected me under their roof again, and sure enough, for whatever reasons, I would end up there.

In 1980, Papa and Grandma often took me on long fishing trips. I was only six years old, but Papa never went fishing without me. He patiently taught me how to put hooks on my line and how to bait the hooks. We always used shrimp as bait, and sometimes we used live shrimp. Grandma would sit back and smile, but whenever we went fishing on a boat, she never smiled. Grandma considered herself to be a serious fisherman, so on boats she took everything serious. Papa never took much of anything serious except when it came to me. He was serious about teaching me everything he knew.

Papa almost never gave me butt-whippings, but I recall once when he did. I was about nine years old, and he bought me a BB gun. He always trusted me, so he placed cans in the backyard and told me only to shoot the cans and nothing else. "Shoot the cans only, you hear me?" Papa said. "Yes, Papa," I replied, "only the cans."

Bored with knocking the cans down, I took aim at a very old car in the backyard. It had been there for so long that I figured it was just junk. I took aim at the tires first, but when I struck them with my BB gun, or air pistol, as some people call it, the bullets came back full force. I realized I could do no damage, so I took aim at the car windows. At first, when I shot at the windows, nothing happened, so I continued. After repeated firing, the windows in the door shattered with a resounding crash. I stared at the window for a few moments, then shouted, "Papa, something happened to your window!" Papa came back outside. He said nothing, but picked up a switch off the ground and headed in my direction. I smiled at him as he approached, but he did not smile in return. I knew then that I was in trouble, so I took off running. Thinking that I could out run Papa was a mistake. He caught me before I had gone ten yards, and he proceeded to give me a butt-whipping that went down in my book as "The Greatest Butt-Whipping of All Times."

Oh no, the butt-whipping was not the end of my punishment. He took the BB gun into the garage and disappeared for a while. When he came back, he handed me the gun. "Here you go, Meathead," he said. I looked at my new gun, but it was no longer new, the barrel of the gun was pointed back at me when I held it in my hand. The lesson was, if I wanted to shoot something, I'd better think twice about it, or I would shoot myself.

I WAS SMILING AS I walked back into the tank. Duck was sitting at the table in the dayroom watching television. "Why you smiling, L.A.?" he asked. "You had a good visit with your peoples, huh?"

"Yeah," I replied. "I had a good visit, but I was just thinking about something as I was coming back."

"So, did you find any news about when you go to court?"

"Tomorrow morning."

"Well, I don't want you tired and shit when you to court, so I'm going to let you make it up on them push-ups," he said magnanimously.

"Wow!" I said. "Thanks for the fuckin' favor." We both laughed.

"Seriously, I hope you get some good news," Duck said. "I left the Ellis Unit a few weeks ago, and I went to court, but I don't think it went too well."

"Why did you come back to Harris County?" I asked.

"I'm trying to get a new trial, but you know how that goes. No money, no trial, no justice," he said, his frustration showing by the scowl on his face. "Sometimes I feel like the only crime I've committed is being born black. Don't get me wrong. I'm black and proud of it, but America doesn't give a fuck about black men. Most of us are either dead, working for slave wages or rotting in prison."

"Hang tough, Bro, that's all we can do sometimes," I told him.

"I've been hanging. Now, I'm about to be hung if I don't get some good legal counsel. They appointed me an attorney who doesn't come to see me and basically acts as though he thinks it would be best if I was dead."

"No shit."

"No shit, man. You know how it goes. Texas has been lynching us legally and illegally. I can no longer tell the difference. Texas commits a gross miscarriage of justice toward every black man, rich or poor. Hell, they seem to have designed the system that way! I've been looking at television and every criminal, pimp, gangster, 'ho, prostitute and every other bad guy is black. That's our role in their eyes—being the bad guy, and they act as if we should be happy to accept it," Duck sighed deeply.

I knew what Duck was saying. Tee, Li'l Dez, Y.L., Rogers-el and I had talked about this same thing for years. *The American dream should be called the AmeriKKKan Nightmare*, I thought because that's what life sometimes felt like. We all had to find a meaning to live, but it wasn't through any dreams America tried to sell us. That bottle of illusions was dry.

"Man, I've been locked up so long, hell, I already feel like I've served a life sentence," Duck said morosely.

"Not me," I responded. "Under the laws affecting me, I would have to do forty years flat before I even became eligible for parole." The warm glow of childhood memories was fading for me as I pondered the situation. What kind of country was America when the color of someone's skin was an automatic denial of justice?

"That's too long, but not for me. When I got sentenced, I believe then a life sentence was only fifteen years. I'm more than halfway there now." A deputy came to the cellblock calling, "Rack up time, gentlemen." And with that, we headed to our cells to await the morning.

I sat on my bunk, thinking about what a life sentence would be like, and I realized that the thought of that disturbed me more than a sentence of death. *Why?* I thought about it more and more as the night wore on and sleep would not come. *What would tomorrow bring for me? What future would I have? Or would I have any future at all?*

For many death row prisoners, a life sentence would mean seeing another tomorrow, although tomorrow is never promised to anyone. For those who are guilty of the crimes they were charged with, a life sentence would be much better with the benefits it brought. They would be allowed to work, and they would not be bound by shackles, cuffs and chains. They would, with good behavior, eventually be allowed to have contact visits with loved ones. They could take school courses and work on crafts and have many other things to occupy the years. Everything, that is, except a real hope of freedom. *Very importantly*, I thought, *their families would not have to endure the stress and the ups and downs of years of appeals, and they would not have to anticipate their execution.* Even prisoners who are truly innocent of the crimes they have been convicted of have to take time to think and consider and weigh the pros and cons of such a life sentence. There are innocent prisoners who plead guilty to a crime they did not commit in order to get a life sentence and escape death on the gurney. They may feel that suffering indignities, a few beatings or whatever else is offered by a prison that does not practice rehabilitation, is worth it just to go on living. They can attest, "Hey, man, at least I'm still alive."

Before I was wrongfully convicted of capital murder, I, too, was offered a life sentence. Although my attorney believed me to be innocent of the alleged crime, she asked me to seriously consider taking a life sentence instead of risking a trial and being condemned to death. Needless to say, I did not take it, but did I consider it? *Hell no!* I was no choirboy, and yes, I was guilty of many things, but I was not of killing anyone. I refused to accept being condemned to death as a killer when I am not a killer, so living a life in constant agony is my punishment for not bowing down to the power-crazed state authority that condemned me.

However, even though I never considered a life sentence an acceptable alternative to escaping death on the gurney, I did try to imagine it. The thought has caused a scar on my mind that will be with me always. For me to exist in a general population prison setting would mean that I would have to tuck away my pride and my dignity. It is true that pride is sometimes a downfall for a man, but dignity should never be considered a downfall. If anyone, man or woman, can claim to have something that can never be taken from them, it should be their dignity. That is one thing that should always be everyone's human right.

Any prisoner serving a life sentence is expected to suffer indignities. All prisoners must suffer indignities. What if a guard struck me? Am I to turn the other cheek, file a grievance that would be automatically denied and just keep hoping it would not happen again. I believe Jesus was a strong man, but I am not Jesus. If any man hits me, I will strike him back as hard as I can. No one, with the exception of my parent figures, ever has the right to strike me, and no one ever shall. All prisoners are told to bend over and spread their ass cheeks, in order to submit to the degradation and humiliation of petty tyrants who thrive on and build up their own egos with such commands. I have been beaten, placed in solitary, and physically restrained while guards attempted to physically spread my ass apart for their viewing. They say this is a mandatory part of security, and that this is the rule in prisons all across America. I do not doubt this for a moment, but it is an extreme violation of a person's dignity.

Prison officials allow the guards carte blanche in dealing with prisoners, and all that unrestricted authority includes the degradation and humiliation of prisoners. To spend my life in general population would mean living in a super segregation prison, which is equivalent to permanent solitary confinement. I would have to serve forty years of a sentence under those permanent conditions with no human contact, no visitors, no personal property, no television, with nothing at all except my dignity. Yet, would my personal dignity be worth that kind of hell? Yes, because at least I could live with myself. I would rather take my chances fighting for my life under a sentence of death. Then, at least, I would die with my only possession, my dignity. Even more so, I would die while still proclaiming my innocence to the world instead of rotting in a cell for half a century sick with myself for accepting a life sentence for a crime I did not commit.

The night passed, and the following morning I was on my way to court where I would struggle for my life, for my family and for the spirit of all people whose existence has meaning. If I had to endure this same struggle a thousand lifetimes, I would do it in hope. Hope overcomes all, conquers all.

16

THE LEGAL EAGLE

I WAS ON MY way to court at last; a part of a chain of other prisoners who also had court hearings. We emerged into the busy street of downtown Houston from a tunnel in the basement of the Harris County jail, herded by deputies carrying shotguns and a cigar-smoking bailiff toting a large pistol. To citizens on the streets, we must have appeared to be aliens materializing from somewhere beneath the Earth's surface.

"Everyone please move out of the way," a deputy told people on the streets on their way to work. Most moved quickly and went about their business, paying scant attention to us, because our walking chain gang was a common sight to them, but others felt compelled to stop and examine us, watching as our hefty chains dragged along the concrete sidewalks.

I did not sleep at all the previous night. We were taken before five o'clock in the morning and placed in a holding tank for several hours before court bailiffs came to get us. It was now about eight in the morning, and by the time we entered the 248th District Court, I was extremely weary. We were herded like animals into a large elevator and moved to our respective floors. Weariness and deep concern were etched on everyone's faces, except mine. I wasn't worried at all. Hell, I already had the worst sentence imaginable—the death penalty. It wasn't as if I could get another worse sentence that would matter. I could only die once. The reality was, however, that I could receive good news, too, so I was overwhelmingly optimistic. American jails are filled to capacity; perhaps my freedom would lessen the load. My family, friends and supporters were extremely hopeful as well.

In the court's holdover unit, there were two small holding tanks within a bigger one. Since I was under a death sentence, I was placed in a holding tank alone, and the hefty chains were removed. This holding tank was no bigger than a small walk-in closet, so I sat on the small bench inside as the other prisoners were chained to a long bench outside my holding tank. They were either not aware, or didn't care, that I was kept separate because of my conviction. Those other prisoners had worries of their own as they waited to be arraigned for their alleged crimes. Their attorneys shuffled their way to the back, trying to get signatures from them for plea-bargains to avoid the cost of a trial and, as is the case with most court appointed attorneys, avoid the expenditure of very much of their time. Everyone seemed to have court appointed attorneys, which simply meant that the attorneys worked for the courts and not for the best interests of their clients. Such attorneys are often referred to as "public pretenders," since they spend more time pretending to represent indigent clients than they spend actually representing them. Many of them had their jobs down to a fine art. They pretended to listen to their client's version of events (if the version was quick and short), secondly, they attempted to get their client to a sign plea bargain, and then they moved on to the next client. It was much like an assembly line law practice.

Decades of oppression started in little court holdovers like this one, where lengthy sentences are signed up for on plea bargains, thereby dodging much longer sentences that might have been handed down at a trial. Eventually, after years of incarceration, prisoners realize that they are just a number, not an individual who has a family to feed and bills to pay. Once sentence has been passed, the prisoners are no longer even considered to be poor, third class citizens. They are not citizens at all. They lose the right to vote and other civil rights that should belong to all human beings. They become numbered, no-name slaves of the state.

I was halfway on my feet when the door to the holdover clicked, and the bailiff looked through the small slit in the window. He escorted my attorney into the holdover. To my surprise, he locked her inside with me and left. I had not been alone with a woman for six and a half years. I felt nervous because I no longer knew how to respond, except with a quick nod of my head and a hello.

My attorney was an British woman named Helen, and she was much different than the other court appointed attorneys I had in the past. She was articulate, thoughtful, dedicated, and strikingly beautiful. She was small, with dark brown hair, deep set, sparkling eyes and a curvaceous figure that drew second looks from most men.

"Hello, Nanon," she said softly.

"Uh, hi," I stuck my hand out awkwardly to shake hers.

"Give me a hug," she said embracing me.

I did not actually embrace her back though I would have liked to. It had been so long since someone outside my family and friends had treated me as a human being, that I had forgotten how to respond. She made me feel human again, and although I liked to believe I was still human, blows to my mind had rained upon me from every side for so long and had scarred me, making me uncertain of how to behave anymore. Was I supposed to sit or stand, follow what she did next, or what? I wanted to behave like a gentleman, but maybe I had forgotten that too? Gradually, after speaking about legal matters, all I could do was be myself.

Most court appointed attorneys did not do much on their client's behalf, and initially, I was not fool enough to believe that Helen was any different. Yet, it turned out that she was. Unlike most attorneys, she traveled a few hundred miles, as often as she could, to update me on my appeals, and when she did not visit me personally, she wrote letters telling me of any progress she had made. In truth, I never paid much attention to what she said to me concerning my appeals; I just pretended to acknowledge what she said because I believed that all court appointed attorneys were simply moving through a formality until the time came for the state to kill us. In time, Helen proved to be different; one of the rare court appointed attorneys with a heart, strong principles and compassion. Perhaps that is because she was raised in England where there is no longer a death penalty and where racism is not as prevalent as it is in the United States. Perhaps, I mused, she was an angel fallen from the sky to fight for me. I wanted to believe this. Even more touching, Helen seemed to believe in me. She believed in *me*—a prisoner condemned to death, a vicious murderer, or at least that is what I had been labeled. Yet she believed in me.

It was September 22, 1998. Helen was dressed conservatively, yet with fashionable flair and good taste. She smiled, but her eyes were tired and lines of tiredness showed clearly across her face. Apparently, like me, either she had not slept or she was worried. The friend in me wanted to tell her not to work so hard and push herself beyond her limits, but the death row prisoner in me was proud to have her as my attorney. Before me, I saw an attorney who had spent sleepless nights working on my appeals, and who had sharpened her mind to do battle for me in court. I was impressed. Words can never describe the good feelings I had as I stood looking at her. I never asked her to be my champion; I only asked her to do her best. Helen gave me more than her best; she gave me hope for the future and belief in people again. From that day forward, I knew we could never lose, even if death by execution would eventually be my fate, because I had already won.

We briefly discussed what we were going to present to the courts, then, at that, we made our way to the courtroom. I had to be handcuffed and shackled again, so I hobbled behind her as the bailiff led the way. I was dressed in a standard, bright orange, Harris County jail jumpsuit, and as I entered the courtroom I resembled a giant, walking carrot.

In the courtroom, I saw my beautiful mother smiling in the front row of the public seats. She blew me a kiss, and I returned her smile. Beside her stood my Grandma and Papa. Grandma waved and Papa gave me a thumbs up sign. I winked back and then acknowledged other friends and supporters who were present. It felt great to see so many people who loved me altogether in the courtroom. This was a good day, a great day.

Court began, and the bailiff spoke, "Everyone rise, the Honorable Judge presiding." We all stood. "Please have a seat." And the court proceedings began. For two days, testimony after testimony was given.

> Nanon McKewn Williams, currently confined on death row in the
> Texas Department of Criminal Justice, asks this Court to find that
> his conviction for capital murder and his sentence of death be vacated

and recommend that the Court of Criminal Appeals grant a new trial.

Nanon was arrested and charged with capital murder in 1992. At that time, Nanon was but a juvenile, a 17-year-old kid who still attended high school, played on the football team and was a rising star. College recruiting scouts offered many scholarships because of his athletic ability, until he was accused of being one of several individuals participating in a large drug transaction that turned ugly. Another drug dealer, among all the others involved, was shot and later died.

Three months later, Nanon was arrested. He was read his rights, and he exercised that right to remain silent until he was provided with an attorney. That request was granted a year and a half later. What happened during that year and a half? He was held by his home state of California, which later extradited him to Texas. Nanon waited three years and one month in jail to be taken to trial, in which such lengths of time awaiting trial is unusual. During this time, Nanon was offered a plea bargain. Being innocent, he refused the plea bargain. He would not plead guilty.

The courts had no physical evidence linking Nanon to any crime. In fact, the witnesses, who were convicted felons and directly involved in the drug deal, never identified Nanon as having pulled he trigger of the gun that killed the deceased.

Nanon has not lived the life of a choirboy. He was reared in Los Angeles' toughest ghettos, where drugs, gangs and brutality are commonplace. Nanon sold drugs as a juvenile for reasons beyond recognition to the courts. Perhaps this is why he was the main focal point of an indictment. His father was a known drug dealer and was killed when Nanon was a growing boy. To the courts, he was summed up to be just another generation of drug carriers, and therefore, his life meant nothing. He is not a killer, he has never killed, but he received the sentence of death, to die by lethal injection until he is dead, dead, dead!

In my original trial, no one said they saw me kill anyone. No one. Others just said I was there, as were they, and that I was counting a few thousand dollars before the shooting took place. The prosecutor's star witness was also charged with the capital murder, but he received a ten-year, non-aggravated sentence in payment for testifying against me. Even in trial, he never once said he saw me shoot anyone. He too, along with others, said there was no motive to why the shooting took place. The courts acknowledged something went awry, but what that was no one knows.

During the entire trial, my attorney and my family believed I would be found innocent. At worst, they believed I would be given the same ten-year sentence as the state's star witness. I was convicted. Why? The prosecutor did whatever it took to rid the nation of another drug dealer, the state of Texas did whatever it took to rid the nation of another black man—me—so they put me on death row.

Years later my attorney, Helen, found new evidence and a judge granted me an evidentiary hearing on the sole claim of innocence. At the hearing, Helen presented evidence of physical proof that contradicted the state's case against me. Even more, it contradicted the state's star witness against me. Such hearings as this one are rarely granted.

How Helen found new evidence that proved I was not a killer, well, I am not sure. I must say that her dedication to seeking true justice was a motivating factor. She found out that the state's star witness against me was arrested with a firearm, but the state never mentioned ballistic tests. My original attorney never had ballistics testing done because, being an ex-prosecutor herself, her mind worked as a prosecutor, and this is highly likely the reason she was appointed to me. But, whenever anyone is arrested with a firearm, the state is certain to check and see if the firearm is stolen or has been used in a crime. This is done with ballistics testing.

In a capital murder case, running ballistic tests on a firearm found on an arrested suspect is one of the first procedures in an investigation. This physical evidence helps seal a prosecutor's case. Likewise, it should be a factor in determining innocence, but that requires money for high-priced legal counsel. Therefore, to say the state never ran this test on the firearm found on their star witness at his arrest is evidence of corruption.

When Helen filed a motion to get funds granted by the courts to do a ballistics test on the firearm, the judge granted the funding, against the prosecutor's objections. And yet prosecutors claim to seek justice. The test came in and revealed that the firearm in question was the cause of death to the victim, yet this very same firearm was found on the state's star witness. In all fairness, I wish I could say that this was a rarity in my particular case, but that is not so. It is standard practice among prosecutors in Harris County, Texas.

At the evidentiary hearing, it was obvious that the judge himself was shocked. Furthermore, on a tape recorder, the state's star witness admitted to firing the initial shots that started a shootout because he was spooked. However, the very same audiotape in which the state's star witness admitted to the shooting mysteriously came up missing, although the tape existed in court records. Yet, I was convicted of the murder and sentenced to death while he would serve approximately four years and be set free. He is still free, and the state cannot revoke the plea bargain he was given as payment for testifying against me.

After six years, prosecutors called a new witness to speak against me at the evidentiary hearing. This new witness' testimony was impeached because he was obviously lying and was put up to testifying falsely. He claimed he knew me well, that we were friends and that he drove me to the drug deal. His testimony contradicted the other state witnesses. Helen's co-counsel, who did an excellent job, asked the new witness what my name was and he did not even know my name. The courtroom erupted in laughter and all the prosecutors could do was bow their heads. When closing arguments were heard fifteen days later, the state just presented their theories and had little else to say. Helen presented physical proof that I was innocent and gave me my life back—maybe.

According to the law, the judge would write a recommendation to the Court of Criminal Appeals, and it is there that a final decision would be made. As the hearing ended, I was allowed to hug my mother, my grandparents and my supporters. Seeing their genuine smiles made my heart beat with a rhythm I had never felt before. To me, the most important victory was that, if my mother had ever harbored any secret doubts, she now knew that I was truly innocent. Papa also hugged me so tightly and was the happiest I had seen him in a long time. I felt human again as I touched and hugged those I loved. Even the court bailiff smiled and said he could not believe all that he had heard in court, but I just looked on.

Dear God, I thought, *man, thanks!* I uttered this little prayer to myself as I was escorted to the court holdover once again. The other prisoners had been taken back to the jail, so I welcomed the quietness of the holdover. The hearing took two days, and closing arguments lasted fifteen days, and during that time I knew my life was changing. Helen proved not to be working for the state's best interests. She proved to be the thorn in their side that prosecutors probably have nightmares about. Yet even though the prosecutors had a seething hatred toward her, I could also see admiration and perhaps a hint of jealousy that they had never triumphed as she had. As I watched and listened to her present my case, I often found myself thinking, *Go on with yo' bad self then.* It became the case of the Legal Eagle and I.

17

RUN, RUN, RUN

SEVERAL DAYS PASSED SINCE closing arguments at my hearing, and I still felt high on hope. Every waking chance, Papa came to visit, and we smiled lovingly at each other through the glass in the visiting room, sometimes not even speaking, but just enjoying each other's presence. Helen became a frequent visitor too, and we talked and talked for hours. After each visit, I went back to the holding tank, and Duck and I played dominoes the rest of the day.

"Domino again, L.A.!" he would yell, stretching his arms out in a peacock-like strut.

"Man, sit your ass down, and let's play another game," I would tell him, not because I really wanted to play again but rather to distract my mind from constantly obsessing on the judge's ruling.

One day shortly thereafter, a Mexican prisoner named Felix, who had received a death sentence, was brought to the tank. He seemed nervous at first, but Duck and I soon put him at ease with some joking around. I found a towel for Felix to clean his cell with, and I even offered to help him clean it.

"Si," he told me, "that is muy bueno that you would help me clean the cell. But maybe later. Right now I am watching these very beautiful women on the television."

"Man, leave Felix alone so he can watch some ass," Duck said. "That cell is not going anyplace and neither is he. Ain't that right, Felix?"

"You got it, Truck."

I started laughing and Duck said, "My name ain't Truck, Holmes, it's Duck. Like rhymes with 'fuck.' You know?"

"Oh, I misunderstand," Felix said. "And your name is L.A., right? That is short for Louisiana, no?"

"No," I corrected him. "It's short for Los Angeles. People call me L.A. because that's where I'm from."

"Are you Puerto Rican?" he asked me.

"Are you Puerto Rican?" Duck mimicked Felix playfully.

"Fuck you, Duck," I said. "I'm not Puerto Rican, Felix. I'm black, but I'm mixed with French, Indian and maybe some English. I am Creole."

"What is this Creole?" Felix asked.

"Well, it is a member of the French speaking communities of Louisiana who are mixed with black and often Native American ancestry."

"So you are from Louisiana?"

"So you are from Louisiana?" Duck mimicked Felix's broken English again.

"Duck, you real funny, huh?" I said. "No, Felix, I told you I'm not from Louisiana. However, my mother and grandparents are. In fact, most of my father's relatives are as well. But race makes no difference to me, although I am proud of who I am."

"Me too," Felix said. "I am from Mexico. I am proud to be Mexican, but you too could pass for Mexican, no?"

"Yeah, my Mexican brother!" Duck exclaimed. "You look like a vato to me."

"Fuck you, Duck!" I said again. "You're real funny today."

Since Duck was being the comedian today, I walked to the back and disappeared for a second and motioned for Felix to follow me. I filled up a bucket of water from the shower as Duck continued watching the women in skimpy bikinis on television.

"What are you doing, Louisiana?" Felix asked.

"I told you, I ain't from no Louisiana, man. Just watch and see what I'm going to do."

Felix watch me fill the bucket full of water. I walked toward Duck who was sitting on a stool obviously hot and bothered from watching the sexy women on television.

"Damn, look at Ms. Puerto Rico! Mmmmm!" he murmured to himself, then called out, "L.A., they got one of your relatives on TV!"

I knew he was being funny again since Felix thought I was Puerto Rican, so I whispered Felix, "Go to the back, and come out when I tell you to."

"Okay," he whispered, and was gone.

I drew back the bucket, which was used to scrub the showers and drenched Duck with water. "Now, funny man, that will cool your hot ass off!" I said, laughing.

Duck tried to get up, but he was stunned as water covered him and the floor. "Holmes, I'm going to get you—" He was trying to say, but he slipped in the water and fell back down.

I rushed over and held him down on the floor, but I too slipped. "Now, Felix!" I shouted.

Felix hurried from the back with more water and doused both of us with it. He slipped in the water that covered the floor and suddenly there were the three of us, grownup men, death row prisoners in a tank at the Harris County jail, floundering around, soaking wet, on the floor, laughing hilariously.

"You guys are alright," Felix said, still laughing. "I never expected being around two death row prisoners would be this much fun. You two are crazy. Loco!"

A few more weeks passed and Duck, Felix and I found something to smile about every day. I was still waiting for a ruling from the judge, but none had come yet. Duck was eventually sent back to the Ellis Unit and Felix asked me question after question about the Ellis Unit, the notorious prison farm that housed Texas death row. Sometimes he asked so many questions that his fear would build up to a climax.

Some days it was difficult to find something to smile about, but I still answered his questions as best I could. It was hard for me to tell Felix the raw reality of death row. At times I wondered if it was best for him to gradually allow his own experiences to answer the questions. I had learned that the mind can only handle so much.

"Mail call!" Deputy Daniels called.

I went to the bars and greeted him, which was uncommon. I was not usually friendly toward any law enforcement officer of any kind. However, Daniels gave me extra time whenever he was working on the floor, and that extra time with my grandparents meant a great deal to me.

I looked at the single envelope Daniels gave me. It was from Emerson Rudd, the Young Lion, or Y.L., as many of us called him for short. I tore open the letter, glad to hear from my comrade, fellow death row prisoner and most of all, my friend.

> November 2, 1998
> My Dear Brother,
> When I was a kid, I hardly ever cried. Mainly, because I had picked up
> on that false sense of manhood that taught us crying was a characteristic
> that did not fit the male species. Therefore, each time I felt like crying,
> I would think, after all these years, I should have been able to conquer

this knock-like feeling.

Truth be known, that old knock-like feeling I've been talking about, is my throat, as I struggle to write you these few lines.

Since coming to this house of stone—death row—I have seen many brothers come and go. Some left lasting impressions, others I have no memories of. You are one of the few brothers that have entered my life and left not only a lasting impression, but a positive impression.

This is one of the reasons that I'm elated at the thought of you seeing the outside world again. We brothers on the row need young, intelligent brothers on the outside, brothers who understand and can articulate what it means to live in a perpetual state of anger, frustration and fear, each being brought on by a serious of questions: Will I be executed? Will I ever see the outside world again? Will I ever get the chance to hold my mother in my arms again? Will I have the chance to sire a child? Will the world remember me as simply a killer?

These are questions that we've all asked ourselves at one time or another. And when we cannot answer these questions, anger, frustration and fear begins to set in. It begins to set in, not only in our minds, but also in the minds of our mothers, fathers, and children. The people who love us, in fact—no man, woman, nor children—should be forced to live in such a state. Yet, this is exactly what's happening.

Every letter that we receive, every visit that we have, are seen as symbols of love, hope and happiness. And rightfully so! However, on the other side of all that is good is that which is bad. Every letter we receive, every visit we have are also symbols of pain, frustration and longings to be near those whom we love.

After being incarcerated for more than ten years, having been beaten down physically by racist guards, beat up psychologically by the subhuman conditions in which we are forced to exist, and beat down again by the continuous murdering of our young brothers, you would think that the Novocain would have taken affect by now. It hasn't! Every time I see brothers like, Stick, Tee and Mad C., it is a painful experience.

Brother, I am tired of sitting around watching a ruthless organization brutalize our people. I tire of hearing about organizations marching to the capital in protest, when the state has shown a willingness to kill and kill again. Then we have those who are always talking about the battle or the war against the establishment. When I hear such things, the words of these brothers come to mind: Martin Luther King, Jr. Said, "A man that has found no reason to die for—is not fit to live!" Sun Tzu said, "When preparing for war, prepare to die. For, only then —are you truly ready to kill!"

And I would like to think, without being conceited, that these men were agreeing with me when I said, "Life itself is a struggle, and when there is no struggle, there can be no life."

Man, the life that we have lived and the pain we have endured, I wish on no human being. Therefore, it is my sincerest hope and wish that you will one day sit at a home, and you will be able to answer these questions with a certain amount of certainty. And when you get home, give your mom a warm, long-lasting hug. You and her deserve that and so much more.

This is where I am going to close. That old knock-like feeling is pushing its way into my throat again. Yes, I will write again soon. All the brothers send a mixed array of love and greetings.

From one warrior to another, may your heart forever beat strong like the bongos of Africa. In the Spirit of Shaka Zulu.

Your Brother,
"The Young Lion"

After I finished reading this eloquently written letter from my best friend, I too felt choked up. In fact, tears in my eyes wanted to flow, but I would not let them. This place was not worthy to feel my tears splash against its floors. So I just stood there, unflinching, as I thought of Y.L. The years sometimes had a way of taunting the mind through constant isolation that caused physical pain, and I often asked myself the same questions Y.L. asked.

"What you reading, L.A.?" Felix asked.

"Oh, just a letter from a good friend."

"I thought maybe you got some bad news because your face looks like a mask of iron, but your eyes seem to be holding back—well, um, tears."

"Why were you watching me, Felix?"

"I wasn't, really, but you just don't look right. I guess you don't feel like being bothered," Felix said, casting his eyes to the floor.

"I really don't at the moment," I told him, trying to be polite. "But maybe I'll beat you in a game of chess later on."

"Okay, later then."

Later that day we played chess, and that was the one board game I was good at. We played chess every day, just Felix and me, but no news from the courts or Helen came. Perhaps none would come soon, perhaps never. I began feeling on edge, and I was no longer sure if I was going to return to the Ellis Unit or stay at the Harris County jail. I began spending more of the days trying to show Felix how to write in English and how to read, but I wasn't much help to him because I could not stay focused.

Even when I talked on the phone to my little sister, it seemed freedom was just a fading dream. I would listen to her talk about college, going to parties and everything else. Each word she said just saddened me more because I could not accept the fact that she had grown up so much during my absence from the family. She was a little girl when I left home, and now she was starting an adult life of her own.

"Hey! Come here, L.A!" Felix interrupted my telephone conversation that evening. "Come hurry, and see this!"

I quickly said goodbye to my sister and hung up the phone. "What is it, Felix?"

"They're going to say something on the news about death row any minute!"

"That's all?" I was disappointed and a little put out that I had ended my telephone call before it was necessary. "There's probably just something about an execution date or some new guy getting the death penalty."

"I don't think so. It's something bigger than that!"

An emergency news update came on to the television screen. "Seven death row prisoners escaped from Ellis Unit Thanksgiving night around eight o'clock," the media person said, a quiver of excitement in her voice. "All but one of the prisoners have been recaptured on prison grounds of the Ellis Unit. A massive manhunt started moments ago, searching for the escaped killer who got away."

"Oh shit!" I breathed aloud.

Felix looked at me curiously. "Death row is not that secure, no?"

"It is! Very much so. That's why I'm shocked."

As the night went on, I lay on the bunk in my cell thinking that maybe Y.L., Tee, Li'l Dez, Silo, Kamau, New York or some of the other guys I considered my friends tried to escape. "Maybe the Young Lion was the one still free," I whispered to myself. "Maybe, just maybe, we would be free together. I got on my knees and prayed that night that if it was Y.L., he was okay, and if not, whoever it was that they had not yet been captured, would finally escape the executioner. I could only pray for the best of outcomes.

Run, run, run ... I thought over and over to myself as I drifted off to sleep.

18

THE GREAT ESCAPE

LIKE THE MANY OTHER prison farms across the state of Texas, like the Harris County jail, like prisons anywhere in the world, confinement is basically the same—the loss of liberty is just one consequence. I was returned to the Ellis Unit, to death row, and once again I witnessed the many traumatic experiences death row has to offer.

Perhaps it was a bad sign that I was returned to the Ellis Unit, but no news had come from the courts about my case, and I was returned to death row because of the investigation being conducted regarding the escape. I knew the participants and had resided on the same cellblock from which it occurred. I left Felix behind in the Harris County jail, his fears only heightened by the prospect of his own imminent arrival. I had been back but for a day, ten days after the escape, when I was placed on the cellblock wing, which meant that prisoners whom the prison administration judged as not a security risk were allowed to work in the prison garment factory and were given a few extra privileges that lockdown prisoners were denied. However, since the escape, all of death row was locked down. Texas Rangers, considered the highest ranking and most brutal law enforcement in the state, roamed the prison cellblocks interviewing prisoner after prisoner, in an attempt to discover how escape from a maximum security death row could have been accomplished.

On Thanksgiving Day, November 30, 1998, the most daring escape in Texas history took place. Nothing like this had occurred since 1934 when Raymond Hamilton, a member of the infamous Bonnie and Clyde gang, escaped from death row cells at the Walls Unit along with several other prisoners. I originally hoped that it was the Young Lion who got away but to my surprise he was not involved.

Seven death row prisoners, five black men, one Hispanic and one Basque, cut through a chain link fence leading to the rooftop of building H-17. Since it was a work capable wing, it offered prisoners housed there more freedom of movement. Before the prisoners made their initial move, they created dummies of cloth and placed them in their bunks to give the impression that they were in their bunks sleeping. They spent hours on the rooftop while the guards made their hourly head count, passing by the dummies on count after count, finding nothing suspicious or out of the ordinary.

At about midnight, tower guards apparently noticed movement on top of the building, sprayed their high beam flashlight across the place where movement was sighted, and shortly thereafter, the prison was awakened with the rapid crackle of gunfire. As told to me by other prisoners and the news reports, more than twenty rounds were fired in an attempt to kill the prisoners. Six of the seven prisoners were recaptured on the prison grounds after the rifle assault, but one lone man, the Basque, scaled two razor wire fences amidst the gunfire and ran for freedom.

Shortly afterwards, prison officials conducted a more thorough head count, and the escaped prisoner was identified as Martin Gurule. I was surprised because Martin was a quiet and reserved man, very religious, and he got along well with the other prisoners. He was not considered a troublemaker. If he was, he would have been housed on J-21 where the classification committee placed those considered to be hardened convicts and security risks. Hell, I, Y.L., Li'l Dez, Tee and so many others were not hardened criminals, yet we had been placed there because we refused to meekly surrender our dignity and our humanity to them.

The Ellis Unit, approximately twelve miles outside of Huntsville, sits amid a thickly wooded countryside. Martin ran into a wooded area under a hail of gunfire and while the other prisoners were being apprehended, he got away. All through the night he must have run fearlessly, making his trail that much harder to trace. Over five hundred Texas Department of Criminal Justice employees, assisted by Walker County deputies, searched endlessly for the spirited prisoner. Martin's will to gain freedom overcame the swarm net that encompassed miles around the Ellis Unit. A few days later, a car was stolen in the area and abandoned in Dallas, and law enforcement agencies assumed their worst fears had been realized—that Martin had escaped the area and was free. However, the search relentlessly continued and a five thousand dollar reward was offered for information leading to Martin's arrest.

Felix and I rooted for Martin's freedom while we were together in the county jail, and needless to say, prisoners on the Ellis Unit, both death row and general population, rooted for him too, as well as many of our friends and supporters in the free world. Before I was taken from the county jail, news reports stated a body was found floating in a creek a mile or so from the prison, but that the body had not yet been identified. At last, the report came that the body was identified as Martin Gurule. Our fervent hope that he had gained freedom was gone. On death row, it seemed that with the news of his death, all our hopes for freedom were gone along with Martin's.

I read in a newspaper after I arrived back at H-17, that two off-duty prison guards who happened to be fishing in the area discovered his body. "Bullshit!" I said aloud. "Total bullshit!"

"What's up, L.A.?" a prisoner named Khallid called from the cell next to mine.

Khallid was a massive youngster about my age and a devout Muslim who took no shit. He was the kind of man who was always on the side of the prisoners, no matter what the consequences, and he would face the system with you. He too was often housed on J-21 with the rest of us, but it had been a long time since I had seen him.

"Oh, I'm just reading the newspaper about the escape," I told him. "An article says that two off-duty prison guards found Martin floating in a creek while they claimed to be fishing."

"Why do you say 'claimed'?" Khallid asked.

"Get this! They were fishing in the search area."

"How can that be? Supposedly, all TDCJ employees were involved in the search for the full seven days unless they were working at the prison."

"That's right," I said. "Whenever a massive search takes place, the immediate area is cleared of all civilians so no harm will come to them. Two off-duty TDCJ employees would be considered civilians if they are off duty, right?"

"I'm not following you."

"Now, ask yourself this: Why would those two guards be allowed time off, and even more so, have the privilege of fishing in the middle of a search area, while everyone else was working their asses off?"

"You make a lot of sense." He paused in thought. "I think they probably caught him and beat him to death, then the prison made up the story of the fishing expedition just to cover their asses for murdering Martin."

"Right on," I said. "That's my point! Being that TDCJ was embarrassed by his escape, I personally have no doubt they cleaned up their mistake by killing him just like the slave masters in this same region once killed runaway slaves who got caught trying to escape."

"That's more than likely what happened, L.A. You know Texas has always prided itself on having secure prison systems. It's got the reputation as one of the baddest prisons in the country. Did they give a reason or a cause of his death?"

"Well, yes and no. One paper I have says an autopsy report doesn't know the cause of death and that he apparently wasn't shot by any gunfire. Another paper says Martin drowned in the small creek."

"How could he have drowned? You knew Martin, man! He was in great shape. He ran every day on the yard!"

"I know, Khallid. This one paper goes on to say that Martin wrapped cardboard all around himself to scale the razor wire without getting cut and that weighed him down when it got wet from him crossing the creek, causing him to drown."

"That's bullshit!" Khallid exclaimed once again.

"That's what you heard me say. After several days, in fact, as soon as he got in the wooded area he would have taken the cardboard off so he could run faster."

"You damn right! That's common sense."

"I see it this way: They probably would not want him alive because when he was brought back here, you know the media would have wanted to talk to him," I said. "Martin could have then told them of the subhuman conditions here and the constant witness of death caused him to feel more and more depressed."

"Yeah, a man can only take the psychological and physical abuse so much," Khallid said with a sigh. "All the contributing factors that would force any man to make such a desperate attempt should tell society something."

"It should, Bro. In Martin, they just found a prisoner who wanted to be free one way or the other. He obviously lost his faith in the judicial system, but we would all be a fool to have any faith in America's judicial system."

"L.A., at least Martin died a free man. He died outside these prison walls, so that counts for something," Khallid said softly.

"Yeah, it does, Bro. He overcame the bondage of his incarceration and showed the world that chains, bars or even the hail of gunfire could not confine the human spirit. Martin died in struggle, and that's how I'll always remember him."

"Me too, man. I'm going to remember him for being the courageous soul he was. But you know what else?"

"What?" I asked.

"They probably beat them other guys real bad after they caught them."

"Where are they now?"

"I'm assuming they're all in solitary, but I know those Texas Rangers are harassing the hell out of them. The governor called for an investigation of the prison system to find out how and why the escaped occurred."

"I saw some of those Texas Rangers upstairs when I went to shower."

"They called me to the office yesterday," Khallid said. "They asked me what did I know, and I told them I didn't know nothing and to take me back to my cell."

"That's what you was supposed to say," I told him.

"They may even call you down there today. They have been interviewing every prisoner, regardless of whether they were over here when it happened or not."

"Well, I ain't going down there to the office. Fuck them! I wasn't here, and even if I was, it ain't none of my business." I looked up and Mrs. Milly was standing at my cell door.

"Déjà vu, it must be," Mrs. Milly said.

"Déjà vu, what?" I asked.

"I was sent down here to come and take you to the office to talk to one of those Texas Rangers. Don't be mad at me, Williams," she said. "Baby, I'm just doing my job."

"You heard me then, Mrs. Milly?" I said, shaking my head. "Tell all of them I ain't coming down there!"

"Okay. I'll tell them," she said, "but they'll be back."

"Let them come then," I said as she walked away.

I put on my shoes, put the newspaper away and got fully dressed. I knew Mrs. Milly was right and that any minute they would be back.

"L.A.!" Khallid yelled.

"What's up?"

"I told you they was coming back. They've done that to everyone who refused. That's why I told them as soon as I saw them that I had no statement."

A few hours passed, and I thought they would just leave me alone since I wasn't here when the escape occurred, but I was mistaken. The same toothpick-thin sergeant who hated me appeared in front of my cell, smiling.

"Welcome back, Williams," he said with a toothless grin.

"What do you want, pig?"

"The Texas Rangers have requested to speak with all inmates, and like it or not, that means you."

"Let me say this to you," I said. "I have no statement and that's my right. But call my attorney and have her present. She can repeat the same thing to you."

"You sure think you're smart, don't you, boy?"

"I'm not your 'boy,' pig! But I'm requesting my attorney to be present."

"Well, turn around and be handcuffed," he barked the order at me as if his barking tone of voice was an assertion of his own dubious manhood.

"I told you, I'm not going."

He looked down the tier and motioned for three other guards to come to my cell. "Are you refusing to get handcuffed so I can search your cell?" the sergeant asked in front of his three biased witnesses.

"No, I'm not refusing to have my cell searched," I said, knowing he was trying to provoke an incident. Knowing that I had so much going for me on my appeal and that an assault case would harm my chances, I knew I had to keep my cool.

"Turn around then and be handcuffed, boy," the toothpick-thin sergeant snickered.

I bit my tongue until I could taste blood and turned around to be handcuffed. After the cell door was rolled open, I watched the sergeant and his goons tear my cell apart in search of nothing. His main purpose was just to destroy some of my personal property and scatter my legal papers everywhere so that I would have to clean up the mess. He then placed me back in my cell, still smiling up at me with toothless glee. To my own surprise, I found myself smiling back at him so as not to give him the satisfaction of knowing he had gotten under my skin.

When he removed the handcuffs, I merely said, "Thank you for tearing up my property. I appreciate it."

"No problem," he said, his nasal redneck voice dripping with sarcasm.

"I don't see my pen and paper. You seem to have misplaced it somewhere within my cell," I told him. "Is it okay if I borrow yours?"

"Hell, no!" he said. "For what?"

"I want to write something for you to give to the Texas Rangers."

He looked at me for a brief moment, considered that I was willing to cooperate with an authority higher than him, and he handed over his pen.

I took a piece of paper off the floor and wrote my attorney's telephone number on it, then handed it the sergeant. "Here you go," I said, smiling.

He read the number and said, "What the hell is this, Williams?"

"It's my attorney's phone number so you can call her and request her to be present while I am being interviewed by the Texas Rangers."

His face turned a pinkish red, and he heard Khallid laughing at him. "You're an asshole, Williams!" he said, storming off. I just laughed while dreading the task of cleaning up the mess he made in my cell.

I began to wonder why he had not requested to strip search me before I exited the cell, as that was a tactic that was often employed to throw us off balance. No matter how many times I was ordered to strip, it was something I could never get used to. Our nakedness literally made us feel like we owned nothing, not even the underwear that had the state's trademark in big, bold letters—Property of TDCJ—stamped on it. The only material thing I could claim that was mine alone were the glasses I now wore. I lost vision in my left eye three years ago while being gassed and kicked by steel boots over and over again while I was handcuffed in solitary.

I tried to wear my glasses proudly, but they became a painful reminder of the beating. To me, the glasses represent a permanent scar and every time I put them on I imagine a steel-toed boot crashing against my skull. Sometimes I can almost feel the sensation of unconsciousness creeping over me.

The psychological scars are very deep. Sometimes, I wake up in a deep sweat, shaking, having been awakened by my own scream, although I have never screamed aloud, nor will I ever. Sadly, I know a man can endure practically any pain, but with a show of honor we try to laugh off some of the pain with each other to lessen its impact upon our minds.

Over the years when people have asked me, "How do you do it?" referring to the will to survive under such mind-boggling circumstances. I never tell them the truth. I have often lied to myself, "Oh, it's nothing. Just another day." But there have been times that I have wondered if dying would be much easier. Each time my mother, my Grandma and Papa have visited, I smiled so they could see that I'm well, but I know my eyes deceive me. Perhaps true courage is the ability to just openly cry and let the pain flow away in a river of tears, and hope that time will heal the pain like my body hides the scars. But no, I have to be strong. My loved ones have carried us all on their backs for too long.

"I must stay strong!" I told myself aloud. The anger seemed at times to be my only ally. It gave me a surging strength when nothing else did. But even the anger took on an existence of its own, at times abandoning me and being constantly re-born into a destructive state until I waged a battle within myself to tame it. I sometimes failed. I sometimes stumbled to overcome my own failures sprouted from the seed of oppression that clouds life's images, showing me with strong intensity the horrible reality before me. For Martin, I knew he escaped the pain that still reflected in my eyes, and the eyes of so many others.

19

A REASON TO LIVE

I RECEIVED A WARM welcome when I returned to the Ellis Unit, although my friends wished the best for me and that meant hoping I would not have to come back. Of course, I did not want to return either, especially under the strictest conditions I ever experienced with all of death row on lockdown. I wanted to be free, yet I often wondered, if freedom did come, what would it mean to me, knowing that so many of those I called "friend," "bro" and "comrade" were still here, facing each day with death hovering, circling them like a hungry shark in turbulent waters?

On H-17 we had the privilege of being un-handcuffed as we went to the showers, to recreation and to the visiting room. We preferred that our families and friends not see us handcuffed. Who would ever think that not having one's hands and feet bound would be considered a privilege?

Khallid and I became close friends, and we often exercised together and held endless discussions, jumping from one topic to another. Sometimes we argued just like so many others and even ignored each other for a few days, but our bond grew stronger. We began to take on problem after problem that the other had; the guards knew this. In fact, our cells were searched much less often because the guards knew they would have a problem with both of us, even if they bothered only one of us.

We constantly bounced thoughts off each other in hopes of learning, but just as we exercised our desires to educate ourselves, we physically exercised together to relieve tension and frustrations, and in doing so, we both became bigger.

"Keep your head up, Khallid, now do twenty-five more push-ups," I urged him on.

"Damn, L.A., it's your turn." He got up from the floor. "Head up, now go!" Khallid began counting. "One, two, three, four," and then he stopped and ran to the window.

"Khallid! Come on, man, let's finish these sets of push-ups," I told him while he stood staring out the window.

"Say, L.A., they just rolled somebody down the hall on a stretcher, and he was covered in blood."

"Oh, yeah?" I jumped up. "Who was it?"

"I don't know, but whoever it was, was still alive because several pigs were struggling to hold him down."

We were concerned, so we searched for further information. I went to the door of the recreation yard and motioned for Mrs. Milly, who was the guard working on the wing. She came to the dayroom when I beckoned to her.

"Say, Mrs. Milly, they rolled somebody past the dayroom window just now, and Khallid said he was covered in blood. What happened?"

"Jesus, let me tell you," Mrs. Milly said, as her eyes grew big. "This one inmate earlier this morning cut both of his wrists open and blood poured from him like a fountain. He wiped his own blood all over his face and then wiped it all over the walls. I went over to J-21 to see what happened about an hour ago, and the cell looked like someone crucified himself, but the inmate in the cell just stood there cutting on himself with a razor he got out of one those shaving things." She stopped to catch her breath. "Other guards were scared to open the door because they were saying he might have AIDs, or he might try to cut them."

"Well, apparently they finally got him out of the cell," Khallid said.

Mrs. Milly went on. "When I saw him, I hurried up and left J-21 because the sight of blood makes me very sick to my stomach. He even started cutting his face, and he wasn't screaming, or wincing in pain or anything. I mean, nothing at all." She was shaking as she spoke.

Khallid and I tried to finish our exercises, but we couldn't. The afternoon grew older, and we returned to our cells without a word passing between the two of us. Viktor E. Frankl said, "Apathy, the main symptom of a second phase, was a necessary mechanism of self-defense." The famous Jew who was a survivor of the Nazi concentration camps said this because when one deals with so much pain, all of one's emotions center on the preservation of one's own sanity. To say that Khallid and I were trying to preserve our own sanity was true, but to say we were lacking any emotion toward a fellow prisoner was not true.

If we were honest, most of us had entertained thoughts of suicide at some point, but to hear that someone had actually tried to take his own life or had succeeded in doing so, hit many of us like a spear in the heart. Even on death row, we had to find a meaning to live, and when we did find a meaning, that became the breath that kept us alive. To realize that another human being could find no reason at all to live—not a single reason whatsoever—caused me to reevaluate my own reasons to live.

Even when we could see no light at all and hope seemed to elude our grasp, we still stumbled in the darkness searching and searching for some inkling of hope to grasp onto. Sometimes we could still hear the cries of the damned calling out to us, along with the cries of the forsaken who once roamed these very same halls trying to find a reason to keep going, to keep searching, to keep living. There was never any way to retreat from the terrible surroundings of death row unless we chose to dwell in a quiescent state where illusions became our companions.

For many, there were two groups of thought: either the safeguarding and preservation of our sanity, or facing the reality of a living hell that inflicted pain and the promise of pain continually in the future. Each of us calculated just how much we could take, but pain is never particular. It is seen through different eyes, felt through different traumas, and strikes with a deadly blow to the very core of the mind, at the process of the thought that struggles to overcome it. At times, we tried to become apathetic in order to suppress our emotions, but this self-defense mechanism eventually fails.

I will never forget the dead who once lived, who once existed in my shoes, even if I can no longer remember their individual names. Those lives engulfed my own—the child molester, the kidnapper, the serial killer, the innocent who had done nothing wrong and the other teenage boys like myself who grew into manhood inside this dungeon, leaving the boy in themselves dead.

As I sat thinking about the prisoner who cut himself with a razor, I wondered if fate would offer me a similar chance after so many experiences? With every slice of the razor he inflicted upon himself, I felt it. I felt the screams rise up in my throat, but none came out, only the echoes that bounced off the soundless walls, blasting my eardrums in denial. It could never be me, yet I envisioned him as clearly as I saw myself. *Look at your wrist!* I thought to myself. I stared at it and touched it ever so gently, seeking the vein that pulsed with life. I felt the pressure of the blood that moved with the rhythm of my heart, throbbing, moving ever so thickly through my body and sustaining my life. And then, just as he must have done, I picked up a razor as though mimicking him. Going forward in the same violent motion to relieve the pressure in my veins and to relieve myself of this pain. But, unlike him, I stopped. Rapid warnings attacked my mind, reminding me of so many reasons to live—my beautiful mother, Papa and Grandma, my brothers and sisters, my stepmother, my friends. Did the other prisoner not have such warnings begging for a second chance? Did he not have family and friends as I do?

In my heart, I knew I was too much of a coward to ever commit suicide, although my careless regard for my own life had shown otherwise at times. I believed in fighting back against all the odds I faced because the only odds that exist are those we create in our own minds. For me, I tore down the odds, and I sought out brief moments of happiness to sustain me and become food for my soul and strength for my spirit.

Time taught me that everyone had to have a goal in life. A man who does not have a goal has a short-lived existence. Although I was am in no position to plan for the future, every second that ticked away had to have a purpose. I knew I had to use them however I could utilize them best.

The psychological makeup of the death penalty, I believe, is to destroy the prisoners' will to live. Although death is final and may be relatively easy to accept, the true punishment seemed to be the stripping away of hope, rendering our desires hollow.

During the latter part of one's existence on death row, hope creeps back up on the scene, causing conflicts to arise amongst the realities, the circumstances and one's will to concentrate on saving his life, even after it was too late. This often happens when an execution date is only weeks away. In order to make this observation clear, one tries to believe in the spiritual aspects of their religious belief in an attempt to compensate for the loss of hope.

No outsider can truly grasp how a death row prisoner feels, but I knew I had to gain an understanding for myself in order to avoid becoming apathetic as a defense for the preservation of my sanity.

"Hey, L.A., what you doing over there?" Khallid called out from his cell next door.

"Just a little writing, that's all," I answered.

"Writing about what?"

"About life for us, hope and my reasons to keep on living."

"I bet you were thinking about that other prisoner who cut himself up today, right?"

"Yeah, how did you know?"

"Because I've been thinking about the same thing. I guess we all want to believe it will never happen to us, trying to kill ourselves, I mean. But everyone eventually tells himself that."

"Have you ever thought about killing yourself, Khallid?" I asked.

"No, not really. I have to stay strong for my mother, but if my Queen Mother ever died, well, I would probably give up my remaining appeals. My Queen Mother is all I have."

How well I understood where he was coming from. "Me too, Bro. If my Mama wasn't suffering as I am, trying to gain my freedom so we could live together as a family again, I can't say I would have the desire to live either. My Mama is the voice that whispers 'All is well,' and I believe her. All is well as long as I know her love exists for me."

"We feel the same way then, L.A.," Khallid told me.

"Right on. At least me and your big-head ass agree on something."

"Yeah, I hear you. I'll rap to you later. I'm going to write my Queen Mother now."

"Alright. I think I'll do the same. Tell your mom I said hello."

"You do the same, L.A.," Khallid said.

I ended the day writing my Mama, letting her know I love her and that her love is my strength and my salvation. "Mama, I love you with all my heart," I ended the letter. "Love, Your baby boy, Nanon."

20

WORDS OF ENCOURAGEMENT

THE SKY WAS ALL I could see as I walked hand in hand with my thoughts. It seemed as though I was never truly alone. Some thought was always with me, waiting to comfort me when I was sad, or throwing a weed on a furnace to inflame my anger. I was never alone. There was always so much to be done, but never enough time to do anything. I tried to accept each day on its own, trying to understand it with the hope it would bestow a certain amount of wisdom, to plant roots for a more promising future. However, there was no time to wait for it. The future for me was in each moment, as was the past and the present, each of them attempted to take me beyond my physical boundaries.

A sound with great intensity slammed against my eardrums as a horn blew, bringing me back to reality. My thoughts were gone, off into the skies, moving with the clouds that passed above my head.

"Count time, count time!" a guard yelled through the window. "Number, please!"

"My name is Nanon Williams," I replied.

"I only need your identification number," He glared at me.

"9-9-9-1-6-3," I said.

"Are you the only inmate on the yard?"

I ignored him. If he needs to get a correct count of prisoners, he would have to do so on his own. I would not assist him. After all, he only saw me as an "inmate" and as a number. With the exception of Mrs. Milly, I disliked all other guards. At least Mrs. Milly respected us.

"Well," said the guard, "thanks for your help." He stormed away from the window.

Those were my exact sentiments! Thanks for your help in assisting to drag fellow prisoners to the execution chamber. Thanks for your help in breaking our bones with the force of a baton. Thanks for seeing me as a number instead of the name my Mama gave me. "Thanks for nothing, you punk!" I yelled at him as he hurried away.

I wanted it to be clear that I didn't consider myself to be an "inmate." Most dictionaries define "inmate" as someone who dwells in the same place, and to me that wasn't an accurate description of the circumstances in which I was forced to live. I was a prisoner. I was being held against my will, and I wanted this to be clearly understood. If I willingly participated in my own incarceration, only then would I accept the term "inmate."

I always kept myself aware of the fact that I was not a number. The purpose of giving prisoners numbers is not to keep an accurate account of us; it is designed to strip away our humanity and make our individuality non-existent. Being just a number seemed to make it easier to treat us as animals, or to bury us, not as human beings but as some irrelevant non-entity. I would never even give an identification number, but if I didn't, I wouldn't get recreation, letters from those I loved, or even visits. For security reasons, they would claim to not know who I was and deny all of those things.

I believed I could deal with anything, even the everyday life of prison, but I wouldn't accept it. The one thing I could never get used to was how my family dealt with it. When my younger brother was still a little boy he would ask me at visitation, "Big brother, when are you coming home?"

I would look at him, smile and lie to him. "Soon, little brother. I'll be home very soon." And he would get excited and try to prove to me how much he had grown up. I could never look at him and be truthful. How could I tell him, "Little brother, I am here to die, until an executioner draped in a hood tells witnesses I am dead, dead, dead!" So I shamefully lied to him again and again. "I'll be home soon, so get big because I'm going to beat you up like I used to," I always told him playfully. Mama just smiled and encouraged me. She told me, "Look how big he's gotten," and she knew the truth too, but she remained strong for the both of us.

While I continue walking the yard alone, all I ever had were my thoughts and my memories.

"Williams!" the guard shouted as he came back to the window. "You have a visit. What's your number?"

Ever so consciously, I recited the number once again like a rehearsal in a play, and then I was escorted to the visiting room without handcuffs. I had no idea who was coming to see me. Hell, I never knew. I just got there in a hurry, glad someone cared enough to visit me.

That day, in the midst of the other prisoners, I was placed on a side of the visiting room where there were no individual cages, where I was normally locked, so I sat on a stool with only plexiglass separating me and my visitor instead of all the other metal restrictions. I just sat on the stool and waited for someone to appear on the opposite side of the plexiglass, waiting.

Suddenly my Grandmother appeared before me and sat down, no smile of acknowledgment coming forth. She just sat there. Then moments later Mama appeared, and she wasn't smiling either.

"Hi Mama," I said. "Hi, Grandma."

"Hello, Baby," Grandma finally said, "how are you doing?"

"Oh, I'm doing fine. I'm just surprised to see the two of you. It's been a little while," I said. "When did you fly to Texas, Mama?"

"I came in last night, Sweetie."

I was wondering why they both came without Papa. It surprised me because Grandma and Papa always came together, always. "Where is Papa?" I asked Grandma.

No response came. Something was wrong. I asked Mama, "What's wrong? Where is Papa?"

Finally Mama spoke, "Sweetie," she said softly, "Papa died two nights ago."

"Where is Papa?" I asked again, not sure what I had just heard.

"He died of a heart attack while talking on the phone," Grandma said slowly. "You be strong. Papa lived a long life, praise God."

From that moment on, nothing seemed real. I could not pretend I was strong for the sake of my family. Tears came, one after the other, and I bowed my head.

"It's okay," Mama said as tears rolled down her cheeks too. "Just let it out."

Grandma, however, didn't cry. She just sat there, being strong. Maybe she was still in shock. I was too caught up in my own pain to understand which. After a few minutes passed, I got up and made my way toward the back to the restroom area to retrieve some toilet paper. We are supposed to acknowledge the guards during visits if we get up to go to the restroom, but without care or thought, I went anyway, as fellow prisoners stared at me, whispering among themselves.

In escaping to the restroom, I rounded a corner and a guard hurried behind me. He grabbed my elbow with force to stop me, and without hesitating, I spun around, grabbed him by the throat and felt his Adam's apple crush beneath my grip. We were facing each other, tears streaming down my face and fear etched across his, as I had him penned against the wall. I couldn't determine how hard I was gripping his throat, but he was pushing against me in panic. I vented so much rage and pain that I nearly collapsed, and at precisely the right moment he broke loose and scampered out of my sight, back into the open visiting room.

I finally got some toilet paper and wiped my eyes. I didn't care that more guards would rush to the back and take me down. I just blew my nose and splashed water on my face without concern. When I was done, I went back to the visiting room. Other prisoners stared at me, and several guards motioned for me to sit down and continue my visit.

I sat down and Mama again asked me if I was alright. I was supposed to be the strong one in our family. After all, I was now the oldest male. Mama told me she had arranged a special visit with the warden, and we had extra visiting time. The extra time did help. We talked and talked, even mustering an occasional smile. But what we talked about that day, I don't remember.

After the visit was over, Grandma blew kisses through the glass window, and I caught them and planted them on my cheek. After they left, I sat alone in the visiting room. No one else was there but several guards. I didn't move, nor did they. I just sat there trying to figure out exactly what I was going to do next. I suppose I figured that if they wanted to give me a severe beating because I had grabbed a guard, so be it. I would welcome the physical pain as a substitute for my bleeding heart. No confrontation came, however. Later, one of the wardens came to the visiting room and escorted me back to H-17, with several guards following along behind us. Not a word was passed between any of us, and apparently none would. I was just placed in my cell and left alone. I didn't receive an assault case or any harassment. Nothing at all. In fact, I didn't care.

A good friend named Marion tried to talk to me and shelter some of my pain, but I was in no mood to talk. I just sat in my cell rocking myself back and forth as the tears came in abundance. All through the night I rocked on my bunk and let my memories slowly heal me if they would. I thought of my own father and remembered how he was shot over and over again on a street in Los Angeles, over drug territory. I remembered being a boy of eleven and going to the funeral, watching hundreds of people, it seemed, lay flowers on his casket and kiss him. My father just laid there, very pale, his eyes closed, stitches closing his wounds. There was no life in him, and I stood above him, staring at first, and then I laid my head on his chest crying and begging him to wake up. "Please wake up, Daddy!" I begged him, but he didn't move nor would he, ever again. Someone pulled me away, I don't remember who but later, my stepmother just held me as I cried on her shoulder. She just held on to me, holding me together and letting me know she was there and that she would love me just like my daddy did.

Even prison could never erase the memories of my father. Fourteen years after his death I would sometimes wake up with tears streaming down my face, missing my father. Now Papa was gone. He had tried to fill my father's shoes as best he could. He attended all my football and baseball games. He refused to miss even one. He could be seen yelling in the stands, "Go get 'em, Meathead!" And he would give me the thumbs up sign. Whenever I earned the game ball, I proudly gave it to Papa, and he would put me on his shoulders and move around in circles. The first time I made the junior All Star team in baseball, he got a shirt made that said, "That's my boy #1" and that was my jersey number. When I received my trophies for every sport I played, I gave it to Papa so he could be proud of me.

Now, there would be no other chances to make Papa proud. I wouldn't be allowed to attend my grandfather's funeral and this caused me more pain than anyone could imagine. I would never have a chance to look into his face again, to see him smile, hear his words of encouragement, or to say goodbye. I sat down and I wrote the following for Papa. I would not say goodbye.

Words of Encouragement
When I was a kid,
We would laugh, wrestle, and hang out together
And you never seemed to get bored with me.
Even when I knew you were tired,
And needed to rest for work,
Or whatever other responsibilities I knew you had.

How you came up with all the energy to keep up with me,
Well, I never really knew,
But it was obvious your love was true,
As it reflected in everything you would do.
And as I took strides toward adolescence,
You were always there with words of encouragement.

You were the reason that made everything matter,

As I created goals in life.

And dreams that were formed just so I could tell you,

Because I envisioned your face,

Gently smiling with the same encouragement.

But now, things have changed.

Gone are those smiles and words of encouragement,

That once made everything matter,

Because unexpectedly you left,

Leaving me all alone with not a dream,

As they now rest peacefully with you in another place,

Like that of a sleeping rose, resting forever.

You were not just someone to call friend,

Or someone to hang out with,

You were the rhythm of my heartbeat,

That created the pulse in everything I did.

But now that you're gone

I have no words of encouragement,

Because only you could give me that, Papa.

Dedicated to my beloved Grandfather, Emmett Oliver Lymuel, March 25, 1999

After Papa died, I realized out of all the deaths I had witnessed, the pain I felt was nothing compared to losing a loved one. My own death would be much easier, but for Papa I had to remain strong. I still had so many others who needed me, so Papa had to live in me and together we had to stand tall.

For many days I laid motionless on my back, but Papa's words of encouragement reached out to me, and although it took months for me to actually regain my composure, the pain never left. Perhaps I didn't want it to leave me. At least the open wound kept Papa alive, every day, every minute, every second, I wrote with the stroke of my pen. I knew so many other prisoners, and people around the world who suffered like I did, but we must get back up and keep going. The Young Lion once told me, "Even the great runners of Kenya get tired and must rest, but they get back up and continue the journey. Even we get tired and must rest, but we too must continue the journey."

My life may not have been what I wished it to be, but still I had to live it, and go on just as we all must. I spent the next few months learning from Marion, a fellow death row prisoner who had the spirit to find happiness wherever he could. If I ever believed a prisoner to be innocent, it was he because it was reflected in how he treated others. He was a generous soul, and he helped with those same words of encouragement Papa had given me, only this time the words came from a friend.

Because of the Thanksgiving Day escape, we were all to be transferred to a new super-maximum security prison called the Terrell Unit. Young Lion and a few others whom the prison administration deemed as the worst of the worst were taken there ahead of the rest us, but we would all eventually be transferred. My name was on that list, so I thought to myself, "Well, at least I'll be around other soldiers." Sometimes that was how I saw it, that we were soldiers in the middle of the battlefield, armed only with our weapon of courage. "Forward, March!" we would say as we clashed against our oppressors.

21

SOMETHING REAL

NIGHT HAD FALLEN AND I had already packed my property and given it to the guards who had come to collect it. I was told that in the morning I and a few other selected prisoners would be transferred to the Terrell Unit. The Terrell Unit was built in 1993 and was initially designed for the purpose of holding the most violent of prisoners, but before the escape, that had not meant death row prisoners. Other prisoners occupied the Terrell Unit. We were to be put to death, and yet other prisoners were considered more violent than we were so they were housed in the super-max facility.

The minute I finished packing, I resigned myself to standing at the cell door, staring out the window. Unlike J-21, I could see outside and let my eyes roam upward into the stars for as far as the eyes could see. I had no plans for sleeping. The Ellis Unit, although it had been another hell for us all, was the only place I had known for most of my adulthood. Would I miss it? Hell, no! I would miss the memories of individuals who became my friends, like Rogers-el, Da'Oud, Billy Joe and so many others; so very many others, in fact, that all the faces of those who had been executed seemed like they were from two lifetimes ago. As I looked up at the moon hovering above the prison, I remembered how Da'Oud used to watch the night whenever we were at recreation late in the evening. He saw the night as another world, even better than day. He said the stars were like the eyes of God watching us. On nights when the moon was full, he said it was unlike the sun, in that the beauty of the moon was in watching it change and knowing it would do so. On this particular night, my very last night at the Ellis Unit, I was the moon's acolyte as Da'Oud had been for many other nights.

We sat together all night, my memories and I, but nothing had really changed—just the years. Time and time again the memories would come and then abruptly leave, tonight was just peaceful for me. When the moon finally disappeared, so did the dark blue light it gave.

"You still up there?" Marion asked me.

"Been up all night," I said.

"I'm going to give you some food and stamps to take with you because there's no telling when you'll go to the prison store over there." Marion's kind and generous offer was his way of saying goodbye.

"Right on, I appreciate that." I knew I would need those things; the sharing and giving took the place of sentimentality. I didn't really say very much to Marion, but I knew him in Harris County before I ever went to death row. Then, we were both just waiting for trial, both of us believing that justice would prevail, although it did not for him or for me.

"You ready?" he asked.

"Go ahead."

A bag skidded down the tier way directly in front of my cell. Inside the bag were fifty stamps, a pair of new gym shorts, a few bags of peanuts and some colorful chewable candy.

"Thanks a lot," I said gratefully.

"It's no big deal. When you get there, just write me and let me know how it is."

"I will, as soon as I get there."

I saw a guard approaching on the tier way. "The bus is out back, Inmate," he said. "Take off your jumpsuit." I did as he told me. "Now shake it out for me," he said.

"That's it?" I asked.

"No! Let me see your shoes." He grabbed them and shook them together. "Come to the bars, and I'll handcuff you in the front instead of the back," he said. When I did so, he put the handcuffs on me.

While the door was being opened, other prisoners yelled over the tier saying goodbye, and one guy even said more words to me in one minute than he probably had said in a whole year. "Alright, Khallid, see you later, Bro," I told him.

"Be strong."

"Alright, Marion," I said as I walked past his cell, carrying the bag he had given me.

"Be cool," he said.

When we got to the end of the tier, I looked back, taking one last look at the cellblock, and I turned facing the hall. As we walked down the hall, Mrs. Milly came up with a sad look and stopped us.

"You don't get in no trouble over there, Williams," she said. That was her way of saying goodbye. She could not say much with the other guards on each side of me.

"Keep treating people the way you do, Mrs. Milly," I nodded my head at her and kept moving.

Something in the way Mrs. Milly stressed my last name seemed as though she was going to cry. She was a prison guard, which was something I disliked, but Mrs. Milly still managed to make me see her just as a person, because that's how she made me and so many others feel.

Moving further down the hallway, the door to solitary was flung open as several guards wrestled with a prisoner from general population. "That's enough," the general population prisoner screamed, but a sadistic guard ignored his pleas and kicked him so hard in the ribs that he doubled over in pain, just as the door slammed shut.

"Move it, Williams," the big, burly guard told me when I stopped and witnessed the assault. "Move it!" he said again, shoving me with some force.

As I refused to move, Mrs. Milly appeared out of nowhere and spoke to the big, burly guard.

"Okay," she said. "I got him from here."

"Let's go," the other guard said, and Mrs. Milly encouraged me to move to prevent problems.

Without giving the other incident much thought, I reluctantly moved. Mrs. Milly held onto my elbow and led me out the door to a large concrete platform where more than twenty guards were lined up, chains slung across the ground, and two small white buses stood in the background with doors open.

"I got to go now, Williams," she said. "Don't give these other guards the satisfaction of hurting you out here, because they will," she sighed. "This is considered the highest security move in the state of Texas at this very moment. They will not hesitate to knock you unconscious to get you on that bus. Do you understand what I'm telling you?"

"I hear you, Mrs. Milly," I said. "Thanks."

"Thank me by keeping your cool." And with that, she walked away. I knew that we had seen the last of each other and that I would never meet another prison guard like her. Nor did I want to. It was easier to keep the battle lines drawn with the enemy.

The captain, who carried a baton, had his white hair combed back, with each wisp of his mustache nearly in line with the other.

"Get on your knees!" he barked.

I looked up and thought about what Mrs. Milly said. I slowly got on my knees. Within seconds, shackles were clasped around my ankles, almost crushing my Achilles tendon. After the shackles were secure, a rusty four-foot chain was wrapped around my waist, and I was jerked to my feet.

"Relax," a different guard said somewhat civilly. *But,* I thought, *what man was supposed to be civil in return when you were being wrapped in chains and given orders with the threat of a savage and brutal beating hanging in the air?*

The guard picked up another chain, the chain was looped around the chain connecting each shackle around my ankles and then pulled up and reconnected with the chain around my waist, causing me to have to squat down until I was no longer standing upright at all, but slouched over like a gorilla and expected to walk like one. After suffering this kind of treatment over a period of time, some prisoners just passively accepted being treated inhumanely. The years wear down their resistance, but it did not wear down mine. I refused to let it. I wanted these fucking pigs to know that I didn't accept nor like the way I was being treated. I suppose they wanted me to say, "Thank you, Master," like I was a slave willing to accept such treatment.

"Move, Inmate!" the captain shouted.

"Fuck you!" I told the captain as I moved, slouched over like a gorilla. As I moved slowly, lifting one foot at a time with my hands almost crushed between my legs, I had never felt more humiliated in my life. No matter what, handcuffed or not, I always walked with my head held high, but I couldn't walk upright; in fact, it would have been much easier to hop like a frog than to walk.

"Name and number," a blond, female guard said at the entrance of the bus.
I just ignored her, and I knew they would think me to be dangerous had they seen the expression on my face. It didn't make me a bad person because I had dignity, so at that point, I refused to give a number if I wasn't getting mail, recreation or a visit,

and so I had nothing to gain by demeaning myself.

"Nanon Williams," I said.

"What's your number, Inmate?" she scowled, demanding the response she wanted.

"I don't have a number, My name is Nanon Williams," I said through clenched teeth.

The captain saw progress halted at the entrance of the bus, and he walked up to me as if he thought he was God himself.

"What's the problem?"

The blond female shook her head as she answered, "This inmate won't give me his identification number."

"That's Williams. His number is 9-9-9-1-6-3. Now put him on the bus, so we can get rid of his kind."

"I'll be glad to get away from your racist ass," I told him, knowing that the words "his kind" was simply another way of calling me "nigger." I had heard him use the term "nigger" before in casual conversation among the other guards when they thought no one else could hear them.

The shackles restricted the movement of my legs due to the chain that held my feet only inches apart, so that I couldn't climb the first step. Two guards lifted me up the first big step, and then I had to almost crawl up the remaining two. I was hurting, not from the pain of the chains, but from the pleasure I saw in the guards' eyes as they smiled at our discomfort.

As I finally stood upright in my gorilla like stance, I made my way to a seat where other prisoners were, near the front of the bus. The first person I saw was Tee, and he seemed happy to see me.

"What's up, Bro?" Tee asked, trying to nudge his glasses back up on his nose. "I knew once they told me I was on the list to be transferred, you was on it, too."

"I thought you were on the first transfer with Y.L."

"Nah, I was still left on J-21," Tee told me. "I knew that you made it back more than ten or eleven months ago, after your hearing. How did it go, man?"

"It went very well, but still there's been no ruling."

"No news is good news."

"For some, maybe. I want to get busy living, or get busy dying! If fighting back causes me to die quicker rather than patiently rotting in a cell and putting up with this bullshit, then so be it!" I said. "So be it!" I repeated softly.

"I understand what you mean, L.A.," Tee said as we watched Silo get onto the bus.

It had been almost two years since I had last seen Silo. He stood on the bus, refusing to sit. Then he began stamping his feet strangely like I always heard him do in solitary.

"Silo! Good to see you," I told him.

"Did you ever see any ghosts?" he asked me, throwing me off.

I thought about all the stories he once told me when we were in solitary, about the Walls Unit and Ax Man. Silo had not changed a bit, and I just laughed. "Nah, man, I ain't seen no ghost," I said.

Tee had somehow maneuvered his way over to another prisoner, Gary Graham, known as Shaka Sankofa. They got caught up in conversation, and I just sat still, rubbing my wrist as the other prisoners boarded the bus. It seemed as if everyone who came on the bus was black and Hispanic, and sadly, that was true. I knew virtually everyone, and we all acknowledged each other. Then I just sat looking around me at how the bus was designed. To me, every new surrounding was worth investigating, even if it was only temporary.

The outside appearance of the bus was white with bars crossing each window. It was a half-size bus like the kind of bus teenagers laughed at that carried disabled kids to school. Only this time, no one was laughing—nothing seemed funny at all—except the guards, but even a few of them were on edge. The inside of the bus was steel with metal reinforced bars crossing the inside of the windows and making escape impossible. There were rows of plastic green seats that had cushions, but were very dusty and smelled bad. However, many prisoners happily flopped down on them to relieve the pressure of the shackles, so I flopped down as well. In the back of the bus was a cage with a stool inside for a guard to ride shotgun. In the front, there was another cage that blocked passage toward the driver's seat and the one entrance where we entered the bus.

"Que Honda, Homeboy?" Someone spoke to me in Spanish from behind me.

When I turned around, I saw that it was a guy I knew for many years, much longer than anyone I knew on death row. His name was Edgar Tamayo, and I briefly knew him in California before I was extradited.

"Que tiraes tu?" I said, meaning, what's up with you?

"Que pasa, L.A. It's been a long time," he said.

"It has been a long time, Vago," I said, addressing him by his nickname. "I'm surprised to see you."

"I can't tell. You said hello to everybody else, but you missed a poor Mexican in the back," he joked. "What the fuck, you don't know me no more?"

"Vago! You know better than that," I said. "We go way back."

"Well, give a brown brother some skin," he said, holding out his hands in the handcuffs.

I shook his hand, glad to see him. "These handcuffs hurt," I told Vago.

"What the fuck, you don't know English?"

"What do you mean?" I asked.

He laughed and said, "You know English, so tell one of these pinche jura to loosen these handcuffs."

In Spanish, "pinche jura" was an East Los Angeles street term meaning "damned police" or "bastard police." Vago used these terms to describe the guards, so I knew what he meant.

"Man, ain't no sense in asking those pigs to loosen these cuffs," I said. "They knew what they were doing to begin with."

"Probably so, but I'd tell the pinche jura anyway."

I slowly rose to my feet, just to make sure the pressure kept my feet from getting numb from the shackles, and then I sat back down.

"Well ese," Vago said, "let me go holler at a few of the other Vato Locos I know, and I'll see you later."

"Alright," I said and turned my head to look out the windows again. I knew Vago didn't much like many people, so when he said "Vato Loco" it meant "crazy dude," but that was his way of saying he respected someone.

Silo was still standing in the way of other prisoners boarding the bus, so someone shoved him to one side, and he finally decided to have a seat. Most of the other prisoners were still shaking hands and probably a little nervous at the idea of moving to another prison. For Tee, well, he had been at Ellis Unit for twenty-three years, so I can't truly imagine how he felt. After being here for so many years, I'm sure he had mixed feelings, yet still, he knew we were moving from one hell to another.

"Everyone have a seat." A guard entered the cage in the back of the bus with a shotgun he pumped once to show it was loaded. At that moment the van roared to life.

Most of the prisoners who weren't already seated sat down, and others ignored the guard as if he did not exist. Besides, he too was now trapped in a cage on the bus like us, so it wasn't like he could do anything about it, even if he did hold onto the shotgun like he was the baddest son-of-a-bitch on the planet.

"Kiss my ass, pig!" someone said, but he pretended he did not hear the insult.

As the van inched forward slowly to an inspection gate, two more guards jumped on to the bus, waving pistols as an act of show, and sat down. While the inspection of the van took place, a large gate rolled open and sheriff's deputies, other prison officials and a few Texas Rangers, all armed to the teeth, positioned cars in front and back of the bus. Then we all pulled out.

"Everything is still pretty dark, huh?" one prisoner in front of me who I didn't know asked me.

I didn't mean to be rude, but I no longer felt in the mood to talk. "You're kind of stating the obvious, don't you think?" I said.

"Guess so," he said. "Your name is L.A., ain't it?" he asked.

"Nope," I lied, not offering any information about myself to someone I didn't know.

"Oh, my bad," he said. "I thought I heard a few of the other prisoners call you L.A."

"Why you wanna know?" I asked the young, skinny guy.

"Ah, no reason," he said, raising his long neck to look at the window. "I just heard a lot of stories about you and Y.L. since I've been on death row."

Evidently he was convinced I was L.A., whether I told him differently or not, but I just continued staring out the window so he could see I didn't much feel like being bothered. I knew he was just nervous and needed someone to talk to, but we all had our own little problems and fears. Like myself, and so many others, he had to learn to get over them.

The bus moved along the dirt road and all the surrounding lights lit up the prison like a giant Christmas tree. Not a word passed from anyone's lips as they gazed out the windows. To my surprise, even Silo stared out the window silently saying goodbye like Tee and so many others. The Ellis Unit was an old, dirty, rat-infested prison, but even all the rusted steel that confined us gave us memories, even though most of those memories were bad. There were still memories.

Shortly after we hit the highway, the bus became loud with chatter as the sun began to rise. The further we got down the highway, the foggier it got, and at some point on the trip, I couldn't see anything out the window. The fog became so thick that it seemed like we were stuck in a giant cloud, but I still strained to see out the windows. All there was to see were trees, but then, about forty minutes into the trip, we crossed a small bridge and there was a large body of water. "Welcome to Lake Livingston," a large, white sign read.

"We're pretty much here," Tee said from where he sat a few seats over.

"We are here," I told him. "This new prison we're being moved to is in Livingston, and we're crossing Lake Livingston right now."

"Hey, L.A.," Vago yelled from the back of the bus, "all that water makes you wish you were back home in California at the beach, no?"

"It doesn't remind me of any beach, but yes, I wish I was back home in California," I replied.

The skinny, new guy looked at me and spoke again, "See, I knew your name was L.A."

"Okay, I'm busted," I said. "I'm L.A., and I hope being him isn't such a bad thing."

"Not at all," he said. "I just heard a lot about you. My name is K.C.," he said, trying to keep my attention. "I'm from Kansas City."

"Well, that's good you got a name, but let's enjoy the view while we can because there's no telling if we'll get another chance."

"Sure," he said. "I understand."

I went back to looking out the window, wondering what the hell he did to be put on death row. I was in my mid-twenties and was still young, but he couldn't have been more than eighteen or nineteen years old. Why they were moving him with the rest of us, I didn't really understand, because most everyone else on the bus had been on death row at least a couple of years.

The sun was rising now, and we made a couple of turns down a few long roads. We passed another thick strand of trees and suddenly, out of nowhere, large buildings loomed beyond a turn-off, and a large sign read "Charles Terrell Unit." To say the prison was big was an understatement. This prison was more than twice the size of the Ellis Unit.

"Goddamn," someone breathed. "This place looks like a fortress."

"You better quit using God's name in vain," someone else said, and it got quiet.

The bus moved along ever so slowly, following the surrounding small cars that led the way. While we crossed some roads, the small cars could be seen ahead stopping traffic well in advance so that the bus never had to stop at all. We passed through stop signs, red lights, and yield signs as though they didn't exist. We had arrived and everyone was silent, drinking in the sight of our new hellhole.

The bus stopped at a large tower and most of the guns were taken off the bus. Then it was driven inside the prison fences while the smaller escort cars stayed behind. Once inside this prison, you could see barbed wire fences, one after another, three feet apart. The bus was inspected again, and we moved deeper into the prison through a maze of concrete roads. The Terrell Unit was on about four hundred-sixty acres of land and buildings consumed a great deal of it. Actually, you wouldn't have thought Terrell to be a prison if it did not have so many fences, razor wire and gun towers. The buildings resembled those of a large university for rich kids.

We traveled through a maze of buildings and stopped. One of the guards quickly jumped off the bus, pressed a button, and hurriedly jumped back on again. What we all thought was a steel wall began to move very slowly, and once it was fully opened the bus inched forward and stopped while the steel wall closed again. The bus took us to a prison within the prison. Nothing moved, but the voices of other prisoners got louder and louder.

Outside the bus, there were more than thirty prison guards, most of them suited up in riot gear as though they expected trouble. Still, none of us were being moved. I opened the bag Marion gave me, since it had surprisingly gone unchecked. I opened two packs of peanuts and passed them around to some of the guys because I didn't really want them anyway.

I saw K.C's mouth tighten because I didn't offer him any peanuts, so I opened the bag again and took out the colorful chewable candy.

"Here you go, youngster," I said and tossed him the bag of candy. I even laughed at myself for calling him "youngster" like so many others once called me.

"Thanks," K.C. said. "I sure do like candy." He tore open the bag, not offering anyone else a piece of the candy, but most of the others had their mind on what would happen next and not on whether or not K.C. shared the bag of candy.

Two guards got back on the bus and surveyed the scene as prisoners moved from seat to seat talking to each other.

"Inmates, listen up!" one of them shouted. He wore a wide-rimmed cowboy hat and had spurs hanging from his boots. He looked like a throwback from some western movie. "One at a time, I want each of you to slowly move off the bus!"

"Okay, you fucking cowboy son-of-a-bitch," someone said, and the bus erupted with laughter.

Vago had maneuvered his way back into a seat across from me and he said, "Que jodida!"

"What does that mean?" I asked.

"In English it means, 'what a fucked-up situation,' because this place ain't right.

This place is something real and shortly the others will realize this is no picnic."

"You got that right. This place is certainly something real, and we're in a for a big change," I said. "Give me some skin my brown brother." I stuck out my hand.

"Alright ese," he slapped my hand. "Take care because who knows, we may never see each other again."

"I won't say goodbye, because we'll see each other again. How do you say 'see you later' in Spanish then?"

Vago smiled and looked at me. "Say, 'hay te wacho."

"Hay te wacho, then," I said. I made my way off the bus as the guard wearing the ludicrous cowboy hat signaled for movement. "Alright. Tee, Shaka, K-Deuce, ya'll take care. And you too, youngster." I nodded at K.C. and got off the bus.

When I hobbled to the concrete in my gorilla-like stance, two guards rushed to my sides and grabbed my arms. One of them was a large black woman three or more inches taller than me. Other guards stood ahead holding batons, shields and pepper spray, as if itching for a problem to arise so they could use their cowardly weapons, but no problems arose. I hobbled inside a building that was all white and clean, and there stood many more guards.

"On your knees," the large, black woman said.

I shook my head and reluctantly obeyed her command. She removed the shackles first, then the handcuffs, and finally the other chains.

"Strip," she said.

I took off the prison jumpsuit, boxer shorts socks and shoes. I then dropped what remained in the bag, and I stood there, butt-ass naked as the day my Mama gave birth to me.

The large, black woman grinned, "Run your fingers through your hair. Okay, now lift your nuts. Now turn around and spread 'em."

I ran my fingers through my hair. I lifted my nuts as she stared openly and unmercifully at me. But then, we came to a roadblock.

"I ain't spreading nothing," I said, standing up straight, no longer conscious of my nakedness.

Her face softened, and she smiled. "It's my job, Inmate," she said.

"Well, it's my dignity," I replied.

"What's your name?" she asked as other guards moved closer, wondering what the hold up was.

I was surprised that she didn't ask for my number too, so of course I did not offer it. "My name is Nanon Williams," I said.

"What's your number?" she asked. "Oh never mind, I found it."

I was just standing there as more prisoners came in behind me and were also told to strip.

"Is there a problem?" another guard asked.

"There's no problem," she said. "Go ahead and get dressed, Williams."

I got dressed too quickly, but I was glad she didn't press the issue of me spreading my ass cheeks apart because I was not going to do it. I didn't want any problems, and apparently she didn't want any either, so I appreciated that. After I was dressed, she handcuffed me again, and we moved on while another guard followed behind.

The hallway was long, but we walked in strides. The inside of the Terrell Unit looked as big as a shopping mall, but this was just one building. When we turned another corner, a large metal door said "D-POD" in big, bold black letters, and I was gently pushed toward the door. Inside there was a large glass enclosed structure with buttons and lights. Inside was another guard who controlled all these buttons.

"Hey, picket officer!" the guard said. "Hey, picket officer!"

"How can I help you?" a man asked through a slot in the window.

"I have an inmate here named Nanon Williams, 9-9-9-1-6-3. What cell am I supposed to put him in?"

The picket officer looked at a piece of paper and said "Put him in A-section, number thirteen."

We entered deeper into D-Pod. This cellblock had six sections: A, B, C, D, E and F sections. Each section had fourteen cells with metal doors, not bars like the Ellis Unit had.

"Pop the door to A-section," she told the picket officer through a speaker in the wall.

We entered the door. This section was like a giant cell with bars draping around the structure like an extra security net, but there were no bars on the cell doors. We ascended some steps and went to the second to the last cell on Two Row.

"Pop thirteen cell," she said and the door popped open.

She slid the door open and slammed it shut. Then she took a bar, opened a slot in the door and removed the handcuffs, then slammed it shut too.

"Damn," I said to myself, "this is it?" There had to be more, but there wasn't.

Inside the cell everything was white and very clean. There was a steel bunk with a metal box welded underneath, a large concrete ledge hanging near the bunk that acted as a desk, and a toilet. The cell was six by nine feet, but it did seem slightly larger than the cells on the Ellis Unit. In the back of the cell, at the very top, there was a window, but when I stood on the steel bunk to look out, there was nothing but a wall. A wall and nothing more.

I went to the door and looked through the long slit, but I could see nothing but the picket and a small dayroom area with a pull-up bar. With nothing to do, I sat on the bunk, knowing that this place wasn't going to be easy at all. "This is something real," I said aloud, remembering what Vago said on the bus. "Something really fucked up."

22

MEMORIES ARE
MADE OF THIS

YOU NEVER EXPECT TOO much change, but Terrell Unit was too much change for most prisoners. In all honesty, I wish I was never transferred there at all, although at times I fooled myself into believing otherwise. After a few weeks passed, I had all my property and tried to develop a schedule of sorts. I normally spent the days and years as I always had, but even the things I once did at the Ellis Unit were limited here. Hell, everything was limited here except the total isolation. There was plenty of that.

Inside the cells everything was cold, so very cold it made you want to stay wrapped in a blanket all day. In fact, that is what other prisoners did. It was not by happenstance; it was by design. One reason is that cold air makes a person restless and even drowsy with not much on your mind except keeping warm, almost wanting to go into hibernation like a bear. By making prisoners want to sleep all day and stay warm, guards heard less noise, which made the atmosphere seem more passive.

The cells were pretty much soundproof, as much as possible, so the only thing one could hear was silence. That silence slowly drove some prisoners insane. The only way we could talk to other prisoners was through a side crack in the door and every word that was spoken sounded like an echo in a canyon. However, you could speak to one of your neighbors through the air vent that connected the cells, which allowed you to hear at least one person very well. Surprisingly, my neighbor turned out to be Vago, and we always stayed at the vent or at the cracks through the door talking late at night.

Most of the prisoners were used to watching television all day, but not at Terrell. There were no televisions. Staring at televisions all day allowed many prisoners to keep updated with current news events and to see the world as best they could. Others, well, all the sitcoms and movies allowed them to escape their reality and dive into a world where sex, adventure and happiness seemed alive again. There was also no human contact of any kind, so we could no longer play basketball together, play dominoes, shake hands or even fight, for that matter. Most of the time fighting never benefited anyone, but even friends sometimes fought to relieve their frustrations, but not at Terrell. There would never be contact with another being's skin again, in any fashion, unless a guard's hand brushed against your own while being handcuffed through the metal slot in the door. Otherwise, we were further separated from other people as though our being human was finally erased completely.

When the door slammed shut behind you after going to recreation for an hour, five days a week, that door slammed with a finality that none of us missed. Even recreation wasn't much different than being in the cell. The open area in each section was considered to be the dayroom, at least that's what they called it. In the small open area, there was only a pull-up bar, nothing else. Some prisoners did pull-ups so much since there wasn't anything else to do, that a few even cracked jokes about it. They would say, "Man, I did so many pull-ups today that I couldn't even wipe my ass! When I took a shit my back arms hurt so bad." Those who were standing at the doors of their cells listening would burst into laughter. There was also a sixteen by twenty outside cage that was considered to be a recreation yard, though how, I don't know. There were so many bars crossing the top that we couldn't get any sun, and the walls were solid concrete. Everything was quite similar, except unlike the dayroom, the recreation yard had a basketball goal with a flat backboard. Other than imagining we were playing one on one with Michael Jordan and actually beating him, push-ups were the only thing we could do. Afterwards, back to the cell we went.

Everything was so disused that you couldn't even feel like a statistic anymore. Nothing was in use except for one's mind. If we wanted to do anything, we either read a book, wrote a letter, or drifted so deep into our mind that we hoped never to come out. If one could see some of the men sitting in their cells, some would have their head leaned against the wall smiling and staring into nothingness. Others would be doing the same thing except that they would have blank expressions. Occasionally someone would just start screaming over and over again.

"Kill me! I'm tired of this shit!" a little guy named Nuncio screamed. "Get me out of here!" He banged on the door and then there was no sound at all, nothing.

Several days later I learned that Nuncio stuck his pencil into his eye and tried to dig his eyeball out. My only conclusion is that he didn't want to see anything anymore. After all, at the Terrell Unit we had only our imagination and plenty of darkness when the lights went out. If we weren't careful, our imagination could swallow our perception of reality, and we would just sit in the cell like a babbling fool uttering things that weren't even comprehensible anymore. I've heard some men talking so casually when you walked by their cells, that you would have sworn they had a cellmate. Sometimes when guards did a count, they checked some prisoners' cells to make sure they were alone.

"Hey," Vago yelled out his door to a guard, "bring me a roll of toilet paper, or a clean towel, pinche jura. I have to use the restroom."

I laughed when he said that, so I went to the vent. "Vago!" I yelled.

"Que Pasa?"

"You crazy, man. I heard what you told that guard."

"I have to take a shit and those pinche juras always ignore us like we don't exist."

"Here comes a female guard up the steps."

"Okay, don't say nothing, but watch this," he told me. "Go to your door and listen."

When the female guard came to Vago's door, she opened his metal slot and handed him a roll of toilet paper. The woman looked damned good to me. She had long black hair, a pretty face, nice flared out hips and was about six feet tall.

"Is that all you?" Vago asked her.

"Is what all me?" the female guard asked.

"Is all that ass yours in the back, because damn, you're fine," he said in broken English.

Thinking that she would storm off, I just laughed, but to my surprise she just smiled and stood talking to Vago, so I got away from the door. Vago thought himself to be a playboy, so I gave him a bit of privacy since he obviously had the woman's attention.

Since prisoners are sexually deprived, whenever a prisoner could get the attention of a female guard they lavished in whatever response they got, as did many of the female guards. Even the ugliest of women could come to prison and feel like a beauty queen because the years had a way of making a woman look better and better. Some female guards knew they looked absolutely terrible, yet they would strut down the tier in their tight gray slacks and have the nerve to switch their asses and have an attitude. Let them tell it, and they knew they were sexy. In fact, many female guards teased some of the prisoners on purpose just to get a rise out of them, and some of the prisoners stood at the door with nothing on but their socks waiting for a female guard to pass by their cell. Some people are natural voyeurs, but a certain amount of sexual deprivation will make most people voyeurs.

"Okay, see you later, baby," Vago told the female guard.

She just waved at him and walked away smiling, and I knew that made his day. It even made my day because he was obviously feeling like he was Don Juan himself. We ended up talking about the female guard all through the night.

"Let me ask you a personal question, ese." Vago said.

He used the term "ese," meaning dude, guy, man, basically just addressing another male. I knew he was going to ask me another question about women, so I braced myself. "Okay, shoot. What's your question?"

"Have you ever been in love?"

"I'm not sure," I said. "I came to prison at such a young age that I haven't had much experience."

"Well, I've had a lot of experience. I've done some things with women that you can't even imagine," he bragged. "What woman would you say captured your heart the most then?"

"There was one girl. Her name is unimportant, but even today I think about her."

"Why do you think about her?"

"For many reasons, I suppose. She made everything matter for me," I said, reflecting on my memories.

"Well, tell me about her. And start from the beginning because we're not going anywhere."

"Man, I don't need to tell you about any woman in my life! For what?"

"Just tell me, ese," he said. "Come on."

"Alright, man, I'll tell you, but if you laugh one time, I'm stopping."

"I won't laugh, L.A. Go ahead and tell me." Vago waited for me to begin. "Ese, a cat got your tongue, or what?"

"Well, I don't know where to begin."

"Where did you meet her?"

"At the high school we attended."

"Then start there."

"I had just turned sixteen years old and walking to school was a thing of the past for me. My mom had just bought me a truck, and I invested every dime I earned into that truck to fix it up so I could catch all the girls' attention. I wanted to fix the truck up with all the latest car rims and all the other accessories that made the truck look good and that was expensive. Needing money more and more, I started to sell marijuana after school to some of the gang members who lived in the neighborhood. Before you know it, I was running around with them, making money where it could be made. I was the star football player on the high school football team and was rapidly becoming the neighborhood fuck-up.

"When I wasn't at school or a football practice," I continued, "I was out making money and soon selling marijuana became petty change. I began selling harder drugs so I could give my family money to buy whatever they needed. I guess you could say I was trying to be the man of the family by bringing home what we needed, but we were doing okay as a family. Mama made ends meet the best she could, and I had no business selling drugs.

"At school, like you, Vago, I could always be seen talking to different girls in between classes and sometimes ditching school to be with someone. I was starting to explore sex, but I never actually dated two or three girls at a time. I always had one girlfriend at a time, although no relationship seemed to last long. I never mistreated a woman because I had two beautiful sisters, and I thought of them often. I tried to treat girls the way I would want some guy to treat my sisters, so I guess you could say I treated the girls well, although I did flirt with a lot of them.

"There was one girl at school who was very reserved and quiet. She had long braided black hair, ebony colored eyes, strong facial features and soft brown skin. She had a knockout body, but she dressed conservatively, unlike other girls at school. I often saw many of the other guys at school trying to talk to her, but she was just polite to them and never paid much attention to them. She was always focused on her schoolwork and trying to graduate, so because I was an underclassman, I never really bothered talking to her. Back then a senior wouldn't dare associate with a underclassman because it was like some unwritten rule. Kind of like the ones we have in prison.

"At the beginning of a new semester, I was transferred to another class. This class was job training by working in the attendance office. I'll tell you her name, Vago, but don't ever be funny and mention her name to me again.

"What's her name?" Vago asked.

"Her name was Shanice," I told him. "After working in the attendance office for a while, I did my rounds and went from classroom to classroom picking up attendance rosters. As I went to the last building, there was Shanice. She was at her locker exchanging books and hurrying to get to her next class. While she was at her locker, I walked up to her, kind of cool like, and asked her what her name was, although I already knew it was Shanice. I started to tell her what my name was, but she cut me off. 'I know your name already, Nanon,' she told me. 'Everyone knows your name.' I was about to burst with pride that she knew my name. I got a little bolder and asked her if I could have her telephone number so I could call her sometime."

"What did she say?" Vago asked.

"She told me that I was a troublemaker and walked away from me without saying another word. I wasn't really used to being rejected, so I just stood there and tried to regain my composure, you know. I mean, the male ego is really something else and mine was wounded. I couldn't get over the fact that she rejected me so politely and yet insulted me at the same time by calling me a troublemaker. Maybe it was known around school that I sold drugs, but I wasn't a troublemaker.

"Weeks went by, and I saw her around school, and she even started to wave at me and occasionally say hello to me, although she never encouraged me."

"You're a man, ese," Vago interrupted. "You got to take control."

"Let me finish telling you what happened, Don Juan."

"Okay, please continue."

"One day I went to the school parking lot with a friend of mine so we could go home, and there was Shanice, sitting on her car that was parked beside mine. I gave my friend my keys and told him to go ahead and drive my truck home since we lived in the same apartment building anyway. He was so surprised that I would let him drive my truck and so excited by the thought of driving it that he didn't even ask why I was letting him do it.

"I walked up to where she was sitting on her car, and I asked her why she was just sitting there. She told me she was waiting on her friends, but she also let me know it was none of my concern. She then asked me why I let my friend drive my truck and leave me there. I smiled and told her that I was hoping I could hitch a ride with her."

"Did she give you a ride?" Vago asked.

"No," she told me, "'Boy, I'm not taking you home.' And when she said that, a big smile wreathed her face, and I knew she meant it. I asked again for her phone number and at that moment, her two friends appeared, and they all got into the car. I got the hint, so I started walking out of the parking lot. I only lived a few blocks from the school. Walking wasn't any big deal. As I was walking along, to my surprise, Shanice's car stopped beside me, and she said, 'Boy, you are something else,' and handed me a piece of paper. Then she and her friends drove away, and her friends were laughing. I felt really foolish before she stopped.

"I looked at the paper she gave me, and it was her phone number. That made me feel much better. The walk home seemed well worth it to me.

"In the next few months Shanice and I often talked on the telephone and spent a lot of time together. When summer came, we were inseparable, and for a while, I even stopped selling drugs. Shanice graduated, but by the time she did, we weren't really a couple. We spent time studying together, but I wasn't really interested in studying, although I never made an intimate move toward her.

"Shanice wasn't like the other girls. She didn't care for going to movies and things like that. She preferred picnics on the beach. Sometimes she would make a lunch, and we would eat sandwiches side by side and stare into the sun. Sometimes we wrestled playfully in the sand, and I would let her pin me down, and she would kiss me real soft and slow. I would savor the moment like it was my last breath.

"The last day of summer, before she started college and I began my senior year, I picked her up and carried her into the water at the beach, and we splashed water on each other for hours. It started to rain, but we didn't leave. We just held hands and walked along the beach in the rain, as if the rain did not matter. Nothing else in life mattered to me as long as we were together.

"During the school year, she had a day off, and I decided to skip school against her protest. We ended up going to my apartment and no one was home. We didn't plan to do anything, but she slowly undressed me and I undressed her. I had never made love, but feeling the curves of her body against mine did not seem real. I felt the unmistakable swelling between my legs and before I knew it, man, I felt myself between the softness of her flesh, and she was a virgin. It wasn't just sex, it was as though we truly and literally became one. The way she laid on my chest and cried afterwards washed me clean. They were tears of joy; I remember each tear as clearly as seeing the morning sun rise, and at that moment my nerves made me actually shake. Why, I don't know. I just don't know.

"To make a long story short, life took a drastic turn for me, and I ended up here with you in prison. At first, Shanice stayed by my side, but I pushed her away because I felt she deserved more than I could give her. A friend told me he believed she was pregnant, but she got an abortion. I can't say that I believed him at the time, but the thought that I could have been a father hurts me more than any pain death row could ever inflict. If I ever failed anything in my life, it is my family and Shanice. When I pushed her out of my life, it may have been the most foolish and insensitive thing I have ever done. I just wanted her to have more than I could give her, because to me, she will always deserve so much more than this life I have.

"Sometimes at night, even now, I can feel her fingers cupping my face, kissing me softly, as tears pour down her cheeks. All I can do now is put my dreams on a star and think about the good times we shared together. I cherish my memories, but sometimes they make tomorrow that much harder to face, because today won't leave. I promised myself if I ever knew love, it was then, and if so, I never wanted to explore its depths again."

"It sounded like love to me," Vago said. "Luckily I got a fresh roll of toilet paper because you're breaking my fuckin' heart over here," he said, laughing softly.

"Holler at you tomorrow," I told Vago.

"Go ahead and think about Shanice," he said. "I know the feeling, ese."

I did just that, but how I fell asleep I don't know. The memories were no longer comforting; they created an ache that never left and perhaps never would.

23

THE NEW MILLENNIUM
ARRIVES IN HELL

NIGHT FELL AND DARKNESS filtered through the window as I stared at a newspaper. I read, dissecting each word for the lies they told. I didn't need the words to provoke images in my mind. I could see his intense eyes, and his face scored with a mask of rebellion, and his body rigid as he embraced the impact. There was no crying or moaning. There were no tears to burn away the pain, but instead a single man robed with spirit in his defiance of death.

Desmond Jennings, known to the courts as a convicted killer and not worthy to live a natural life, was executed. To me, he was known as Li'l Dez, my fellow prisoner, my comrade, my friend. I was struggling to accept that Li'l Dez wouldn't be around anymore, because I never really got a chance to say goodbye. I didn't even know he had an execution date. Instead I have his face splattered across the newspaper before me. The title of the first page read *Defiant Inmate Executed After Resisting Guards*. I was left to struggle with my emotions while pretending to be strong. I have experienced moments like this before, yet there is no script I could follow or a fundamental reaction that could lessen the pain. It was as though I have wounds that were stitched up, ripped open again, and then had salt thrown over the blood that poured out. Why this repeatedly happened, well, I've grown tired of trying to figure it out.

Li'l Dez always told me if they ever tried to execute him, he would fight back with everything he had, and true to his word, he did just that. I received a letter from a fellow prisoner describing to me what took place, regardless of how the media portrayed it. Guards clad in helmets, mask, shields and chest gear, the so called extraction team, stood at Li'l Dez's cell while the warden repeatedly sprayed him with pepper gas because he refused to walk to the death house at the Walls Unit. He refused to go like a lamb to the slaughter. "You can't break my spirit!" he yelled at the warden. Realizing that he wouldn't surrender and come passively out of his cell, the extraction team of five guards eventually ran in and beat him until he could be restrained and dragged from his cell.

The newspaper told the story differently, of course. A journalist wrote that Li'l Dez had warned prison officials that he would not cooperate, and at least that much was true. "I won't do this," they claimed that Li'l Dez said, and fifty-two seconds later he was removed from his cell without being gassed. Knowing Li'l Dez as I did, and knowing other prisoners who retold what really happened, I knew that Li'l Dez did what he had said he would do; he fought back. He told me more than once that if he had any right at all, he had the right to fight for his own life by any means necessary, and who would dare say that no man had that right?

The media accused Li'l Dez of being responsible for as many as twenty slayings, yet that wasn't what he was convicted of. Li'l Dez never confessed to being innocent or guilty. I am not God, so I accepted him for the man I knew him to be. It was the first time in one hundred ninety-three executions carried out by the state of Texas since capital punishment resumed in 1982 that prison officials claimed to have used force to move a prisoner to the death house. But I doubt very seriously if that is true. I can only remember Li'l Dez for the spirit he had, because he would not want anyone's tears. He would want us to remember him as the fighter that he was.

I will never forget the way he always asked me, "Man," he would say, "what good books you got to read?" And I would send him some philosophy book, but he would just complain and tell me, "Don't send me that trash! Send me something that I can relate to, like Malcolm X, George Jackson, or even that Cuban dude—what's his name?"

"You talking about Che Guevara?" I would ask.

"Hell, yeah, that's who I'm talking about!" Li'l Dez got excited. "Send me something with spirit!"

Later that night, after he was gone, I placed those exact words in my newsletter because I remember them all too well. I wrote that he should be remembered with the identity synonymous with spirit, and all I can do is hold on to that.

Sometimes it seemed like I was awake, but still somewhat unconscious, until the sun died with the night. Sadly, the night doesn't always display everything in plain view, so eventually I too, would escape reality in my own way. I tried to select only what I choose to feel among all the conflicting emotions. In a sense, it's like opening a closet door and looking at my wardrobe. I try to make a logical choice of what to wear, but it is always an adventure.

You see, life never promised to be easy. No. Not for anyone. Even when things seem to get easier, and you can relax a bit, there's always a hard slap in the face that will let you know it will only get harder. Li'l Dez knew—as do so many of us—that we are all only flesh and blood, we have thousands of experiences in only one lifetime.

I stood, flicking the cell lights on without an eyelid fluttering from the brightness. And moving toward the sink, I removed all my clothing and then neatly folded them on the steel bunk, so that the floor would not add dirt to them. I then laid out a fresh pair of boxer shorts, a brush, razor and other things I would need.

Turning on the sink, I took a torn sheet that I used for a washcloth and bathed myself, almost as though I was baptizing myself and cleansing my soul. I wanted to wipe away the pain and start over as the millennium was coming to an end, while midnight brought another millennium that only a privileged few of us here on death row would ever see.

Then I took another piece of clean sheet, drying only my face, and then I lathered my face with soap. When I grabbed the razor and looked in the mirror, it was the man/child I saw in the reflection, the boyish grin erased with time, his hair dripping with wet black curls, and the scars, each telling a story of its own.

With each movement of the razor, the stubble was removed, and my hands shook uncontrollably. My face had changed and small creases gave their own answers to why they were there, but I needed no explanation. I realized anger was changing the lines that gripped my face; perhaps they would destroy me.

When I was done, I got back fully dressed, tying my brown prison boots very tight. I wasn't planning on going anywhere, of course, but midnight was only minutes away now, and there was no telling what the year 2000 would bring. Some said the human race might simply vanish, leaving everything behind. Others believed the coming of the rapture would occur, and God would come to reclaim His people. If Christ should come and take his own I wonder, will I go with my family? And if so, I wonder if Li'l Dez, Rogers-el, Da'Oud, Billy Hoe and hundreds of others who are dead, will be there? Or are they burning in an eternal furnace?

Others believed some computer bug called Y2K would possibly start a world war, or just cause enough chaos that planes would crash, traffic would gridlock, banks would lose all the records of peoples' finances, people would go berserk, grab a gun, and scatter their brains out in the middle of the street.

Many death row prisoners didn't know what to think. Their goal was just to make it to the year 2000. But selfishly, I don't care what they thought. I only thought about those whom I love, and they were not in prison. Other prisoners like Silo, well, he probably believed something alien was keenly studying him, or maybe he was so zoned out that he didn't even know the old millennium was ticking away. Outside the cell door, screams and shouts were thrown about concerning the approaching new year, but I couldn't decipher exactly what was being said. At the end of time, whenever it comes, we will all know the answers to everything. At least, that is what I believe.

Knowing the time was about near for the year 2000, my left hand fumbled as I grabbed my watch and placed it back on my wrist. I then quickly said a prayer for my family and friends, hoping if something horrible was going to happen, they would be safe. My alarm on my wristwatch beeped, and I began my countdown toward the new year. Five, four, three, two, one, but there was no burst of "HAPPY NEW YEAR!"

24

STILL HOLDING STRONG

THE YEAR 2000 ARRIVED, yet nothing drastically changed except my moods and thoughts, which swayed back and forth. At times I felt a physical pain inflicted by my heart that left me doubled over, but my pain was perhaps a blessing in disguise. It taught me and constantly awakened me. When it seemed I went deep into the coldness with the temperature feeling well blow zero, it warmed me and stripped away the numbness, although that pain was the very cause of those feelings.

At the beginning of the new year, some of us prisoners engaged in a massive hunger strike to protest living conditions at the new super max security prison, and, yes, it was hard. We all went on for weeks without eating a single morsel of food and my body weight slowly disappeared like a single drop of water in the middle of a furnace. Yet many of our spirits were fed in order to endure this psychological war.

The prison officials denounced the hunger strike, denying to the media that it even took place, down playing our protest so that no light was shed upon it that would reveal our inhumane living conditions to the public. Still we gained a victory. We stood strong with each other as best we could and those struggles created bonds that would endure past the test of time, even though that time was swiftly running out for us all.

The conditions at Terrell were so atrocious prisoners began to take desperate actions. Two death row prisoners held a guard hostage and held her well into the night, not for any personal gain or because they believed they might get free. Indeed one of them, the courageous and spirited Ponchai "Kamau" Wilkerson had a serious execution date scheduled for March 14, 2000. Kamau (which is the African name that means "Quiet Warrior") and L.D., a young man of courage, staged this protest in a last-ditch effort to shed light on the brutality and inhumanity suffered by all of us on death row. Their efforts did gain media interest and helped to expose the criminal brutality of the Texas prison system to the public.

Kamau was involved in the great escape of Thanksgiving night, 1998, running for freedom with the odds heavily stacked against him. He was involved once before in an escape attempt that went awry, but he never gave up. He was a warrior, a man who would not, who could not simply sit idle as the state committed atrocity after atrocity. When Kamau and L.D. took the guard hostage, they had no intention of physically harming the guard, nor did they. They brought light to the barbaric savagery of their fellow prisoners. Before that staged protest, Kamau was summoned to the courtroom in Houston to be given an execution date; summoned, I might add, because the judge who played God and took it upon her sanctimonious self to condemn him to death, felt that it would be "cruel" not to tell him in person the exact date and time of his murder. There in the courtroom, with media present, Kamau stood up and faced the judge. "I will not walk away pretending there is justice and fairness in this court," he said. "I have been wronged by this court." He went on to talk about the corruption and bigotry of the judicial system with regard to African-Americans and the fact that racism is still miasmic and prevalent in the country today. Then, in protest of the wrongs done not only to him but to his fellow man, Kamau refused to walk meekly like a lamb to his own slaughter. He dropped down and forced them to remove him from the courtroom.

Kamau never claimed to be an innocent man. He knew that he had done wrong. But instead of doing nothing, he spent the years of his imprisonment on death row educating himself and helping to educate other young brothers, trying to make a difference in this world. It was his way of healing himself and those he had hurt.

On March 14, 2000, after one final, brave and outrageously ingenious protest, Ponchai "Kamau" Wilkerson went to the Ancestors, but his spirit is with us still.

He left for all of us, a legacy of fierce pride, of struggle for what is right, and an overwhelming love for his family and friends.

I decided to write a living testimony, not for myself, but for the people who are reading these words at this very moment. These are words for victims everywhere, not just for death row prisoners, not just for their victims and their victims' loved ones. These words are also, perhaps especially, for forgotten victims—the family, loved ones and friends of death row prisoners everywhere, that forgotten segment of citizens who receive no support from a society bent on punishing them for continuing to love someone who is on death row. I can make no apologies for anyone else's acts, but it is my hope that people of the world will change. Our world is a beautiful and wonderful place. It is people whose actions corrupt and destroy the beauty and horde the generous bounty in it.

IN THIS BOOK I chose to use curse words and to share my own thoughts as honestly and as accurately as I remember them with each experience. My words often reflect an angry young man. Indeed, as an innocent young man imprisoned for a crime I did not commit, I am often angry. My anger is sometimes the motivating factor in what I do. I have attempted not to misdirect my anger but rather to direct it toward something positive. I know my own anger well, as I have lived with it day and night, and I can honestly say that it originates from my great love for my family, my friends, for this beautiful world that is so wrongly corrupted by some people.

As I brought this book to a close, I was still a young man of twenty-five years of age. I had been incarcerated eight years already. At the time, I was in dread that I would soon see a full decade inside prison walls. I have now been incarcerated twenty-one years, and I continue to abhor the fact that I know the ways and means of prison life more than I know the free world. I was a teenage boy, barely past my seventeenth birthday, when I entered prison's gates. In 2005, the U.S. Supreme Court deemed it unconstitutional to execute individuals whose alleged crimes took place when they were juveniles, and so although my death sentence was commuted to life, my youth and my remaining innocence were executed the moment I entered this place, as I heard the first resounding crash of metal doors slamming shut behind me. Perhaps I further destroyed the boy I was by trying to cram as many years as possible into my memory bank because suddenly my lifetime changed from a long stretch of years to look forward to, to a brief time that could be and might be ripped away from me far too early.

Each year I have lived behind these brick walls has been a year of watching others being destroyed. I have seen more than three hundred men executed. I have watched kids grow to be men inside this place. I have seen developmentally and intellectually disabled prisoners suffer confusion and torment, as well as abuse, because they did not have the mental capability to understand why they were there. I have seen two women murdered by the state. Beautiful, young Karla Faye Tucker-Brown, who became a true Christian and suffered deep and sincere remorse for the crime that sent her to death row. Karla would have been willing to live out the rest of her life in prison helping others, yet she was strapped to the gurney and murdered on February 3, 1998. Betty Lou Beets was neither young nor beautiful, and therefore did not rate the massive media fanfare that Karla's execution did. Betty had been a lifelong victim of abuse and at her execution on the gurney on February 24, 2000, she suffered the final and ultimate abuse.

I know death like I know the structure of my hand, and no, you never get used to it. Some days you just don't feel anything, and other days you feel like someone is trying to rip your heart out of your chest.

The reason I named this book *Still Surviving* is that it is the only thing any of us can do when the obstacles of life encourage us to give up. Giving up is too easy, and survival is the oldest instinct known to mankind. We must all rely on that instinct, and whether we are religious or not, we have to pray that we can keep on going. That is survival.

A friend once told me that I am like a flower in middle of the desert, but I have learned that is what hope is, to bloom under circumstances that are not ideal. Inside each of us, that flower only needs a little water, and it will give the breath to our soul that prepares us for whatever may come.

We must create our own formula to keep that soul intact and not lose it, because, due to human nature, someone will take it away from us if we let them. Viktor Frankl, a Jewish man whom I admire greatly, said it best. "So, let us be alert in a twofold sense: Since Auschwitz, we know what man is capable of. And since Hiroshima, we know what is at stake." There is no chance to avoid realizing that humanity is at stake when we exact vengeance on each other, and the death penalty is pure vengeance. It has been proven time and time again that vengeance is the only thing the death penalty accomplishes. It is Hiroshima waiting to happen when we give up on human life, when we give up on each other.

My belief is that one day I will be a free man. I believe I will sit down to dinner with my family, that I will smile lovingly at a wife and have my own children on my knee. However, the reality of my life, at times, doesn't allow me to see past today. For those on death row, tomorrow may never come. Still, as the great Dr. Martin Luther King once said, "I have a dream." My dream is that our hearts will one day be like the color of the rainbow and that the spirit of struggle will embrace us so that we can all live together in this world in peace.

Perhaps even in my struggle, I may become to the world only like so many others who have died on death row—a number soon forgotten by all but those who love me. Or I might become a legend like others I have been honored to know, struggling courageously to the last breath. Or maybe, just maybe, the future will have me in it someday. Maybe someday I will be free. Free at last.

Still Surviving

When the steel baton strikes,
Causing me to bleed,
I watch my blood run.

When the chains bite,
Tearing into my flesh,
I feel the pain.

When the days pass by,
Creating another week,
Another month,
I count the years.

Yet still holding strong,
I keep on striving,
To be a better man, because
I'm still surviving.

In Hope and in Strength

Nanon McKewn Williams

April 10, 2000

ACKNOWLEDGMENTS

My journey to freedom has, to date, spanned over two decades. I have now lived more of my life incarcerated than free. The journey has been full of heartache, disappointment, loss and countless tears. And yet, I have been tremendously blessed. I have lived for the moments of joy and triumph. In writing this book ten years ago, I did not know if I would live to experience the impact it might have on the lives of others. Against the odds, I am here. Through the first edition of this book, I have had the rewarding experience of meeting hundreds of individuals—activists, students, artists, writers, families of other incarcerated men and countless other people—who have reached out and touched my life. To each and everyone of you, thank you. Thank you for enriching my life with your presence and letting me know my life has affected yours. You have filled me with purpose and inspiration to make a meaningful and significant contribution to the betterment of society.

Thank you to my growing family. My incarceration has had a profound impact on each of your lives. Thank you for your steadfastness and willingness to stay with me and take on each challenge one step at a time. Thank you to all my wonderful friends for growing with me, teaching me about life and daring me to keep believing that we can all overcome any obstacle if we are willing to keep trying.

Thank you to my publisher Robyn Short. You not only had faith in me, you also had the courage to tackle a controversial subject like the death penalty. You could have played it safe with other books, but you took a stand to educate people about the cruel realities of incarceration. To the goodmedia press team: thank you Lindsey Bailey for the cover design and book design, Melody Harstine for hours of editing, Kyle Phelps for the digital book production and Kristin Hazen for proofing all our work. You all welcomed me to the team with open arms. This is our body of work. Go goodmedia press team!

Thank you to Elyse Short for the many hours you spent retyping this book. Without your willingness to recreate this manuscript, this second edition would most certainly have been delayed. It is very meaningful to be able to re-release it on the tenth anniversary of its original publication. Thank you for making that possible.

Thank you to Dr. Betty Gilmore, my co-author of the forthcoming book *The Darkest Hour: Shedding Light on the Impact of Isolation and Death Row in Texas Prisons.* Although written primarily for an academic audience, this book will no doubt have a tremendous ripple effect throughout the social justice community and beyond. Thank you for your countless hours of work, thorough research and courage to ask some tough people some very tough questions. Thank you for your tenacity in searching out the truth, when those who guard it were not very forthcoming. With a family and a demanding career, you went above and beyond to invest so much of your time to our book. I am honored to be your co-author and so proud of you.

There are many activists, abolitionists, writers, teachers and students who have inspired me. I owe my vision and dedication to making a meaningful contribution to social justice to you.

To the hundreds of men I saw executed, many of whom I am proud to have called friends, to my loving grandparents and to my father—I know you are all with God. May you watch over us all.

ABOUT THE AUTHOR

Born August 2, 1974, Nanon McKewn Williams grew up in Los Angeles amidst the violence and poverty that plagued the city. As a teenager, Nanon stood out for his academic and sporting achievements and dreamt of a career as a football player. He was an All-American and the recipient of over seventeen athletic and academic scholarships. In 1992, when Nanon was only seventeen years old, he was wrongfully convicted of murder and sentenced to death by the state of Texas.

As a young boy on death row, Nanon discovered a passion for writing and committed his life to being a voice for those who have been silenced. He began with poems, which he published in 2000 under the title *The Ties That Bind Us*, and continued on to write numerous essays as well as several books—*The Darkest Hour: Stories and Interviews from Death Row* and *Still Surviving*, all three now in their second edition. In 1997, Nanon began publishing *The Williams Report* as a contribution to the debate against the death sentence and to provide an international voice for incarcerated individuals. Readers interested in subscribing to *The Williams Report* may do so at www.NanonWilliams.com.

In 2005, as a result of the U.S. Supreme Court's ruling in Roper v. Simmons, Nanon's death sentence was commuted to a life sentence. With his transition to general population, Nanon was able to study for and complete his GED in 2007. He then began college courses offered through Trinity Valley Community College. He earned an associates degree in Liberal Arts and Science and also took trade courses in Horticulture and Cognitive Intervention. He is currently working towards his Bachelor of Science in Behavioral Sciences through University of Houston-Clear Lake.

Through writing, Nanon has found a way in which to endure daily life in prison and connect with and enrich the world beyond prison walls. Nanon's message is a message of peace and nonviolence. He actively works to bring attention to the atrocities that routinely occur behind bars and seeks to be a voice for those who have been silenced while offering a platform of education for those who may learn compassion and kindness for a population of people who are all too easy to shun and turn our backs on.

While Nanon continues to live a life of service to others, it is the hope of his publisher and loving community of family, friends, fans and followers that his work be a force of change that will bring him justice and freedom so that he may continue to be a force for peace while living freely in the world.

Learn more about Nanon M. Williams on the web at NanonWilliams.com. Write Nanon through his publisher at Nanon@NanonWilliams.com.

The Darkest Hour: Stories and Interviews from Death Row

The Darkest Hour: Stories and Interviews from Death Row by Nanon M. Williams emerged from a deep and dark despair in a place where the thought of suicide often holds more appeal than the thought of living. The hopeless ones live below the line but not Nanon Williams. Williams reached high beyond despair with outstretched hands and on tiptoes. He took a firm grip on the branch of hope and hoisted himself up above the line. While on Texas' death row, Nanon was an inspirational voice. This work, now in its second edition, has expanded his inspirational influence beyond prison walls to men and women everywhere. His voice reaches others who measure their lives by an hourglass and do not see enough sand remaining to do anything of importance with their lives. We all learn from Nanon Williams that we can race against time and win.

The Darkest Hour: Shedding Light on the Impact of Isolation and Death Row in Texas Prisons

"... this book will inspire you to view all people through the lens of empathy and compassion ..." ~ book foreword by Susan Sarandon

The Darkest Hour: Shedding Light on the Impact of Isolation and Death Row in Texas Prisons (sequel to *The Darkest Hour: Stories and Interviews from Death Row*) by Dr. Betty Gilmore and Nanon M. Williams sheds light on the widespread impact of extreme isolation experienced by thousands of incarcerated individuals in Texas prisons—many of whom will be integrated back into society. This book presents an in-depth view of the Texas prison system with a specific focus on death row and solitary confinement. The impact of living in severely restrictive conditions is examined through a multi-disciplinary lens that incorporates scientific research and expert opinion and includes powerful narratives from men who have been incarcerated for ten or more years and the people that surround them. Factors such as childhood history, attachment, biology, poverty, race and other social influences are explored in relation to the events that led up to incarceration and the subsequent ability to obtain fair treatment throughout the legal process.

In-depth stories of trauma, survival and growth guides readers through the experiences of these men, and the efforts made to preserve their own dignity in the face of adversity.

CPSIA information can be obtained
at www.ICGtesting.com
Printed in the USA
BVHW071941300620
582653BV00001B/131